W9-CUX-420

Black Cats
and
Dumbos
WWII's Fighting PBYs

Mel Crocker

AERO
A division of TAB BOOKS Inc.
Blue Ridge Summit, PA

To Rockina

FIRST EDITION
SECOND PRINTING

Printed in the United States of America

Reproduction or publication of the content in any manner, without express
permission of the publisher, is prohibited. The publisher takes no responsibility
for the use of any of the materials or methods described in this book, or for
the products thereof.

Copyright © 1987 by TAB BOOKS Inc.

Library of Congress Cataloging in Publication Data

Crocker, Mel.
Black cats and dumbos.

Includes index.
1. Catalina (Seaplane)   2. World War, 1939-1945—
Aerial operations, American.   3. World War, 1939-1945—
Naval operations, American.   I. Title.
UG1242.R4C76   1987   940.54′4973   87-1460
ISBN 0-8306-8391-7 (pbk.)

TAB BOOKS Inc. offers software for
sale. For information and a catalog,
please contact TAB Software Department,
Blue Ridge Summit, PA 17294-0850.

Questions regarding the content of this book
should be addressed to:

Reader Inquiry Branch
TAB BOOKS Inc.
Blue Ridge Summit, PA 17294-0214

Chapter-opening illustrations by John Kirkpatrick.

Contents

Preflight

Rain spattered down out of a gray overcast, and wind swirled it in slanting skirmishes along the shore and out onto the bay. The watchers at the water's edge peered out at the murky sky and wondered if the plane would make it in this weather.

"Here she comes!" A familiar silhouette materialized out of the rain clouds to the north, low over the surf line that marked the reef. The PBY came in parallel to the shore, made a tight turn, and again passed the watchers grouped at the edge of the bay. As it came abeam, a stream of bright flowers tumbled out of the tunnel-hatch and drifted down to the surface of the steely gray lagoon.

It was December 7, 1981. The place was Kaneohe Marine Corps Air Station, Hawaii. The PBY, in its scruffy paint job, was a familiar and nostalgic sight to the people gathered on the long-unused seaplane ramp. Many of them had been in that very spot years before.

The PBY was the property of the University of Hawaii. The flowers were dropped in memory of comrades and shipmates who had lost their lives there the morning of December 7, 1941. Kaneohe was then a Naval Air Station, a base for seaplane patrol squadrons and for the practice landings of Pearl Harbor-based carrier aircraft. Here had actually begun the dreadful "Day of Infamy," marking the active entry of the United States into World War II. The Japanese bombing and strafing began here some five minutes before the first terrible explosions wreaked their havoc at Pearl Harbor, Hickam Field, Wheeler, and Schofield.

On that Sunday morning in 1941, some of the PBY flying boats had been at moorings where now the leis and blossoms floated. The first strafing runs of the Japanese planes had caught them in a bloody splatter. Other seaplanes, lined up on the ramp and in the hangars, were flamed and shattered like ducks in a shooting gallery — a gallery whose targets had not yet been set in motion.

The small crowd that gathered on the ramp and at the hangars on December 7, 1981, had come to dedicate a memorial marking the events of that Sunday in 1941, and to remember those who fell there in sanguinary sacrifice.

Here, then, is the story, mostly in the words of the participants themselves, about a very special airplane and the men who flew it — some to ride it into battle and come home safely — and about some who never came back.

Lt. Comdr. Ercell Hart, USN, retired

Acknowledgments

No author blending nonfictional, historical data into a comprehensive story the magnitude of this writing could possibly claim credit for its contents. Literally dozens of individuals — former military and civilian — museums, government historical departments, libraries, authors and publishers have contributed to the making of the Catalina Story.

In the following pages, I want to gratefully acknowledge each of these people and the cause, department, or organization they represent.

My brother, Glenn, gave me the idea and incentive to begin research on the book when he tired of my frustrations in fiction writing. He reminded me of my naval service and my continuing fascination for the PBY Catalina flying boat of World War II.

My wife, Rockina, never wavered in her support and encouragement, even as expenses mounted and results seemed vague or unreachable. In the final months of meeting contractual requirements, her physical effort and advice helped pull us through.

Sometimes, a large, close family is drawn closer by a happening that involves members of that family. This is such a case. While each family member supported the project and volunteered their services, I really do not believe this story could have been finished without the guidance, professionalism and devotion to the cause offered by our son Gary, and the help provided by his wife, Lynda.

Our son, Douglas, sister-in law, Jane, and niece Sheri Kontra spent hours on map research and tedious line drawings.

Many former PBY pilots, crewmen and naval aviation enthusiasts contributed countless hours of research and memory-jogging to provide individual stories of the aircraft's naval service from the late thirties to the end of World War II. All deserve mention, but three former PBY pilots and one former chief petty officer must be singled out for their strong, continuing, and sincere support of this project.

Thomas Benton, Santa Ana, California
William A. Barker, Marshall, Texas
Norris Johnson, Ventura, California
Ercell Hart, Kaneohe, Oahu, Hawaii

My sincere gratitude is extended to Ray Wagner, Archivist of the San Diego, California, Aerospace Museum. His knowledge of naval aviation in general, and the PBY Catalina, specifically, straightened out a number of bends in my story. Admiral Samuel Eliot Morison's History of United States Naval Operations in World War II — Fifteen Volumes — provided reference. Specifically referenced was Volume Seven: Aleutians, Gilberts and Marshalls, June, 1942 – April, 1944; Copyright 1947© , revised 1975 by Samuel Eliot Morison, reprinted by permission of Little, Brown and Company in association with the Atlantic Monthly Press.

Invaluable data, in the form of naval historical facts, stories, photographs and advice, came from the following sources:

Naval Historical Center, Department of the Navy, Washington, D.C., Dean Allard, Head Historian.

Naval History Division, Audio-Visual Archives Division, National Archives, Department of the Navy, Washington, D.C.

Office of Chief of Naval Operations, Naval Aviation History, Washington Navy Yard, Washington, D.C., Wes Pryce, Historian.

William Wagner, Reuben Fleet and the Story of Consolidated Aircraft. Aero Publishers, Inc., 1976 — Now TAB BOOKS, Inc.

George T. Mundorff; Aerospace Historian, Volume 23, #4.

Department of History, Kansas State University, Kansas.

Naval Aviation News, Washington Navy Yard, Washington, D.C., Bill Armstrong, Historian, Sandy Russell, Managing Editor.

Ray Wagner, Story of the Catalina. First published, 1972, Flight Classics.

San Diego Aerospace Museum, General Dynamics photographs, Ray Wagner, Archivist.

General Dynamics (Convair) San Diego, California. Excerpts from Convairiety, Convair House Organ, Jack Isabel, Public Relations.

Introduction

It wasn't love at first sight, my meeting the PBY Catalina patrol bomber. Hardly! In that moment, I felt fate had dealt me a cruel blow and that my first flight would be my last. It seemed my short Navy career and my life would soon be over.

I was standing beneath the giant wing, and alongside the wasplike fuselage, of a PBY5 model, Navy seaplane which was perched on spindle-legged beaching wheels at the Naval Air Station, North Island, San Diego, California.

A group of 30 or so new graduate aviation radiomen, mechanics and ordnancemen was getting a guided tour of the Operational Training Unit for PBY Catalina seaplane squadrons. From that point, we would enter extensive hands-on development of skills necessary to support two pilots, a navigator and six of us enlisted men in the multiple tasks before us.

A Chief Petty Officer guide, obviously from the ranks of retired World War I veterans who had been recalled to active duty for World War II, must have read the panic in my face as he walked up and scornfully said, "Boy, count yourself lucky! That dear old lady is the safest aircraft in the fleet. If you respect her and care for her, she will take you anywhere in the world, through hell, if necessary, and bring you home safely."

As relieved as I was by the Chief's assurances, my panic returned a few days later when I boarded a PBY for my first-ever airplane flight. As we started to move away from the launching ramp, the sound of sea-water pounding against the aluminum hull grew into an almost deafening roar. I thought, "Surely, the hull will cave in and we will die." But the seaplane lifted into the air and I had my first of many exhilarating flights in a PBY Catalina.

We flew for a short interval, sounded as if we were crashing when we landed, then taxiied safely to the launch ramp. And my PBY career had begun.

The stories you will read here are not my stories. My experiences as an Aviation Radio/Radarman with Black Cat Squadron Twelve, serving in the South Pacific Campaign, while exciting and interesting to me, pale alongside the colorful, humorous, heartbreaking and, sometimes, miraculous tales revealed in the Catalina story.

The story of the PBY Catalina patrol bomber is not just a tale of an ugly-duckling seaplane, scheduled for the scrap-heap, that was pressed into emergency service when the world became embroiled in war; neither is it just a biography of a group of brave, dedicated men whose trust in that aircraft developed into an almost fanatical faith; Rather, it's the incredible, almost unbelievable, true accounting of a naval aircraft, and of the men who flew it.

Together, they wrote history in World War II by defying intolerable weather, and a tenacious enemy, while protecting Alaska and the West Coast of North America from a possible Japanese invasion. Together, they bombed, strafed and torpedoed enemy submarines, surface warships, freighters and troop ships, and were deadly nuisances to the enemy in every naval war zone of the world. Together, they patrolled the thousands of miles of the world's oceans and seas, supporting Allied fleet and merchant vessel movements. And they battled, sometimes successfully, the faster, better armed and more maneuverable German and Japanese aircraft.

But for thousands of men and women throughout the world, the slow, clumsy-looking, amphibious seaplane became a mechanical angel of mercy. Braving impossible seas, and often an hostile enemy, the Catalinas rescued airmen, seamen, merchant mariners, refugees, coastwatchers, and even the enemy.

Rescues accomplished by the PBY and their sister squadrons of PBMs and PB2Ys numbered in the thousands. Little wonder, then, that this angel of mercy became so affectionately known as the Beloved Cat.

1

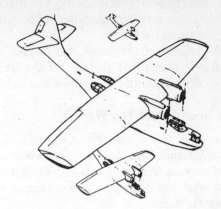

Day Of Infamy:
December 7, 1941

One by one, the three PBY Catalina patrol bombers moved slowly toward the seaplane launching ramp on Kaneohe Naval Air Station. Pilots and crewmen busied themselves with preflight check lists in preparation for an 0600 takeoff. The Dawn Patrol, a routine security mission, would cover certain sectors off the United States' territorial island of Oahu, Hawaii, then return to base about 1000 hours. It was Sunday morning — lazy and peaceful — a day in December, 1941. The only other activity on the base centered in the chow hall where cooks were preparing the first mess of the day. Here and there a solitary guard paced the steps of his station.

Ensign William P. Tanner, in command of one of the patrol planes, was making his first flight as a Patrol Plane Commander. Today he was flying 14P1, the skipper's airplane, and he was concerned with the responsibility. In addition to his commander's aircraft, he was also responsible for the Catalinas piloted by Ensigns Meyer and Hillis. But with the PBYs in the air, and his crew settled into its chores, Tanner's anxieties diminished.

Almost as soon as they were airborne his radioman began receiving messages, most of them requiring his confirmation. He didn't take them lightly, but was well at home with base radio. Previously, he had spent many hours in the co-pilot chair beside Commander Thurston Clark, Commanding Officer of Patrol Squadron 14.

The slow-flying PBY crossed the island and entered the air space above Pearl Harbor a short time before 0600. As Tanner looked down on

1

the bulk of the United States' Pacific fleet, he thought of the full alert status that all Catalina squadrons had been on for over a month until December fourth, when it had been lifted. He remembered, too, that orders to attack any submarine not in authorized sanctuaries had not been changed, and the depth charges on the aircraft were live.

Deepening the tension of the patrol, the skipper had warned the officers of scheduled weekend PBY flights that the United States was entering into a critical period with the Japanese and to be extra alert.

Bill Tanner: One Hour Before The War

Ensign William P. Tanner of Rossmoor, California, a Lieutenant Commander by war's end, remembers the events of December 7, 1941.

"I was already nervous from the group leader role, but if I had had the slightest inkling of what was coming up in less than an hour, I probably would have aborted the flight.

"It was just after 0600 when we got up on the step and lifted off the water in Kaneohe Bay. 14P1 was to patrol south of the island, so I set a heading that took us directly across Pearl Harbor to where our search sector was to begin.

"We were a little south of Pearl when we spotted the submarine. The USS Antares was approaching Pearl from Palmyra with a barge in tow. Riding the wake some 200 yards aft, with its conning tower barely awash, was this submarine — clearly outside the established sanctuaries.

"An old World War 1 class destroyer, the USS Ward, was nearby but we didn't have immediate radio contact with her, so we made a run on the sub and dropped smoke markers. I guess the Ward spotted it about the same time we did because she started bearing down hard. We made as tight a turn as we could and bracketed the sub with our depth charges. But now, with the Ward closing and firing, we pulled up and watched her launch four depth charges from the fantail. The submarine rolled over and sank.

"We filed a radio report of the incident with the base, which was acknowledged, and were ordered to 'continue on mission.' Well, it wasn't quite 0700 yet, and as I set the PBY on course, my thoughts were going wild. This was my first command. What if that submarine was one of ours? It had seemed smaller than ours, and it wasn't supposed to be where it was. But I was a young ensign and how small is small? I hadn't really seen enough subs to know. If it was ours, how many Americans died from our actions? I was sick. Somehow the men in that sub blocked any thoughts of what an enemy at that location might mean.

"A few minutes before 0800, when we were somewhat southwest of Oahu, the airwaves came alive with reports of the Japanese attack. Voice and morse coded messages were too garbled and frenzied to make much sense. This fighter squadron was scrambling; bombers were taking off from Hickam Field and this, that and the other. Later, many of those

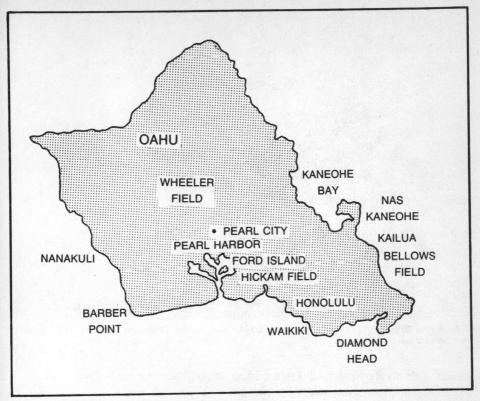

Oahu Island, Territory of Hawaii.

reports proved grossly exaggerated. They were mostly the result of excitement and total disbelief of what was happening. Most aircraft were destroyed on the ground. A few fighters got airborne but, as far as I know, we were the only U.S. bombers in the air.

"About this time we received a coded message from the base to deploy all three aircraft in search of the Japanese carrier, or carriers, responsible for the attack. Since I was flying the Commanding Officer's plane, the message was directed to me. It instructed us to search 30 - degree sectors from 270 degrees to 360 degrees, which would be west, through northwest, to north of Oahu. I challenged the order, using a method we had to verify that a message wasn't emanating from the enemy. It was verified and I advised the other PBYs. About an hour later, Freddie Meyer, flying the 330 - to 360 - degree sector, came under attack by Japanese fighters.

"Meyer, in command of 14P2, was north of the island when he was spotted by Japanese fighters apparently returning from Pearl or Kaneohe. He said he was about 40 miles to the north when he sighted eight or 10 aircraft ahead of the PBY. He carried out the procedure we all had been

PBY-6A final design, amphibious. Manufactured in New Orleans, Louisiana, January, 1945. (courtesy General Dynamics.)

trained in of diving to about 20 feet off the water; there he could keep hostile aircraft from flying under the plane.

"Freddie put his crew on alert, ordering them to man their battle stations and to try to identify the approaching aircraft as soon as possible. Suddenly, the fighters closed and started firing on his plane. It wasn't until then that he knew for sure they were Japanese; he ordered the crew to return fire.

"As he turned back toward Oahu, hoping to pick up support from some of our aircraft, the Japs were hitting his plane pretty hard. However, most of the hits were in the aft fuselage with no control damage.

"During the fight, one of the fighters went into a spiral, smoking heavily, but the crew was too busy to verify whether it went into the water. Probably with an eye on diminishing fuel, the Japanese soon broke off the attack, leaving Freddie to lick his wounds and take stock of the damage. He chose to remain in the air and to continue searching for the carrier task force.

"Meanwhile, we continued our fruitless search of the area west of Oahu while Tommy Hillis was covering to the northwest. We searched all day, coming back at dusk. And, let me tell you, it was a hell of a shock to see our burned-out planes and demolished hangars.

"In retrospect, I have often thought of the hour-plus warning we had, based on the action with the Jap submarine. I've wondered why we didn't better use that time to mount a defense of the island. But I guess nobody — and that certainly includes me — was able to immediately perceive the relatively insignificant incident as a part of a much greater scheme: an all-out attack by Japan on the United States in the Far East and Hawaii."

Bill Tanner's PBY Catalina, 14P1, of Patrol Squadron 14, by attacking the Japanese submarine off Pearl Harbor, became the first U.S. aircraft to fire on the Japanese in World War II. Ensign Fred Meyer's PBY, 14P2, by engaging Japanese fighters north of Oahu, became the first U.S. airborne bomber fired on by the Japanese in that war.

The Dawn Patrol of December 7, 1941, at best a token search of the waters surrounding the territory of Hawaii, began in peace that Sunday morning. It ended with the United States' military forces on the island of Oahu virtually destroyed. By the time Tanner's 14P1 and the other PBYs landed, over 10 hours after takeoff, the U.S. Fleet lay in ruins; the Army Air Force detachments were all but wiped out, and the Navy's PBYs — most of them new — had been reduced from 81 to four flyable and a few repairable. Three of the flyable aircraft were the Catalinas of Ensigns Tanner, Meyer and Hillis.

Whether from the surprise of the Japanese attack, or from a sudden release of long pent-up tensions regarding the possibility of war with Japan, the military forces on the island of Oahu that morning — individually and collectively — reacted with the ferocity and determination of a mother bear protecting her cubs. Collectively, they formed primitive battle stations and fought with grossly inferior weapons. Individually, they faced almost certain death by refusing to seek protective shelter from the exploding bombs and withering machine gun fire of the Japanese aircraft.

One such individual effort was that of Joseph T. Crownover, Coral Gables, Florida, then a Radioman First Class in VP11.

Joseph T. Crownover: Left For Dead

Joe Crownover tells it as he saw it:

"I was awake that morning but still in my bunk at the Kaneohe enlisted men's barracks. I heard machine gun strafing by the first wave of Jap fighters, but thought it was our Army Air Corps going through their mock warfare tactics, which they did occasionally. But Otto Leo Simmons, Radioman First Class, came into the barracks yelling that they were Japs and that they were shooting everything in sight.

"I got dressed, combed my hair, and tried to assume an attitude of, 'Take it easy — here it is — what we expected would happen. Don't get excited.' I don't know how long I held that attitude but it wasn't for more than a few minutes.

"Some 40 of us enlisted men sprinted about a quarter of a mile to the hangar area where we found most of our planes ablaze. We formed fire-fighting parties and pushed some planes, not on fire, away from others. One

PBY-5A at Kaneohe Naval Air Station, Oahu, Hawaii, December 7, 1941. (courtesy Jack Coley file.)

plane on the ramp was tied down to the pad-eyes at four places — bow, tail and at each wing.

"I remember a Lieutenant Delaney taking charge and ordering about 20 men to heave and shove that plane out of the way of the fire. No one could tell him it was tied down. Every time someone tried, he hollered, 'Shut up and push!' A sailor gave me a 30 – cent small-stores knife and I cut the lines. We pushed the plane across the road.

"Number-Ten-Boat, 11P10, was burning when I grabbed the 30 caliber machine gun from the tunnel hatch and tried to set it up for firing. I had about 20 cans of ammunition, each can holding 100 rounds, but I didn't have a gun mount. I held the gun by its stock with one hand and pushed the trigger with the other. The recoil action made it jump around so much my accuracy was questionable. But on one strafing run, I had a chance to open up on them at low altitude. I could see my tracers hit the wings of three planes, and I saw gasoline leaking out of the small holes. Exhaust from the engine set the gas on fire from some of those holes. I saw one plane fly away on fire but didn't see him go down.

"I don't know when I got hit. To this day, I don't know, or remember, much more than I have said so far. I was told some things, though. Seems I fired more than 13 cans of ammunition. I only remember loading the third

6

one into the gun. I was told that I was running around with a face full of blood, helping others put out fires. They said I was placed on a pile of bodies of men considered dead, covered with a tarp and left—forgotten in the excitement. Later, six of those bodies were either moaning or stirring. I was one.

"They sent me to the nearest hospital, which was Kaneohe Territorial Hospital, an insane asylum. I woke up on December 14th, a week later. All my hair was gone and my head was full of stitches. I couldn't remember anything except my name and that I was a radioman in the Navy. Dr. Ralph B. Cloward, M.D., a civilian brain surgeon, who happened to be visiting the island, operated and removed a bullet from my skull. I lost my left eye but it wouldn't have made any difference if that doctor hadn't been there just at that time."

Jack Coley: "I Saw The Big Red Circle . . ."

Jack Coley, Chicago Park, California, explains the patrol squadron procedure at Kaneohe during the weeks prior to December 7, 1941. He provides one substantial lead as to why the PBYs were not out in force that morning and relates his experiences.

"The way they worked the patrols and such in the days before the Pearl Harbor attack was to have one squadron take all the ready-duty for a week. That squadron took all the patrols, stood the wing-duty and wing-ready. On December 7th, VP14 had the duty and three of their PBYs were airborne.

"At the time, Commodore P.N.L. Bellinger was in command of Patrol Wing Two, headquarters for all patrol squadrons based in Hawaii. He had asked for more fuel so as to provide long, 700–mile searches. When they turned him down, he pulled in the patrols to cover shorter distances, reducing coverage to the Hawaiian area. This, of course, eliminated any possibility of an early air warning.

"I remember Lieutenant (jg) J.O. Cobb, who was one of the academy guys, discovered a Jap submarine on the surface just off the west tip of Molokai several days before December 7th. He made a pass and it immediately submerged. While the doctrine said that if a submarine was in our territorial waters we were to attack, there was enough ambiguity in the order that we weren't sure whether they would back us or hang us. So he didn't attack, reporting it instead.

"Officially, I was on leave the morning of December 7th, but was staying at the BOQ, cramming for an exam on augmentation into the regular Navy. I was supposed to take the exam on Wednesday and had been up, finished breakfast by seven, and was back in my room hitting the books when the Jap fighters first came by.

"I looked out and my first reaction was, 'The damn Army Air Corps is playing around again.' They had been out on maneuvers for the entire preceding week and a big coast artillery organization had moved into Fort Hase, outside the gate of the Naval Air Station at Kaneohe.

"I was just settling back down to study when a guy from down the hall came running and said, 'It's the Japs!'

"Oh, you're kidding."

"Naw, I saw that big red circle on the side.'

"We dashed over and looked out the window just as a Zero came by, strafing the cars on the apron.

"Of course, the typical reaction in terms of what to do: I changed into the uniform-of-the-day because those were Navy regulations. Lieutenant Carlton Clark came by and we started out the front door of the BOQ to drive down to the hangar, but there was a Zero banking in our direction. He cut loose and we ended up all the way back in the galley before we stopped running. After that, we timed it so that just after a Jap made a strafing run, we ran to Clark's car.

"There was a little-used back road to the hangar area, and by using it, we made it there without further attacks from the Japs.

"Everything was in shambles. Airplanes were burning. The injured were receiving help. Men were trying to salvage equipment from burning PBYs and some of us guys organized a group to recover the 50– and 30–caliber machine guns from as many planes as we could. We took the guns to a spot adjacent to a public works compound where we tried to set

PBY-5 at Kaneohe Naval Air Station, Oahu, Hawaii, December 7, 1941. (courtesy Jack Coley file.)

PBY-5 at Kaneohe Naval Air Station, Oahu, Hawaii, December 7, 1941. (courtesy Jack Coley file.)

them up. Here was a real problem. Machine gun mountings in PBYs were just a ring in a mount with a yoke that allowed the gun to pivot and elevate. To accommodate the mounting, we took water pipes and drove them into the ground with big sledges. It worked pretty well. Then we got some vehicles from the compound and made a circle like the old covered wagon trains used to do.

"One sailor, standing next to me, caught a bullet right in the center of his stomach. We drove him to the dispensary in the last drivable vehicle.

"It was all so frustrating. The Jap attack was so devastating, so thorough. We had lined our aircraft wing-tip to wing-tip; nothing could have been more convenient for them.

"I remember some of the silly things. As soon as the second wave was over, and things had settled down somewhat, all the sailors came down to where the hangar had been. They were ordered to go back to their quarters and get into whites because that was the uniform-of-the-day. It was required of a military man when he was fighting to be in the correct uniform. We didn't have combat fatigues or anything like that until much later.

Ruins of PBY hangar following Japanese air attacks, Kaneohe Naval Air Station, Oahu, Hawaii. (courtesy Jack Coley file.)

We were told to get up on the side of the hill and dig fox holes from which to defend the base. There were rumors about parachutists over on the west end of the island — about Barber's Point. An invasion fleet was coming in up on the northwest side. With side arms and rifles, we dug in like Marines holding an important point.

"Someone decided the white uniforms were a dead-giveaway, so they had the guys get all wet and roll in the red dirt. The idea was to camouflage their uniforms. Not happy with that, they boiled the whites in coffee to turn them brown, making them coffee whites, the standard uniform-of-the-day for a month or two before more rational thinking took over. The senior officers were as confused as their juniors at that time."

Otto Horky: Truce With A Mongoose

Otto Horky, San Antonio, Texas, was an enlisted man with Patrol Squadron 11 and on duty the morning of December 7, 1941. His story includes a brush with a member of the wild animal colony of the island.

"I was on the base at Kaneohe when the first wave of Jap fighters hit us. We had PBYs tied up to the buoys in the bay, all peaceful and nice, when I looked up to see what I thought were six of our SBD fighters making a strafing run on them. All at once, one of the PBYs blew up.

"In the excitement I ran down to the water's edge, cursing the Army over at Wheeler Field; I figured it was their doing. Then I saw the rising sun emblem on one of the fighters and knew what was happening.

"It was about 200 yards back to the hangar and I took off for it with a Jap Zero after me and several other men running in the same direction. His bullets were hitting the concrete in back of me and ricocheting every which way. The chips of concrete he was kicking up were flying over my head and falling in front of me. I made it to the hangar, just getting inside and down on the floor, when his slugs ripped big holes in the hangar door.

"Before then, I thought those big hangar doors were made of armor plate. We were never allowed to open or close them with a tractor for fear they would jump off their tracks. We had to push them by hand, and it took nine or ten men to push them. Me, like a damn-fool country boy, I'd push

PBY hangar on fire following Japanese air attacks, Kaneohe Naval Air Station, Oahu, Hawaii. (courtesy Jack Coley file).

my guts out. What I didn't know was that several of the other guys weren't pushing at all, just grunting.

"When the first attack ended, somehow we knew the Japs would be back. So everybody rushed around trying to find something to fight with. All I could find was a regular G.I. pistol and it without a clip. I found plenty of ammunition, in fact, I stuffed my dungaree shirt pockets full. But here I am with a one-shot 45 automatic.

"Figuring the next group would be bombing the hangar, I hunted for a safe place to hide — a ditch — anything. Now, the natural place to hide during an air raid is in a gasoline pit, right in the middle of the high octane aviation gas farm. So much for sound reasoning.

"I jumped into a six-foot-deep pit with concrete walls straight down, and pipes and valves going every which way. Sure enough, the Japs came back with their two-engine light bombers and started systematically wiping out everything the fighters had missed in the first attack. And here I am, down in this gas pit putting in one shell and bam!— firing at the enemy with a one-shot 45.

"Sometime during the attack, I heard something behind me. Looking over in the corner of the pit, I saw a great big mongoose. Right then, I was more scared of that mongoose — they can be vicious — than I was of the Japs. But he was scared, too, and stayed in his corner.

"When the attack was over, I got out of the pit and took off for the hill back of the station where everyone was regrouping. I didn't think of that mongoose for two or three days.

"We worked around the clock to patch up as many PBYs as possible. This day, I was on my way to the mess hall for chow when I remembered the mongoose and wondered if he was still in the gas pit. I checked and found him there. It had rained and some water was standing in one corner of the pit but he probably hadn't eaten anything. I took a piece of timber from our wrecked hangar and leaned it down as a ramp, then I got out of there. That evening he was gone, but I never forgot the incident. Through a common disaster, normal enemies temporarily became trusted friends."

A.L. Dodson: A Ring — Wedding Plans — December 7th

Al Dodson was born and reared on a farm in Cass County, Missouri, and became interested in flying when he took his first flight as a passenger at the early age of 10. He idolized the early barnstormers around Kansas City: Tex Rankin, Bill Long and others. When Charles Lindbergh flew the Atlantic in 1927, Al decided, once and for all, that becoming an aviator was his life goal.

Choosing Naval Aviation, Al tried to make the cadet training program but had only two years of college and the program required four. He got a break, though. In 1939, when the war broke out in Europe, the cadet college requirements were lowered by two years. Al was accepted and sent to Pensacola, Florida, where he trained in the early configurations of the PBY, P2Y2 and the P2Y3. He won his wings and Ensign commission in the summer of 1940 and joined VP14 at San Diego, California. He took his first flight in a PBY in November, 1940, and flew with the squadron to the new Naval Air Station at Kaneohe, Oahu.

In those days, the young Ensigns were required to wait two years to marry and Al's two years were scheduled to end on the 11th of December, 1941.

Commander A.L. Dodson, USN, Retired, Raymore, Missouri, tells his story of December six and seven, 1941.

"I had given my hometown fiancee, Jane Turner, an engagement ring in 1940 and I would be eligible to marry on the 11th of December, 1941. We utilized short wave radio, telegrams, and what have you, to make our wedding plans for the 14th.

"We were to be married in the Methodist Church in Honolulu. All arrangements had been made for a 10–day honeymoon to start on the 15th, with all the romantic trimmings of the Honolulu Island setting. I even had a cottage leased where we were to have Christmas before I would return to duty on the 27th.

"Jane arrived on the third and the rest is history. Our plans were knocked into a cocked-hat. As it turned out, we were married in the parsonage on the 11th, the day I was eligible to marry.

"As Franklin Roosevelt said, December seven was a 'Day of Infamy'. Jane and I had watched the Willamette University play football with the University of Hawaii in the afternoon before and we had gone to Trader Vic's for a party that lasted quite late.

"I was asleep in the BOQ when the attack hit. I didn't sleep long. With some other officers, I tried to leave the BOQ but the Japs had a Zero there, strafing the front door to keep us inside. Some of us went out the back way and made it to the squadron area toward the end of the first wave of the attack.

"My PBY, 14P9, was in the hangar during the first attack and survived damage. However, the other planes were all destroyed on the ramp and at anchor in the bay. 14P9 was removed from the hangar between attacks and Ensign Lev Thurlow tried to round up a flight crew to get it airborne.

"Johnny Black, the enlisted pilot in the crew, and I got aboard just as the second attack began. We manned the 50–caliber machine guns in the waist positions and got off a few rounds. But our ammo was belted — four ball and a tracer — and every time we fired, it looked like the Fourth of July. Naturally, it didn't take the Japs long to spot us.

"A three-plane section came in from our bow, strafing with incendiary bullets, and our old PBY was riddled before we could get out. It was like a burning torch. Fortunately, those 1830–92, Pratt-Whitney, engines up

Aerial view of Kaneohe Naval Air Station following Japanese air attacks, December 7, 1941. (courtesy Leon Freeman file.)

there in the line or fire of fire took all the lead that was meant for Johnny and me. We escaped unscathed.''

The men who formed the nucleus of the first PBY squadrons of World War II came from quite varied backgrounds. Most were selected by the age-old Navy way of offering a preference, then assigning them to the least desired alternative. In the case of PBY pilots, many requested carrier fighter assignments. However, once the initial disappointment was resolved, pilots and crewmen alike took to the Catalina with pride and confidence.

Tex Foret: "The Eyes Of The Fleet"

Tex Foret, Anthony, New Mexico, joined VP23 in November of 1939. He was with the squadron when it was renumbered VP11 and remained through two colorful tours of combat duty. He left only after December, 1944, when the squadron was relieved of duty in the Philippines and returned to the United States. Foret became Aviation Chief Machinist Mate during those years and was a typical example of the men who served in PBY squadrons. A wife seldom feared her husband would stray to an-

U.S. Navy sailors placing leis on graves of fallen comrades, Oahu, Hawaii, December 8, 1941. (courtesy Leon Freeman file.)

other woman, but she learned early on to share him with his other love, the PBY Catalina.

Foret's story:

"I was stationed at North Island, San Diego, when the first old PBY-1s took off for Pearl Harbor, so I got a good look at them early in the game. But it wasn't until November of 1939 that I reported to Pearl for duty in a squadron.

"We did routine duty: patrol, towing targets and the like. The duty was real nice. Hawaiian life style — tropical hours — we worked from 0700 until around noon, escaping the heat of the afternoon.

"In June, 1941, we were happy to move to the brand new air station at Kaneohe Bay. There, I got some of the best quarters, at the cheapest price, on any station in my naval career. We paid about $27 a month for a two bedroom apartment and, after paying those Honolulu landlords, we thought it great. In fact, we thought we had the best duty in the Navy, right up until the morning of December 7, 1941.

"I was born on December 7, 1914 and married my wife on December 7, 1934; so the date was to be a special occasion for us. We had the icebox full of beer and all kinds of picnic goodies, and had a beach party planned.

"I was a light sleeper, had gotten up about daylight, made some coffee, and was sitting on the front porch looking straight up at the Kaneohe control tower. It was on a little hill right in front of our house. I heard some planes off in the distance and thought, 'What are those crazy Air Corps boys doing out this early on Sunday morning? They ought to be in bed, sleeping it off.'

"But the planes kept getting closer and closer. Finally, one of them came up over the house. He was flying on the control tower. Just before he opened fire, I saw the big red meat ball under his wing and I knew what it meant — what was about to happen.

"I ran upstairs and got the wife and kid, a little baby girl, and told them to get underneath the stairwell, to shut the door and not to come out 'till somebody came for them. I ran back outside, jumped into the car and headed for the hangar. On the way, three fellows hailed me down.

"After parking my car under the old hangar to protect it from the destruction that had already hit the other cars around the area, we ran

Graveside ceremony, Kaneohe Naval Air Station, Oahu, Hawaii, December 8, 1941. (courtesy Leon Freeman file.)

16

toward my plane — one of two not torn up or burning. I thought, 'We'll man the guns and see what we can do to protect ourselves'. But when I raised the waist hatch, the smell of gasoline almost knocked me down. There were four to five inches of gasoline in the bilges. We couldn't fire the guns in there as the plane would have blown to pieces from the first spark.

"They wiped out the 'eyes of the fleet', our PBYs, doing quite a job of tearing up that bunch of brand new Catalinas. Then, they came back about a half hour later with light bombers and finished off everything they could see. They roamed free, at will, with no resistance except from a bunch of crazy sailors, firing their guts out with totally ineffective weapons.

"Only two PBYs survived the attacks. One of them was my plane, 11P11, but she was so badly damaged and full of holes that shortly after that they shipped her back to the Alameda Naval Air Station. There, they let young metalsmiths use her as a training ship, putting patches on and taking them off. The poor girl wound up as a dummy in a classroom.

"The other PBY was also damaged but was kept around, restricted to about 800 gallons of gasoline and used for pilot and crew training close around the island. She never got too far from the base and usually her flights were scheduled for around noon. We nicknamed her, 'Noon Balloon'.

"To my way of thinking, there was never a more dependable aircraft than the PBY. I always felt it would out-perform anything else in the air. She was slow, slowest thing with engines, but always reliable. I thought so much of the PBYs and the crews I served with, that in November of 1942, I turned down a commission rather than be separated from them."

George R. Jackson: "Daddy, I'm Scared!"

Most naval personnel caught in the Japanese attack on Hawaii were career men. When not on duty, many lived off-base with their wives and children. The unexpected attack caught families separated, some by several miles, and because of the confusion following the attack, four to five days passed before near-normal family relations were restored.

The traumatic impact on family members from this experience cannot be fully defined. But Chief George R. Jackson, Leonardtown, Maryland, recalls the impact on him and his eight year old son:

"I was Engineering Chief of VP11 and had been with the squadron since before we opened the new station in June of 1941.

"On Monday morning, December eight, the squadron was to depart for a 10 day advance-base operation at Johnston Island. Eleven of our 12 aircraft had undergone minor engine rework; the 12th was scheduled to be completed and ready for flight-testing by 1100 Sunday morning, December seven.

"In Pearl City, at 0645 that Sunday, the Jackson family was having breakfast together. It was decided that my eight-year old son, Jackie, would go with me to the station since we were expected to be back home by 11 o'clock. Mom and Margy, my seven-year old daughter, were to prepare a lunch for an afternoon picnic at Nanakuli Beach on the north side of the island. Since I would be leaving the next day, we all looked forward to a Sunday afternoon together.

"Jackie and I left for Kaneohe at 0715 and it was a few minutes before eight when we pulled into the parking lot across the road from the hangar. Chief Dotson, our Metal Shop Chief, drove up and parked alongside our car. For a few moments, the three of us stood by the front of the car passing the time of day; Jackie was excitedly telling about our picnic plans.

"Our aircraft were lined up wing tip to wing tip and nose to tail outside VP12's hangar to facilitate a smooth launch procedure the next day. VP12 had six PBYs, with crews, anchored in the bay where they were simulating advance base operations.

"'Jackie,' I said, 'we'd better let the crew know we're here.' Then we started for the hangar. At this moment, we heard and saw six aircraft approaching the station from the north; they were flying low and very fast.

"As the aircraft approached the VP12 seaplanes, they opened fire. I turned to Dotson and said, 'I didn't know the Army had any operations scheduled this morning. If they don't, somebody's in for a court martial for waking the Admiral this early.'

"Dotson said, 'Yea, man!'

"Just as the six planes disappeared behind the buildings, a PBY in the bay burst into flames and the men aboard began diving into the water.

"Now the planes came directly at us, strafing both lanes of PBYs. I grabbed Jackie by the hand and ran toward the hangar. Inside the hangar, I pushed him between a paint locker and the wall of the shop and said, 'Lay down close to the wall and don't you move!'

"He said, 'Daddy, I'm scared!'

"I said, 'So am I, but don't you move from that spot; lay close to the wall.'

"We were under attack by six Zeros. They were excellent pilots and knew their jobs. In less than 15 minutes, all the aircraft parked outside the hangar were burning; that, in addition to all the VP12 aircraft at anchor in the bay.

"As the PBYs were obviously their main target, and as they apparently were satisfied that all had been destroyed or put out of commission, they turned their attack on the hangars and any traffic on the roads.

"The Zero attack lasted about 40 minutes. After they left the area, the dead and wounded were picked up and taken to the base hospital which had not been hit.

"When I felt reasonably sure there was a lull in the attacks, I took Jackie from the hangar with the idea of driving him off the base. We didn't have to be told, the Japs would be back. A Jap shell, probably a 20mm, had wiped out my left rear tire and spare but I salvaged a tire from a nearby wreck and took out of there to Chief Surratt's house.

18

"When we got there, many of my buddies' wives were out in the yard wondering what was going on and asking about their husbands. Rather than worry them more, I said I didn't know. Mrs. Surratt said she would look after Jackie and agreed to load the car with as many wives and children as it would hold and get off the station as soon as possible.

"As I turned to leave, I said to Jackie, 'Son, I must return to the hangar.'

"Jackie said, 'Daddy, don't go back there. What if you get killed? How are we going to eat?'

"I didn't know whether to hug and kiss him or kick his little butt. Like any eight year old boy, he was being practical and honest. I didn't see him again until Thursday, the 11th. Then his first words were, 'Daddy, all I had to eat was rice and fish.'

"I returned to the hangar just before the second attack began. Since our leading chief, Byron, had been seriously wounded, it became my responsibility to take over his duties.

"I joined with others in salvaging 30 and 50 caliber machine guns from our wrecked PBYs, then set up a defense perimeter. Our efforts, while noteworthy, fell far short of a planned, well fortified, anti-aircraft battery.

"After the bombs had fallen, and the enemy was gone, I looked around at a devastated air station. Over near the hangar, a fire engine and crew had been fighting the fires; it was no longer there. Crownover, a radioman in our squadron, had been firing a 30 – caliber machine gun — holding it in his arms. He was down and unmoving in a pool of his own blood. I thought him dead. He lost an eye but came through miraculously.

"Almost immediately the rumors began. The Japs were landing on the north side of the island and a host of other stories. We were instructed to dig in on the hill north of the hangars. We salvaged many cement bags from a temporary cement plant that had been set up on the base, and after digging our fox holes, we lined the tops of them with dirt-filled bags.

"But after a long, weary night, the dawn broke with no sign of the Japanese invaders; we started coming out of our fox holes. Soon we answered the call to morning chow and the first day was history."

Whatever the circumstances, whoever was to blame, on the seventh of December, 1941, there were 81 PBY Catalina Patrol Bombers available for patrol duty on the island of Oahu, Territory of Hawaii. Squadrons VP22, VP23 and VP24 were based at Ford Island, Pearl Harbor. VP11, VP12 and VP14 were at Kaneohe Naval Air Station. Only three PBYs were in the air when the attack came. One of those gave a warning of over an hour that something was happening but the warning wasn't heeded.

Days after the attack, it was determined that the Japanese carrier force could well have been detected at least 12 hours before it attacked Hawaii, if there had been full-range, complete sector patrols of the PBYs.

2

The First 90 Days

The overwhelming success of the Japanese surprise attack on Pearl Harbor, Kaneohe and other military bases on Oahu left little from which the battered U.S. forces could draw encouragement. But there were a few shortcomings in their victory. For all the massive devastation the jubilant Japanese airmen inflicted, they failed to destroy Pearl Harbor's repair shops. These were rebuilding and restoring ships, planes and equipment before the fires were out. They missed, entirely, the power plant and fuel tank farm. Had either of these been destroyed, U.S. recovery from the attack would have been severely delayed.

But if the success of Japan's air attack on Hawaii was the result of surprise tactics, their assault on the Philippines, even with the defenders forewarned by some six hours, was every bit as successful. Military forces in the Far East had prepared and trained for over a year anticipating war with Japan, in spite of little cooperation from Washington. But pathetically small U.S. forces, augmented by equally weak representatives of Great Britain and Netherland East Indies, had no more success in the Philippines than the U.S. had at Pearl Harbor.

Brilliantly executed movements of Japanese naval units were made possible in part by their complete control of the air. Undeniable luck also played a major role as Japan repeatedly had strong forces at the right place at exactly the right time. Taking a page from Hitler's blitzkrieg doctrine, the Japanese methodically reduced Allied resistance in the Philippines, Malaya, and Netherland East Indies to a point of virtual collapse by early March, 1942. Even tiny Corregidor, which bravely held out until May 6th, served no more Allied advantage than to build a stronger resolve on the homefront.

One common Allied misconception contributing to Japan's successful lightning-like blows in the opening weeks of the war was that few military strategists felt the Japanese had the capacity to mount more than one concentrated attack at a time. Considering the mobility of modern war machines, there was a dominant feeling that sufficient forces could be brought against the Japanese to stop them in any multi-nation attack. When the Japanese successfully attacked the island of Oahu, then within a few hours, hurled gigantic naval, air and land forces at the Philippines and the Malay Peninsula, it became tragically clear that the enemy presented a formidable arsenal of men and machines.

Japanese aerial bombing of Clark Air Force Base and Nichols airfield on Luzon during the first hours of hostilities, followed shortly by precision bombing of military installations at Baguio and Tuguegarao in northern Luzon, left the United States' Army Air Corps in the Far East with less than 40 fighters and 17 bombers. Then, on December 10, the Japanese all but eliminated effective resistance by simultaneously attacking the Cavite Navy Yard, power plant, repair shops, submarines and support installations at Manila, and Nielson airfield. Between the 17th and 20th of December, the few remaining Army B-17s were withdrawn to Darwin, Australia, thereafter making only one raid before the Allied complete withdrawal.

At the outset of war, two United States PBY squadrons operated from bases in the Philippines. Commanded by Captain F. D. Wagner, under Naval Patrol Wing Ten, VP101 and VP102 were flying, perhaps, the only war-ready PBY-4s in active squadrons.

The personnel of the two squadrons were well-trained professional naval aviators. They were ready for war, using the PBYs for what they were intended: patrolling and bombing. But they were not ready to defend themselves while moored to buoys on the water, or to be singled out while on patrol by swarms of Japanese fighters.

Dawn of December 8, 1941 in the Philippine Islands was just six hours after the beginning of the Japanese attack on the island of Oahu. Sweeping in just over the trees at Davao Gulf, Mindanao, nine Japanese Zero fighters attacked two of the three PBY Catalinas assigned to the seaplane tender Willie B. Preston; the third PBY was out on patrol.

Moored at buoys and unmanned, except for the pilot in one, the two PBYs were the first aircraft casualties in the Far East. The pilot, Robert Tills, was killed as he vainly tried to man the bow gun of his aircraft. He became the only United States casualty of the action in Davao Gulf that first day. The Willie B. Preston successfully withstood Japanese strafing

PBY-4 on takeoff. Typical of model in Philippines as war began. (courtesy National Archives.)

attempts, and dodged the bombs of 13 dive bombers escorted to the area by the fighters. The Preston escaped the anchorage without damage or loss of personnel.

Three of the many men who served in VP22, VP101 and VP102 retraced their memories and recalled the dramatic days of defeat in the Philippines, Malaya and the Dutch East Indies. Their stories reflect the helplessness of the Allied position during the first six months of war with Japan. But they reflect, also, the determination to stop the enemy advance, though all efforts fell short of success and each day reduced their ranks.

Russell Enterline: "Execute WP57 Against Japan"

Russell Enterline, Aurora, Colorado, was an Aviation Radioman flying with VP101 and VP102 when the war began. His story of intrigue and escape is one of the most graphic presented in this writing.

"I joined Patrol Wing 10 in September, 1941, flying with radiomen Dockery, Simpson and Goodikuntz until I was checked out in radio and squadron procedures. We knew the situation with Japan was serious and we flew patrols to the north every day, constantly watching for signs of aggression. With one squadron at Sangley Point and the other at Olongapo, rotating monthly, the radiomen stood ground station watch and flew periodic PBY patrols as well.

"I had the mid-watch at Sangley Point Sunday night, Manila time, December 7, 1941. As I went on shift, Captain Wagner, Commanding Officer of Patwing 10, came by and told me to wake him if any messages came in for our base, regardless of the time. He went to bed as I took over the watch. All was quiet except for a couple of planes in the air.

"At midnight, Radio Cavite suddenly began calling all ships. And, without waiting for response, they sent the message, 'Execute WP57 against Japan'

"Since Captain Wagner had ordered me to wake him, I hung up my earphones and ran to the other side of the building where the skipper was sleeping. When he read the message he said, 'This is it!'

"Still in his white pajamas with lavender polka dots, he ran down to the ground level where he rang the warning bell for all hands to fall-in. He told us we were at war with Japan and to prepare for hostile relations. We didn't know for several hours that Pearl Harbor had been bombed.

"Flight crews hurried to their planes, starting engines and checking them for flight readiness. Our radio loud speakers called out, 'Red Alert!', meaning to stand by for an attack, but from where, we didn't have the slightest inkling. We knew that our ships in Manila Bay had been alerted, so we felt they would give us support, whatever happened.

"Regular patrol flights were let into the water. Beaching gear was taken off and they taxied out for take off. Word was passed that all PBYs were to clear out of the area. Crews were rounded up as planes were gassed

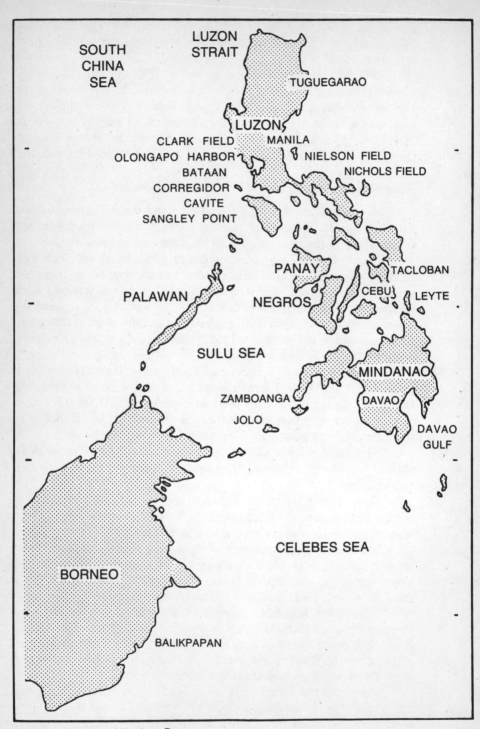

Philippine Islands and Northern Borneo.

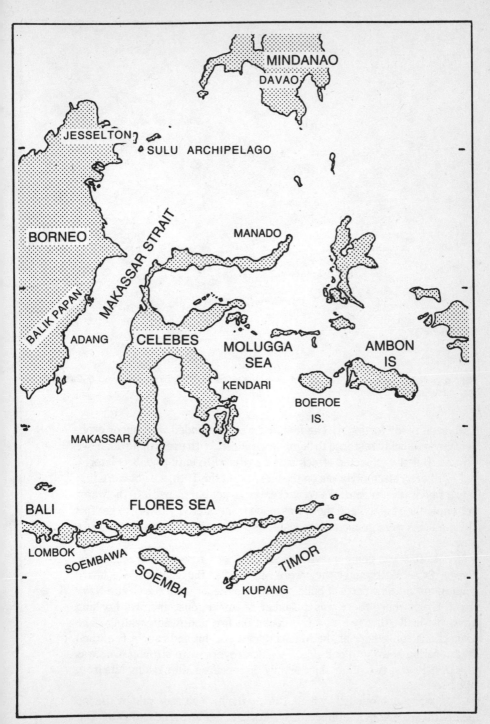

Celebes and Flores Island Chains.

PBY-5 in flight. Typical of first Model Five seaplanes in Philippines following outbreak of war. (courtesy General Dynamics.)

and made ready for flight. The few that were grounded with minor problems were quickly restored to flight-worthiness. With everything done, we waited. But the expected attack didn't materialize until two days later.

"Shortly after daybreak on the morning of the 10th, we got word that an air raid was imminent. We were ordered to get our planes into the water for immediate takeoff and there was much frantic activity trying to get this done. Planes were going into the water as soon as the plane ahead cleared a few feet.

"As this was going on we noticed "Vs" of aircraft in the air, four or five groups. We thought they were our B-17s. But suddenly we heard explosions and saw parts of buildings fly into the air from the Cavite Navy Yard. Everywhere there was a blanket of smoke, dust and fire. Looking toward Manila Bay, we saw the docks on fire and disintegrating. The Canopus, a sub tender at the Manila docks, was hit and caught fire, then began listing heavily to one side. Two destroyers were burning. One was the USS Peary; two other ships simply disappeared after taking hits from the bombers.

"I was dumbfounded by it all. During the high altitude raid by the Jap bombers, our planes continued their efforts to get airborne and away. But now the Jap fighters were coming in low over Manila Bay, shooting at anything that moved, and they found several of our PBYs still in the water.

"I watched as the plane I was assigned to for alternate flights sped across the water, desperately trying to get into the air, up on the step, then settling back down as if he didn't have enough air speed. Again the pilot tried, this time succeeding in bringing the Catalina up on the step and lifting off. But I watched in absolute horror as a Jap fighter picked up my plane from behind. Flying up the wake, his bullets strafed the water before ripping into the tail assembly. As the Jap fighter pulled up, parts of the PBY's tail flew off. The plane seemed to hang still in flight for a second or two. Then she exploded, falling into the water in many burning parts. The same fate was met by several other PBYs that morning, but a couple made it through the attacks and were able to fly clear of the devastation.

"When the fighters finished strafing our aircraft, they strafed the beach areas where I, for one, was dug into the sand. They strafed our barracks, hangar and nose docks, setting them afire. With no resistance, a second wave of bombers attacked Cavite Navy Yard. This group hit our Canacao hospital and our water tower at Sangley Point, causing it to burst with a 10-foot rush of water.

"Then it was over. The Japanese fighters and bombers were gone and the attack had ended. We were left with Cavite Naval Yard and our base afire. Ships in the bay were sunk or sinking. Some were leaving the bay for the open sea with fires burning out of control.

"How could they attack with such reckless abandon? We were told sometime later that our anti-aircraft shells had been sabotaged and were set to go off at 2000 feet. The enemy simply stayed out of that altitude.

"Word came through that Olongapo had been attacked at the same time we were and that most of the PBYs on the base had been destroyed. It was all so disheartening.

"Captain Wagner called the able-bodied together and brought us up to date on the situation. He said that a major portion of our fleet had been destroyed, or severely damaged at Pearl Harbor, that the Japs had hit Manila in force, and the destruction around us was the same all through the Philippines. He told us we were no longer a Patrol Wing or a squadron, that we were all under independent orders. We could go to Corregidor where the Army was, join the guerrillas in the hills, or leave the Manila area in any manner we saw fit. That statement left us standing there looking at each other.

"That evening I went to the mess hall, which was still intact, had supper, then went to a movie in Cavite. I just didn't know what to do. In the middle of the movie the back of the theater blew out, taking the screen with it. I left in a hurry, through the newly opened wall. Sailors were being shot, so I spent the night in a rice paddy. Later, they caught several Filipinos who were Jap sympathizers.

"There was heavy activity on the base the next day. Everyone was in an optimistic mood, having decided the Japs had made a fatal blunder by attacking Pearl Harbor and the Philippines. There was a 'picnic' approach to their preparations. The few Navy wives and many Filipino girls were packing for what they thought would be two or three weeks in the hills. Certainly by then the Japanese would be begging for mercy. Though we in the area had long been aware of the general Japanese intent, the enemy had successfully disguised his war-making potential until he was ready to unleash it. Now the military wives and the Filipino girls would learn the fallacy of their optimism. Many times since, I've wondered what happened to them. Did they escape, or were they taken captive by the Japanese?

"Soon we heard that Singapore had been attacked and that most of the English Asiatic Fleet had been sunk, including two of their best battleships. Our spirits sank lower. The British had been our last hope of supply. All reports were of Japanese successes and our losses were staggering on land, sea and in the air.

"Many sailors left — to where we didn't know — and those of us who remained began to realize it was about time to decide our direction. I chose to stay at Sangley Point, hoping that help from some source would arrive. But as the days went by, and the bad news continued, I knew it was just a matter of time before I would have stayed too long. But we kept getting word that help would arrive any day, either fighting ships, supplies, or both. We didn't know until later that we had been given up for lost, that we were considered expendable and that our supplies and help were being diverted to Australia.

Christmas Dinner: Sangley Point; 1941

"The Japanese shifted their attacks to other areas and for a while we were allowed to regroup. But with Christmas came the news that the Japs were landing all over the islands. Fully aware of our plight, our cook prepared us a final meal of the best he could put together. Christmas 1941, we stuffed ourselves with turkey, ham and all the trimmings. Then we began to scatter to avoid capture by the Japanese.

"I was lucky. I caught the USS Childs, one of our aircraft tenders, as she pulled in to take on oil. The Captain spoke to us on the ship's intercom saying we would remain in Manila Bay that day and evening and would slip through the mine fields after midnight. Once clear, we would head for the open sea with a southerly bearing. He said he didn't know where the Jap Navy was, or of its size. He wouldn't bet on our chances for survival but promised that we would make a damn game run for it.

"It was pitch black that night except for the phosphorescent wake behind us. We moved through the mouth of Manila Bay quite slowly. Clearing the mouth of the bay we headed south, hugging the islands. We spotted a couple of Japanese PT boats along the way, but apparently they didn't see us.

"At Ambon Island we pulled into a harbor that had a PBY base — all dirt and mud. They didn't have flights scheduled but their two PBYs looked in good shape for having escaped the Philippine debacle. While we were helping patch up the two aircraft with parts from the Childs, we got word that a PBY squadron was arriving to beef us up.

"VP22 arrived in groups of three planes, flying new PBY-5s. The crewmen had flight jackets and uniforms, reminding us of a time that already seemed so long past. Their planes had the latest equipment and they were fired up, wanting to know where the war was. We told them they would damn soon find out. They did, and tragically, too soon.

"The first night they sent out a patrol of three PBYs, none returned. The next night, three went out, and two came back. Then the Japs found us and bombed us out leaving the few flyable PBYs to head for Batavia, Java. I remained with the Childs which up-anchored and headed for Surabaja, Java.

"We were about to drop anchor at Surabaja when a Jap air raid hit the harbor. I was heading aft, about midships, and saw a couple of sailors standing under a steel ladder by the deck house. Suddenly a bomb hit. The two sailors, the ladder and the top of the deck house just disappeared.

"After the raid, the captain ordered all passengers to leave the ship at Surabaja. On my own again, I contacted a Dutch Air Force outfit. But they were leery of me without identification or anything to prove who I was. They told me to contact an American outfit in Bandung. I did, and they assigned me to a base radio station at Lembang where I stood watch, working PBYs on patrol in the Java area. It was terrible duty, but it gave me a chance to meet Si Simpson, the radioman who first checked me out in radio and who was now flying PBY patrols in the area. He promised to help me get into his squadron and on his crew. But it just wasn't to be.

"A few nights after talking with Simpson, I was on radio watch and began receiving reports from a PBY flying over a Jap convoy. The radio operator, whom I recognized as Si, sent data as to the convoy's direction, number of ships and their types. Then, after a lull in the transmission, he came back with the word that they were under attack by Jap fighters. That was the last I heard from him.

"After the battle of the Java Sea and the American, Dutch and English losses there, it became obvious that Java itself could not hold out for long. To avoid being overrun, our radio equipment was packed and moved out; all, that is, except for one transmitter, one receiver, and me. As all the personnel were leaving except me, some suggested such things as, 'If you push the Japs back, let us know. Maybe we'll return.'

"But I was left with my radio to hear that Jap convoys were just north of Java, heading south; that the Jap fleet was heading for Java and then that they were landing on Java itself. When I heard that, I decided it was time for me to leave.

"I destroyed everything of value and walked outside, wondering just how to get away. As if by design, or a miracle, I found a 1939 Ford across the street with the keys in the ignition. On my way to Tjilatjap on the south coast of Java, I stopped in Bandung and picked up my communications officer who was also looking for a way out. Along the way the roads were packed with refugees heading south, their few simple possessions on their backs, on carts, or in a few automobiles. Moving north on the same road were Australian, English and American soldiers on foot and in jeeps and trucks. The picture of doom was everywhere, on the faces of young and old, military and civilian. Everyone knew there was little chance of escape.

"I stopped at a gas station in a small village when the Ford's gas gauge pointed to empty. The station was closed and the gas pump had a chain and lock on it. I got a jack out of the trunk and broke the lock. I filled the tank, and we were once more on our way. We came to a bridge over a deep canyon where at Dutch soldier stood in the middle of the road with his sword raised. We couldn't understand what he was saying but it was clear we were not to cross that bridge. However, I caught him off guard, gave the car the gas and we roared across. I was afraid of being shot in the back for a few moments but we soon understood why we were being held by the guard. The bridge disintegrated behind us. The Dutch were blowing it up to stem the Jap advance.

"It was getting dark and we could see red on the horizon ahead. The distance and direction told us that the city of Tjilatjap was in flames. My communications officer left me at the docks saying he was going to check in somewhere in the city. I put the car in gear, stepped out, and let it go off the end of the pier. I learned from some American sailors that the seaplane tender, USS Langley, en route from Australia to Java with a load of fighter planes and pilots, had been sunk; that a tanker, the Pecos, picked up the Langley survivor and that it too was sunk.

"The word was that a couple of PBYs were taking people out of Java to Australia but that they were only taking Dutch. As it turned out, one of them was shot down near Broome, Australia, with no survivors. All submarines and major vessels were already gone and the only ship I saw was a small one tied up to the dock. I ran to it and jumped onto the bow as it was backing down to leave. I learned that I was on the USS Isabel, the Admiral's yacht of the Asiatic Fleet from Manila. Several days later, after a harrowing but safe passage, we arrived in Fremantle, Australia.

"Finally at a safe port, I set about trying to rejoin our Navy. It proved to be an almost impossible task. I was dressed in a Dutch Air Force uniform, with Dutch papers, and absolutely no American identification. At the Navy headquarters in Perth, Australia, I was told to get lost. Trying to comply with instructions, I had a few beers at a pub where I met two other sailors from Sangley Point who were in my same predicament.

"For over a week we tried to find someone who would believe our stories: that we were Navy men who had survived the Java and Philippine disasters. My break came when I managed to speak to the Admiral of Pacific Submarines. I told him my story, my commanding officer's name and the names of pilots who had been at Sangley Point. At last someone believed me. He had me assigned to a radio station at Perth where I eventually made contact with crewmen of PBYs who were gathering to reform VP101."

Gordon Ebbe: Davao Harbor — Mindanao, Philippines — December 8, 1941

Russell Enterline's memories of the first three months of war in the Far East differ little from those of then–Lieutenant Gordon Ebbe, except that Enterline's experiences were primarily on naval bases and aboard ship. Lieutenant Ebbe was a pilot with VP101 and was on duty in the Philippines for two years before war broke out.

Gordon Ebbe: Colorado Springs, Colorado remembers, "We knew war was coming six months before it began. It was no secret. On the night of June, 11 1941, they broke out a bunch of us. We loaded the PBYs with live bombs and just at dawn I was up on the step. I had my targets on Palau and was on my way. But just as we were lifting off the water, my radioman reached up and said the whole operation was cancelled. Two weeks before the war we had exercised our secret war plans, had rehearsed our responsibilities, and had caches of gasoline stored in 50 gallon drums all over the islands.

"On December 8 my PBY and two others were on 'advanced base' with the Willie B. Preston at Davao Harbor on the island of Mindanao, Philippines. I was scheduled to fly a guy, who had developed blood poisoning, to the hospital in Manila. Takeoff was to be at dawn. But the news of Pearl Harbor had come in during the night and nobody woke me until just before dawn. Bob Tills, the pilot of one of the PBYs, and a very close friend of mine, suggested we move our aircraft closer to the shore so they wouldn't be visible to the Japanese from the air. The third PBY was already out on patrol.

"Just after daybreak I had completed moving my plane and was back on board ship when the Japs hit us. Tills was still aboard his plane and was trying to fire his bow gun when they got him. They blasted both of our planes, sinking them and killing Tills.

"For the remainder of the attack, the skipper of that converted four-stacker simply out–maneuvered a sky full of Jap bombers and fighters. the enemy whittled away at our Cats on that first day but he couldn't hurt the mother ship. That came later.

"Several PBY crews joined us from Manila and we pieced together a small patrol force. We started flying patrols from several Philippine bases:

Davao, Jolo, Zamboanga and Lake Lanao. But with our main naval base at Cavite all but wiped out in the first few days of the war, it wasn't long before we were scattered all over the island chain. They picked us off one or two at a time until finally those few of us left made one last rendezvous at Lake Lanao and began pulling out for Manado in the Celebes, East Indies. From there we flew to Balikpapan, Borneo and on to Surabaja, Java. Several of us wound up in Ambon, a Dutch Naval Base off the west coast of New Guinea.

"On the day after Christmas we gathered six PBYs together for a raid on what was supposed to be a Jap cruiser and two destroyers at Jolo. Instead, we found half of the Jap fleet. Two of us came home. There were six Zeros after our plane but with our throttles full open and doing 180 knots they never put a hole in the plane.

"Of the four PBYs lost in that raid, three of the crews were either rescued at sea or made it back with help from the coast watchers or islanders. Lieutenant Hazelton, who was on my wing, got hit and had to ditch. When I was sure he was in control of his aircraft, I contacted him by voice radio and said, 'I'll come back after you, keep signaling your location.'

"We found them a couple of days later, all quite well, afloat on rubber rafts and in no hurry to be rescued. It seems Hazelton and some other pilots had given their crews a case each of Heinekin beer, packed in straw. When his Catalina went down there were 48 quart bottles of beer aboard. After landing, we pulled alongside their rubber rafts and found them drunker than skunks, sharing a copy of *Married Love*.

"One crew got to Manado. Two weeks later coast watchers radioed that they had walked barefoot across a mountain range but were all right. But Bob Hastings and his crew didn't make it back. They were picked up by the Japs and taken ashore at Jolo where they were grilled for information. From reports gathered after the war, the Japs assembled the people of the island and paraded the PBY crew onto a field. The commander of the garrison spoke to the island people and praised the bravery of the American flyers. Then he advised the PBY crewmen as to how they should conduct themselves when captured. Finally tiring of his game, he ordered each one of the Americans beheaded.

"During the rendezvous at Lake Lanao, I spent most of 48 hours hand-pumping the gasoline from 50-gallon drums into five-gallon cans. We then carried the cans to the wing and dumped them into the Catalina's tanks. The pilots gingerly taxied the planes up to the pier with an anxious eye cast toward a huge waterfall some 300 yards away.

"We almost lost one PBY when the pilot cut his engines too soon and the strong current drew him toward the falls. We were helpless to stop him. He managed to restart his engines just a hundred feet or so from the falls.

"After a couple of days we were ordered to Manado. But the Japs bombed it just before we got there, so we landed at Balikpapan. A few days later we flew to Amboina where the Dutch had a big naval base. From there we flew patrols back toward the Philippines, checking the Japanese advance and keeping an eye on the Makassar Straits between the Celebes and Borneo. Checking and watching was about all we could do. We didn't have a prayer to stop the Japanese.

"During this period, one of our guys was ordered to pick up a coastwatcher who was coming out of the Borneo oil fields. But when the Cat crew got there, the coastwatcher refused to leave his post, opting instead to have the PBY pilot deliver a box to the American Ambassador at Surabaja, East Indies. The pilot stuffed the box under his bunk for a few days before getting a chance to deliver it to the Ambassador. He almost went into shock when he learned the box contained one million dollars in U.S. currency. It was the amount remaining of sums designated to pay for having the oil fields in Borneo destroyed.

Late Night Enemy Air Raid: Fastest Runner

"The Dutch base at Amboina was nice in comparison to what we had grown accustomed to. In fact, they were in the act of building it up when the war broke out. We lived in unfinished Dutch quarters with cots and mosquito netting. In that area it was so hot we slept in the nude or we slept with a 'Dutch Wife.' This was a pillow like object about four – feet long and a foot in diameter. It was covered like a pillow, only pulled down tight with a string at one end. You slept with it clasped to you to keep your arms and legs apart, reducing perspiration.

"One night it was just too hot to sleep and I was sitting on the front steps of my quarters. About 0200 I heard airplane engines and knew they weren't ours. I jumped up and ran around trying to arouse the guys without success. Then as a string of bombs started walking up the hill, the camp cleared in a hurry.

"Our quarters were on a side of the hill. A road with a barbed wire fence and a concrete drainage ditch running alongside was our only access to a big beehive bomb shelter about 200 yards away. I was barefooted. In fact, most everyone else was naked and there were women and children in the group — modesty temporarily forgotten.

"Now I wasn't scared or anxious or anything like that, but one of the VP22 pilots said later, 'I used to be quite a runner in college and even set some records. But after Ebbe passed me that night, I'll never run again.' I paid for my speed, however. You just don't race carelessly on crushed rock. I hobbled around on very sore feet for about two weeks.

"We had been nosing around the southern Philippines one day and were coming back near the Spice Islands when I decided to take a turn around a small island with a big, beautiful bay. Something along the shore didn't look just right so we made another pass. There lay the USS Peary broadside on the beach. The destroyer had been worked over from one end to the other. I don't think they even had their radio working. They were in such bad shape they had beached the ship and were living under the palm trees. Palm fronds had been cut and were covering the ship to camouflage it.

"I landed the PBY all right but the currents through there were so horrendous that the Peary's captain had to send a boat out for me. When I talked to the captain I said, 'Don't stay here. The Japs are moving down on you. Get on your way to Darwin.' No one could have known at the time, but that bit of advice may have spelled their doom.

"There were many rescues, with the old PBY Catalina pulling off one miracle after another. One that hardly could be classified as routine took place out of Amboina.

"The Japs had sunk an inter-island steamer and a PBY crew from VP22 landed beside it, picking up 54 survivors. People were stacked on top of each other from the bow to the tail. The Cat creaked and moaned, but she made it off the water and returned to base.

"But we kept backing up. The Japs were over-flying the islands and it was only a matter of time before landing parties would follow.

"I was ordered to fly to Surabaja, Java to get more PBYs but found nothing. We were down to two aircraft that were in operating order. If we didn't get more we would have to pull out completely.

"Somehow, from out of nowhere, the Dutch came up with two more planes and we moved over to a beautiful little bay at Ende on the tip of Flores. But the Japs found us there, so we moved to Kupang. When they found us again, we hauled ass for Darwin. At Darwin, we flew patrols with three of our four PBYs. The fourth couldn't get enough power in one engine for takeoff and we had no spare parts.

"On February 19, 1942, the battle of the Philippines, Malay and the Dutch East Indies came to an end for the remnants of Patrol Wing Ten. That morning the Japanese, attacking in two groups totalling 242 fighters and bombers, struck the city of Darwin, including the docks, the ships at anchor and the last of our PBYs. They wiped out our four aircraft in brief strafing runs. They sank cargo ships and shot down four brave P40 fighter pilots who rose to challenge them. With no resistance, they systematically destroyed almost everything that moved. I watched them sink an Australian hospital ship alongside our tender, and the crippled USS Peary, the same ship I had persuaded to weigh anchor for Darwin, took a direct hit down the stack and just disappeared. There were 14 ships in Darwin Harbor that day, some of them ours. Most were cargo ships that had escaped the Philippines and Indo-China. Very few got out.

"We had no way of stopping the Japanese by that time. Why they didn't continue on and occupy the west coast of Australia, no one could explain.

"We didn't go unscathed ourselves that day. I had just left the area of the fantail of the Preston, when a bomb hit and detonated 14 rounds of ammunition right behind me. We were an absolute mess. The ammo blew a hole in the fantail and knocked out all the steering. Since there were two of us aviators aboard, and we could read compasses, we steered the ship from back aft. I had a crew of men down in the hatch with a big wheel running the rudder manually.

"In this manner we steamed down the coast of Australia, trying to reach Perth. Along the way, at some 26 knots, we hit a reef. The Preston shuddered over the reef without tearing a hole in the hull. But we lost all but four feet of each propeller. So, at six knots, we struggled into Perth.

"Struggled might be a mild word for those miles. As we pulled into Broome, Australia, we found the Dutch had just landed six PBYs in the bay. They were packed solidly with women and children survivors of the East Indies. But the Japs mounted an air attack just at that critical time. They sank all six PBYs. Each caught fire, burning or drowning most of the people aboard. We could only watch helplessly in horror.

"It does something to you to experience so much death and destruction. We had been forced backward — December, January and February, defeated every time and everywhere."

Ed Aeschliman: "We Sure Didn't Last Long."

Ed Aeschliman, now residing in Kailua, Hawaii, didn't arrive in the Indo-China war zone until January 15, 1942. But he wasted no time tasting the fruits of the American military presence in the area. In fact, his arrival dramatically impressed him with the stark realities of war.

"My plane left Pearl Harbor on January 6, 1942. The end of the line for that aircraft came nine days later near Ambon on the Island of Ceram.

"We were in a two-flight section, flying into Ambon from Darwin, Australia. We had already started our landing approach when Japanese fighters peeled off from an incoming bomber, fighter attack and simply took us by surprise. The other PBY was ahead of us and managed to land and beach itself without being completely destroyed.

"I don't know how many fighters were involved, but I well remember the sound of bullets passing through my hull. They sounded like a tin can full of marbles being shaken, only much louder. My first thought was, 'We sure didn't last long!'

"Somehow we managed to get both waist guns and the forward turret gun firing by the time the Japs came in for their second run. The net result of that effort was that an ammunition box was shot out of our turret gunner's hands while he was reloading.

"Still under attack, we hit the water and taxied as fast as we could for the protection of the trees and heavy foliage on the beach. After reaching shallow water, we left the plane and staggered ashore. Why the PBY didn't explode, with the fabric on the wing afire, and gasoline spurting from dozens of holes, is a mystery I've never figured out. We had no self-sealing gasoline tanks in those early planes. But when we returned to the plane after the raid, we found it so badly shot up that there was nothing left to salvage.

"Although we lost many planes operating in the Dutch East Indies area, we were very fortunate in saving most of our crews. The area was dotted with small islands and, unless a man was dead when he hit the water, chances of rescue were good. My squadron lost several individuals, but never a complete crew.

"We had one Catalina crew shot down near an island already occupied by the Japanese. At the time, we didn't know if there were survivors because their last radio message said, 'Under attack by enemy fighters — going down.'

"Later we learned they were picked up and sheltered by friendly natives. Some of the men were badly wounded and died before making it back to an Allied base. Those who made it hid by day and traveled by night. They were shuttled from island to island by the natives and reached Australia months after they were shot down.

"When the Japanese hit Darwin, Australia, in late February, 1942, I was on the water giving our plane a much-needed check. Three of our PBYs were on the water that day, and all were destroyed. The only plane we had on patrol out of Darwin that morning was shot down with one fatality. He died when the ship that had plucked them out of the water was bombed and sunk later that same day. The plane commander of that aircraft was Lieutenant Tommy Moorer, who later became Chairman of the Joint Chiefs of Staff.

"One of our tenders, the USS Willie B. Preston, was also in the harbor that day. On board, in addition to the crew, were many men from the squadrons whose planes had been destroyed. Her armament had been augmented by numerous 50 caliber machine guns salvaged from badly damaged PBYs. The flight crews jury-rigged these guns along the deck giving the Japs quite a surprise when they came around on strafing runs.

"A few days later, one of our planes landed in Darwin Harbor in search of survivors. I managed to be among those who were flown out the next morning for Derby. There the other orphans and I boarded the Preston as she headed south for Perth.

"The end of VP22 was drawing near. We started from Pearl Harbor in early January with 12 PBYs. We shared six Dutch PBYs with VP101 and VP102, which had been turned over to us at Soerabaja, Java. But by March 7, we had only two planes left.

"Most of the survivors from PatWing Ten made it to Perth and it was there that the three squadrons were dissolved. In early March a muster was held. We were told to line up in two rows, alternating as our names were called. When complete, we were told, 'This row will stay in Australia and fly with the Aussies. This row will board the Mt. Vernon tonight and head for the United States.' I was in the row which drew the Mt. Vernon. We made the trip unescorted, arriving in San Francisco in early April."

3

Coral Sea—Midway: The Turning Point

Historically, the turning point of the Pacific War came with the unqualified United States' naval success at the "Battle of Midway." Except for isolated incidents of naval encounters between Allied and Japanese forces which ended in questionable advantage to either side, the war in the Pacific had moved from one devastating Japanese victory to the next. Timing, whether by incredible genius on the part of the Japanese, or from sheer luck, always favored them. Whether in having the correct naval forces at exactly the proper location at exactly the proper time, or in taking full advantage of their complete control of the air, the Japanese humiliated the American and Allied forces in virtually every battle until June 4, 1942.

But a small chink in the invincible Japanese armor appeared one month before the Midway battle when combined elements of U.S. and Australian Navies engaged the sons of Nippon in a two-day naval engagement that, when over, had effectively blunted the Japanese advance for the first time since the war began. And, although both sides claimed overwhelming victory, the ultimate losers were the Japanese.

The Battle of the Coral Sea, in terms of ship losses — critically needed warships — and the possible future fighting ability those losses could represent, clearly pointed to the Japanese as victors. Their losses totalled one light aircraft carrier, the Shoho, and extensive damage to one of their heavy carriers, the Shokaku. They also sustained major aircraft losses from their heavy carrier, the Zuikaku; losses so severe, it was unable to engage actively for several months — long after the battle for Midway.

The United States lost the Navy oiler Neosho, the destroyer Sims, and the heavy carrier Lexington. In addition, our heavy carrier Yorktown was seriously damaged, and would have been out of action for up to a year had it not been for a near miracle repair role performed by Pearl Harbor repair crews in less than 72 hours after docking, enabling her to perform majestically during the Midway clash.

But the battle of the Coral Sea wasn't just a naval battle, with each side falling back to lick its wounds before returning to fight again. It was the battle for Australia and New Zealand. The Japanese, intent on taking Tulagi and Port Moresby, New Guinea, planned to build airstrips and seaplane bases to support the conquest of Northern Australia, and most importantly, deny the United States access to the Coral Sea. Their plans were well conceived and, properly executed, could have had a profound effect on the outcome of the war.

The Japanese approached the Coral Sea in early May, 1942 from three directions: A strike force of two heavy carriers, the Shokaku and Zuikaku, two cruisers and six destroyers, under the command of Rear Admiral Takagi; a massive invasion group under rear Admiral Kajioka, and covering group of one light carrier, the Shoho, four cruisers and two destroyers, under the command of Rear Admiral Goto.

The United States Naval force, under the command of Rear Admiral Frank Fletcher, consisted of the heavy carriers Lexington and Yorktown, five heavy cruisers, nine destroyers, plus the oiler Neosho and its support destroyer, Sims. British Rear Admiral Crace commanded a support group of three heavy cruisers and two destroyers.

In the early months of 1942, the Japanese did not have radar, even in the primitive form the Allies had developed, and this proved a severe handicap for them at Coral Sea and Midway. As ineffective as it was, our radar picked up a large formation of enemy aircraft in heavy weather trying to find our carriers just before dark on the night of May 7th.

Admiral Fletcher ordered the covering fighters of the Lexington to attack. The confused and disoriented enemy pilots from the carrier Zuikaku were routed, sustaining severe losses. The survivors were scattered, making a successful return to their carrier, after dark, nearly impossible.

Around midday, May 7th, Admiral Fletcher launched some 90 fighters, dive bombers, and torpedo planes from the Lexington and Yorktown to attack what had been reported as two aircraft carriers with supporting cruisers. Finding that the report was in error, Fletcher did not recall his aircraft, and elements of Lexington's attack group eventually located and attacked the light enemy carrier, Shoho. Joined in the attack by Yorktown aircraft, the Shoho was hit by two 100–pound bombs, erupted in flames and sank within a few minutes. Rear Admiral Goto promptly retired to the Northeast with his cruisers and one destroyer.

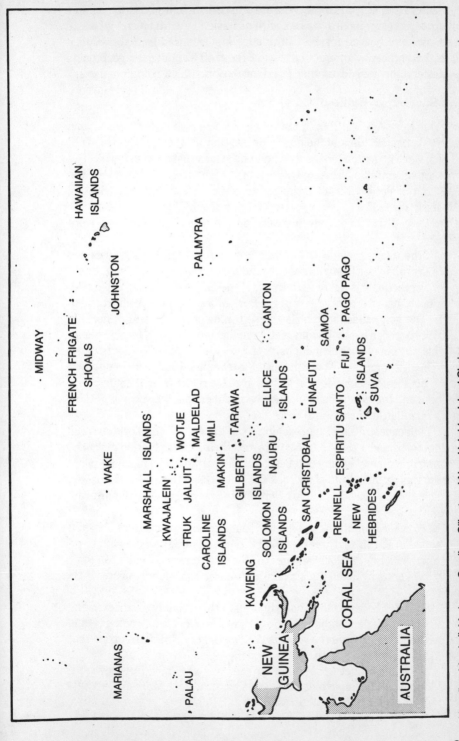

Hawaiian, Marshall, Marianas, Caroline, Gilbert and New Hebrides Island Chains.

Also around noon of the 7th, the Australian-United States support group, arriving at Jomard Passage with a mission to ward off any Japanese invasion force headed for Port Moresby, was attacked by Rabaul-based high level bombers. Admiral Crace drove them off without damage. Finally, he successfully dodged another large formation of high-flying bombers.

The Showdown Battle of Coral Sea

But Rear Admiral Hara's search planes found the oiler Neosho, and escort destroyer Sims standing by on station at Point Rye. The U.S. vessels were no match for the dive bomber attack that soon followed. The Sims broke amidships, sinking within a few minutes of the attack. But the Neosho, taking hit after hit, managed to remain afloat and, after drifting helplessly for four days, was spotted by one of our PBYs. The destroyer Henley was dispatched from Australia, and miraculously, 123 men were rescued.

In the evening of the 7th, Rear Admiral Takagi, having sustained heavy aircraft losses from the abortive Zuikaku mission, and perhaps thinking of protecting his rear, withdrew to the north. This move possibly contributed heavily to the failure of the Port Moresby invasion effort and to halting the general advance of Japanese forces in the South Pacific. Had Takagi proceeded south, he may well have flanked Fletcher, forcing him to fight his way out of encirclement or, at the very least, cut off his fuel supply.

The next morning, May 8th, both Fletcher and Hara launched search planes to locate each other's forces and by 0900 over 175 fighters, bombers and torpedo planes, Japanese and American, were winging their way to the battle of the Coral Sea.

The Japanese attack, approaching from the sun, hit the Yorktown and Lexington around 1130. Both carriers and their escorts battled gallantly, shooting down many enemy bombers, but the battle-tested Japanese pilots pressed their attack. Both ships took the full force of the attack that lasted less than half an hour. Both ships were still afloat and under full power by the time it was over.

Meanwhile, our attack groups had found the enemy carriers Shokaku and Zuikaku, but in foul weather. Yorktown aircraft scored two hits on Shokaku, inflicting major damage to the flight deck. Lexington dive bombers eventually found the Zuikaku and scored one hit, but inflicted little damage.

Both sides believed they had sunk all of their enemy's carriers. The excitement of battle, catching fleeting glimpses of fire and smoke, seeing the carriers listing, made the reports coming out of debriefing certain that the enemy fleets were at the bottom of the sea.

The Japanese fleet won in numbers and tonnage sunk. But they were forced to abort the important mission to capture Port Moresby — a setback which would loom gigantic just one month later.

Japanese Admiral Yamamoto and staff had a number of reasons for capturing Midway Island. Midway could be used as a patrol plane and air terminal from which to harass Hawaii. Capture of it would eliminate the United States' closest land base to the Japanese mainland. But one burning desire drove Admiral Yamamoto beyond all other reasons: he must totally crush the remaining elements of the American fleet. He had missed the U.S. carriers at Pearl Harbor, and he was well aware of the Yankee tenacity when faced with major obstacles. The American Fleet had to be drawn into a showdown sea battle and destroyed. Only then would Yamamoto feel that Japanese complete control of the Pacific might force the United States to sue for a negotiated peace.

Finally the time was at hand for the battle of the Pacific. With the exception of Yamamoto, perhaps, every military officer and enlisted man of Japan's imperial forces, privileged with inside information, was confident of total victory — most to the point of cockiness. And why shouldn't they be? Since the first day of the war with America, the Japanese Rising Sun had been raised on every island, in every country, and over every battle engaged in by its military forces. Well, perhaps not the Coral Sea battle. But hadn't they sunk the mighty American carriers, Lexington and Yorktown?

Between the 26th and 29th of May, Admiral Yamamoto's giant armada of fighting ships, submarines and support vessels began weighing anchor from Saipan, Guam and Hashirajima, Japan. With two occupation forces, Admiral Kakuta struck out for the Aleutians where he was to create a diversionary air raid on Dutch Harbor June 3rd, one day before the scheduled attack at Midway. With him went the carriers Junyo and Ryujo.

From Guam, Admiral Kurita's support group formed up and, at Saipan, the invasion force moved out. Admiral Naguma, with the strike force, and vice Admiral Kondo with the Midway occupation force, departed the Japanese port of Hashirajima, followed shortly by the main force, with Admiral Yamamoto leading 34 ships from his battleship, Yamato.

The combined forces of Japanese Naval vessels totalled 11 battleships, eight carriers, 23 cruisers, 65 destroyers, 19 submarines, scores of oilers, transports, repair vessels, over 100,000 men and some 700 land – and carrier-based aircraft.

Facing this awesome array of naval power, under the tactical command of Rear Admiral Frank Fletcher, were the combined Task Forces 16 and 17, with the patched-up carrier Yorktown, the carriers Enterprise and Hornet, eight cruisers, 14 destroyers and 25 submarines. Aboard the three carriers were a total of 79 fighters, 102 dive bombers, and 42 torpedo planes.

At Midway, under the command of Navy Captain Cyril Simard, were 32 PBY Catalinas from Patwings One and Two, and six torpedo planes. In addition to a small Marine detachment and parts of the 2nd Raider Battalion and 3rd Defense Battalion under Lieutenant Colonel Harold Shannon,

USMC, Midway had a PT Boat squadron, two destroyers and small vessels. The Army Air Force had some high altitude B–17s and B–26s. Under Lieutenant Colonel Ira Kimes, USMC, the 2nd Marine Air Wing had Vindicator Squadron VMF221, with 27 fighters, and SBD Squadron VSMB241, with 27 dive bombers.

Midway: Intangible Weapons In Nimitz Arsenal

With an imbalance of forces of such magnitude, the odds against an American victory were almost astronomical. But Admiral Nimitz had several intangible weapons in his arsenal, though neither he nor his tactical commander, Rear Admiral Fletcher, were aware of a couple at the outset of the battle.

One weapon was the overconfidence of the enemy. On June 4th, as he successfully evaded eight air attacks from Midway and U. S. carriers, that overconfidence may have contributed to Admiral Nagumo's apparent lack of concern at not receiving early and accurate input from the cruiser Tone's reconnaissance plane. When the spotter persisted in sending garbled and incomplete reports on the U.S. fleet's size, type of ships and location, a more cautious commander would have sent additional planes on patrol.

Another intangible happening that contributed to the success of the American surprise at Midway was the failure of a critical rendezvous between three enemy submarines and two seaplanes from Kwajalein at French Frigate Shoals on the night of May 30. This was to be a simple refueling of the seaplanes to enable them to scout Pearl Harbor for evidence of fleet movements prior to the Midway attack. But sitting there at anchor that night was a PBY Catalina. In fact, a U.S. Navy seaplane tender had been on station at the shoals since May 26, effectively, if unknowingly, thwarting implementation of Operation "K", the Japanese code name for the plan.

The significance of the setback for the Japanese can be better understood by the timing of Admiral Nimitz's dispatching Task Force 16, with the Enterprise and Hornet from Pearl Harbor on May 28 and two days later, Task Force 17, with the patched-up Yorktown. Had the enemy seaplanes fueled at French Frigate shoals and scouted Pearl Harbor, they would have reported to Admiral Yamamoto that the U.S. fleet was at sea, not safely at anchor at Pearl. Admiral Nagumo, commanding the strike force, most likely would have been more alert to possible American fleet resistance.

Timing worked against the Japanese when their submarine picket-line around the Hawaiian Islands wasn't set up until June 3rd, missing the sortie of both U.S. Task Forces. This blunder also contributed to the surprise achieved by the United States and, more importantly, kept the Japanese from knowing the exact make-up of the American fleet.

Seaplane Tender Tangier hoisting PBY – 5 aboard. (courtesy National Archives.)

Admiral Nimitz held three more aces over Admiral Yamamoto as the historic battle drew closer. Breaking the enemy code enabled Admiral Fletcher and Admiral Spruance to select a location of their choice for the encounter; the general size, deployment, and ultimate target of Admiral Yamamoto's armada were known for days before the battle. The Japanese had not deployed radar to a point of fleet use in time for the battle; the U.S. Navy used it effectively. Finally, the 32 PBY Catalinas dispatched to Midway toward the end of May, provided long search patterns, most of them remaining aloft for 15 hours every day for better than a week before June 3rd.

Flying 15–degree, pie–shaped sectors, the PBYs each flew daily search patrols of 700 miles out and 700 miles back. Most of these patrols were the typical, tediously boring flights that began just before dawn and ended at dusk; every member of the crew suffered from blood-shot, strained eyes. But on May 30 and 31, four PBYs ventured too close to Japanese patrol planes searching out of Wake Island and, at that stage of the war, Japanese flying skills enabled the enemy to inflict heavy damage on the slow-moving, poorly armed PBYs. All found their way home, but were badly damaged and one crewman was seriously injured.

On June 3rd, the PBYs of Midway were launched at the usual time but with perhaps just a touch more excitement. Intelligence had indicated the enemy most likely would come into range of the 700 mile sectors flown by the Catalinas on that day. And, at 0900, flying a southwest sector, Lieutenant (jg) J.P. Lyle came upon two small patrol boats with a heading toward Midway. flying closer for a better look, he found they not only were Japanese, but he came under fire from anti-aircraft guns. His was the first enemy contact report of the battle.

But Ensign Jack Reid and his co-pilot, Ensign Hardeman, were soon to flash the message that not only would advise their base at Midway of enemy fleet contact, but would alert both Admiral Fletcher and Admiral Spruance who were tuned to the PBY frequency on the Yorktown and the Enterprise.

Ensign Reid was nearing the far end of this sector, which was to the west of Lieutenant Lyle. Extra careful searching by himself, his co-pilot, and duty crewmen had failed to turn up a sign of the enemy fleet. A little after 0900, with the PBY gliding along on automatic-pilot, he decided it was time to change direction for the short leg of his sector. But, scanning the horizon ahead of him with binoculars, he suddenly stiffened and handed the glasses to his co-pilot with instructions to look dead ahead. Ensign Hardeman verified the horizon was black with the outline of many ships.

To the crew of ensign Reid's PBY, the Japanese Transport Group looked like the jackpot — the entire enemy fleet — and he flashed the message: "Main Body!"

Ensign Jack Reid: Shadow The Transport Group

For the next two hours Ensign Reid shadowed the Transport Group, flashing bits and pieces of messages as he dashed from one cloud to another, frantically avoiding Japanese attempts to blast his PBY out of the sky.

On Midway, Captain Simard, confused by the incomplete messages radioed by Ensign Reid and three other PBYs flying the southwest sectors, dispatched Colonel Sweeney with nine B-17s to make the first of several high-level bombing attacks on the enemy transports and strike group — all without confirmation of more than a few near-misses.

However, by now certain facts had become clear: The "Main Body" had only transports and oilers and their escorts, no carriers. The strike-force — that group most concerning the men of Midway — had not been spotted. Somewhere north of the transport group spotted by Ensign Reid and other PBYs from Midway was the true Main Body of the enemy armada. With that force would come the carriers and the inevitable air attack.

But over 1100 miles southeast of Midway, at Ford Island, several hours before Lieutenant Lyle spotted the Japanese patrol boats and Ensign Reid located the enemy transports, a plan was taking shape that would involve the slow, lumbering PBYs in another first in U.S. Naval history.

In the early morning hours of June 3rd, three PBYs from VP24 and one from VP51 were prepared for an 0700 flight to Midway. Ensign Allan Rothenberg was patrol plane commander of the PBY detached from VP51; Lieutenant (jg) Charles Hibberd, Lieutenant (jg) Douglas Davis, and Ensign Gaylord Propst commanded the three PBYs from VP24. Not one of these men nor any member of their crews had the slightest inkling of the hair-raising mission unfolding for them at Midway.

Lieutenant W. L. Richards, the executive officer of VP44, one of the PBY squadrons assigned to Midway, took command of the mission, flying second chair to Lieutenant (jg) Hibberd. Around 2130 they began their historic flight.

Though the weather was clear and the sea bathed in brilliant moon-light, Ensigns Propst and Rothenberg lagged somewhat behind the leaders, Hibberd and Davis. When the transport group was sighted around 0130, Lieutenant Richards had Lieutenant Hibberd circle the ships and begin his attack up the moon path.

Lieutenant Hibberd bore in on the attack, dropping altitude until he was some 50 feet off the water. The PBY slipped closer and closer to the large ship Hibberd had picked as his target; there was no sign of enemy awareness. Finally, at around 800 yards, he released the torpedo and yanked the PBY up and over his target. There was a moment of anxious waiting, then the blister watch called out an explosion and fire in the bow of the ship.

Lieutenant Davis made an additional circle of the ships and also attacked up the moon path, and though he faced no return fire, his target began rapid evasive maneuvering. Dropping down close to the water, Lieutenant Davis waited until he was 200 yards astern of his quarry before releasing his torpedo, flying into heavy anti-aircraft fire as he rose up and over the ship. His plane was riddled with bullet holes but there was no personnel injury or crippling damage.

Ensign Propst came on the scene about the time Lieutenant Davis was clearing out and flew his PBY into a virtual hornet's nest. Attacking in the same manner as his predecessors, Propst hop-skipped over a screening destroyer and released his torpedo at 800 yards, catching the full anti-aircraft barrage of the transport group. How he brought the aircraft through with only a few shrapnel holes defied explanation.

Ensign Rothenberg arrived much too late to effect a torpedo run with much hope of accuracy and was forced to drop in the general direction of the enemy group before turning back toward Midway.

As spectacular and daring as the Navy's first night-air-torpedo-attack was, and though it caught the enemy by complete surprise, the only damage was to the tanker Akebono Maru from Lieutenant Hibberd's first run. The other dropped torpedos simply missed. And the Akebono Maru was patched up and back into formation without delaying the schedule of the transports; but the Japanese hadn't seen the last of PBY Catalinas.

Back on Midway a frantic schedule of activity ground to a halt around midnight. Discovery of the enemy invasion force meant only that an all-out attack by their carrier aircraft was imminent, and that dawn of the next day, June 4th, was surely the time — Midway was the place. All areas had reported ready and a weary Captain Simard meditated the probability of his command becoming another Wake Island.

Lieutenant Howard Ady and Lieutenant Willian Chase of VP23 drew adjoining sectors in the morning PBY search effort of June 4th. Lieutenant Ady's sector was to center on 315 degrees, while Lieutenant Chase's was the next sector south. Flying a few minutes ahead, Ady broke out of clearing squalls at 0530 and saw two of Admiral Nagumo's aircraft carriers some 20 miles dead-ahead.

Howard Ady Report: "Enemy Carriers"

His report, "Enemy Carriers!" brought immediate reaction from Admiral Fletcher on the Yorktown. Waiting only for confirmation from Lieutenant Ady on the main force, the Admiral ordered Admiral Spruance on the Enterprise to launch an all-out air attack. Meanwhile Lieutenant Ady was dodging in and out of clouds, reporting the size and direction of Admiral Nagumo's strike force.

Lieutenant Chase had his own sky to contend with, and a scant five minutes after Lieutenant Ady reported the Japanese carriers, he witnessed the flight of their off springs heading for Midway; his crew counted over 100 fighters and bombers. He radioed: "Many planes heading Midway — bearing 220, distance 150."

Their mission temporarily completed, all PBY Catalinas were ordered away from Midway to French Frigate Shoals or down at sea, but not back to their base.

The battle that began with a devastating Japanese air attack on the two tiny islets of Midway, completely destroyed, or rendered useless, all but a handfull of the 60 odd aircraft defending them. They levelled most of the defenses but killed surprisingly few.

Lieutenant Tomonaga, leader of the Japanese air attack on Midway, realizing they had failed to knock out the landing strips, radioed Admiral Nagumo of the need for an additional strike. The strike never came. Before it could be mounted, Admiral Nagumo's four large carriers and their escorts would out-maneuver — without sustaining a single direct hit — eight attacks by high-altitude Army bombers, Midway and carrier-based dive bombers, torpedo planes and fighters.

But the dive bombers of the Yorktown and Enterprise finally found their range, and in less than 10 minutes time, sent Admiral Yamamoto's prize carriers Akagi, Kaga and Soryu on their way to a flaming death.

However, before the depleted fighters and dive bombers of the three American carriers could sink the fourth enemy carrier, the Hiryu, the Japanese mustered enough of an attack to mortally wound the gallant Yorktown. Then, just as it appeared she would survive once more, the Japanese submarine I-168, dispatched by Admiral Yamamoto to finish her off, fired two torpedoes into her midships. At 0500, June 7th, the Yorktown sank.

The battle was over, but for 10 days PBYs from Midway, Ford Island and Kaneohe scoured the scene, searching for tiny specks on a giant ocean. Back and forth they flew, every daylight hour until Captain Simard was satisfied they had rescued all survivors. PBYs rescued 27 airmen during that 10 – day period. The Catalinas were there at the beginning and were the last to leave.

Allan Rothenberg: "That Little Ensign At The Back of The Room"

Allan Rothenberg, Virginia Beach, Virginia, rose to the rank of Commander during his 20 years of Navy service and along the way proved, quite conclusively, that being a small man physically had no bearing on inner strength and determination. He was awarded the Navy Cross and the Silver Star for service far and above the call of duty.

Rothenberg tells of his nightmarelike first call to action in the Battle of Midway.

"I was the junior patrol plane commander of VP51 when the Battle of Midway began to unfold and, as such, became the only 'volunteer' when the squadron was instructed to send one PBY crew to Midway.

"At about three in the morning, June 3, 1942, they woke me to say, 'You're going to Midway!' Half asleep, I asked, 'Midway to where?'

"Eight hours after departing Ford Island, I landed my PBY-5A on the landing strip at Midway. My crew and I were directed to an underground bunker where we ate and were allowed two hours of sleep before reporting for briefing. I was asking myself, 'Briefing for what?,' but didn't let it sink in right away as I was bone-weary."

"When I arrived at the hangar, there was an ordnance crew hanging a submarine torpedo under the wing of my aircraft; for what reason, I had no idea.

"At the five PM briefing, Captain Logan Ramsey — later Admiral Ramsey — announced that the Japanese fleet had been sighted 750 miles west of Midway and was expected to hit the island the next morning. A decision had been reached to attack the enemy with four PBYs equipped with fleet-type submarine torpedoes.

"Captain Ramsey then advised it would be a volunteer mission: 'Richards and Hibberd, Lieutenant (jg) Doug Davis, Ensign Gaylord Propst, and that little Ensign standing at the back of the room.' It suddenly began to dawn on me that something had gone wrong with my luck.

"Captain Ramsey continued, 'Two hours to takeoff. Plane commanders will stay for briefing.'

"Then came the shortest briefing of my Navy career.

'Around noon today' the captain continued, 'the Japanese fleet was sighted 750 miles to the west. If you depart at 2000 hours you should intercept, by flying on a westerly course, about 550 miles from Midway at about 0100 hours. Find them and attack!'

"Then I remembered the torpedo they were hanging on my plane and I pounded my chest to restart my heart!

"Mine was the last plane to take off and was delayed by a ladder that refused to release, causing an additional time-drag of about five minutes. As a result, the other three PBYs had dropped their torpedoes, were on their way out, and had left a hornet's nest for us to wade through. But we dropped, didn't wait to see the results, and got out of there.

"On our return toward Midway at 0600 to 0630, and about 100 miles from the island, my mechanic, C.G. Lawer and waist observer, C.C. Roberts, spotted a sky full of planes high overhead. Their destination was never in doubt, so I had the radioman send a message, 'Many planes, heading Midway.' We gave statistics as to our location, the Jap's heading and their estimated speed, then we continued on toward Midway. It had been quite cloudy the night before. With some potential cover lingering, we considered the use of those clouds should we run into trouble with Japanese fighters around Midway.

"Then, some 50 miles from Midway, we received a message to bypass the island as it was under attack. We were instructed to fly on to Laysan island, a tiny speck, for refueling. By this time, all four planes were in the same proximity of each other, but not in sight. A big storm forced us to redirect our flight to another small island called Lisianski. Somewhere in between Laysan and Lisianski, Ensign Propst ran out of fuel and had to ditch. He and his crew were later picked up but lost the PBY.

"At Lisianski, we found Davis and Richards had arrived just minutes ahead of us. Our fuel supply was an old Pacific Fleet tuna boat with no pressure pumping system to transfer fuel into the tanks of our planes. We had about 30 minutes of fuel in our tanks and the only fueling method available was with 25 - gallon cans — hand - carried, and passed from the boat deck to the aircraft wing. While loading fuel, crewmen located themselves at various places on the plane manning bamboo poles to keep the craft from ramming the tuna boat.

"We were the last plane to fuel, so we played out the sea anchor and allowed the Cat to drift until it was about a mile from the ship, then cranked her up and taxied back to the spot we started from. If the small quantity of fuel we were nursing didn't hold, there were no contingencies for salvaging the plane. To make matters worse, it was getting later in the day and no fueling could be done after dark. It came our turn with just two hours of daylight left.

"As darkness fell, we secured the fueling, made the plane fast to a snubbing post with a life preserver and prepared to wait out the night. A Lieutenant Glanz, flying another mission, missed refueling and didn't have enough to fly on to Midway. He and his co-pilot chose to taxi near the island and tuna boat all night, taking turns at the yoke. At about 0300, whoever was taxiing fell asleep and rammed into the side of the tuna boat. He then bounced off my plane and sank.

"A damage check revealed that we could not get our floats up, but more than that, he had knocked off our pitot tube, eliminating our speed indicator. But we made it back to Midway the next day and flew the plane for several days in search of survivors of the battle."

Ercell Hart: Action At Last — Search

Ercell E. Hart, now residing in Kaneohe, Hawaii, began his naval career in 1937, rising to the rank of Lieutenant Commander before retiring to the active and inactive reserve in 1946. He piloted PBYs for several squadrons during his active years and served in the Atlantic and in the Pacific war zones. Hart's first contribution to the story of the Catalina presents testimony to the endless hours of frustration suffered by the men who flew her:

"As the Battle of Midway raged, with combatant forces deployed over some 350,000 square miles of ocean, PBYs continued to fly search, rescue and attack missions. However, not all PBY duties were full of action and thrills. VP91's PBY-5As were assigned to fly search patrols out of Barking Sands, Kauai when Japanese intentions to attack Midway became a possibility.

"On June 4th, the squadron was ordered to return to Kaneohe, fuel up for the flight to Midway, some 1135 miles from Pearl Harbor and to arm with as many 500 – pound bombs as bomb racks would carry and fuel load would permit. Action at last! Then came the advisor, 'On arrival Midway, deliver bombs to Commander, Army Air Corps; refuel for maximum search.'

"The squadron landed late the night of the 5th, happily unconscious of the touchiness of coming into a nest of somewhat trigger-happy island defenders who had suffered devastating raids from Japanese carrier planes not so many hours before. After landing, all crew members helped the ordnancemen lower the bombs from the under-wing racks and began the task of refueling with hand-cranked fuel pumps from 55 – gallon gasoline drums. Electric power and fueling facilities had been knocked out by the air raid.

"At dawn the next morning we fanned out on assigned sectors, looking for survivors or possible cripples remaining afloat from the retreating Japanese forces. An almost flat sea and good visibility meant good landing conditions if we should spot survivors. Long hours later, after scanning the surface without spotting so much as a piece of flotsam or jetsam, far ahead we made out something white. What? A lifeboat from either Japanese or U.S. Naval vessels would have been gray. But as we drew closer, it surely looked like a bottoms-up lifeboat. And as we skimmed along almost overhead, black figures in the water waved and splashed.

"My God!, I said, 'They must be all oil covered or burned.'

"It was only as we passed over them that we discovered the 'oil covered people' were albatrosses and other birds. The bottoms-up lifeboat was a belly-up dead whale, probably a victim of depth charges or other explosions of the battle.

"Those were the only 'survivors' our crew found that day, but other planes landed and picked up surviving airmen in rubber boats — tragically few."

Two weeks after the battle, a PBY from VP11 spotted a lifeboat flying the Japanese flag. Investigating, they rescued 35 survivors of the carrier, Hiryu; the sailors had worked their way out of the bowels of the carrier before it went down.

Thirty – four years later, Con Frieze, a machine gunner on the PBY, who had been ordered to shoot if the survivors committed any aggressive action, arranged a reunion in Tokyo with three of the men he helped rescue.

Milton Cheverton And Jeff Blackman: Torpedoes For Midway

During the war in the South Pacific, Milton Cheverton and Jeff Blackman were close buddies, flying for VP23. In a rap-session reminiscing their PBY days, the two former Catalina pilots, still close friends, recalled the Battle of Midway:

Milt: "Blackie (Jeff) was at the Battle of Midway. I had just arrived at Pearl Harbor, after they sent me down to Pago Pago from the states to join VP22. But those of us making the trip knew that VP22 had been wiped out before we left San Francisco. They got it in the Philippine debacle.

"When we arrived, the Swan, which was an old mine sweeper, really, but was considered an auxiliary seaplane tender, had its buoys out and acting as though it had PBYs. This was all a put-on because we didn't want the Japs to know they had wiped out the squadron.

"Then the cruiser Indianapolis came in and we got word that the Midway thing was about to happen, so went at flank speed all the way to Hawaii. When we got to Pearl, the Indy dumped us and led the diversionary group streaking for Alaska to make the Japs believe we had bought their 'main-target' as the northern U. S. territory.

"I was sent to Pearl Harbor and stuck in a great big underground plotting center at Ford Island, going nowhere, decoding messages from all the PBYs. When the squadron returned from Midway, I was transferred into VP23.

"We had a lot of our second pilots navigating for the Army B-17s because the Army simply couldn't find their way on patrols at sea. Unfortunately, they also had some of our pilots go out with Torpedo Eight at the Battle of Midway; that squadron was completely destroyed."

Jeff: "We had an interesting thing occur on the way to Midway. I had been in San Diego with a bunch of men to pick up some new PBYs; our squadron was so badly depleted at Pearl Harbor. About a day after we got back to Pearl, the skipper called us all in and said, 'Gentlemen, I want you to go back to your quarters tonight and say absolutely nothing to anyone. A truck will pick you up at 0300 hours and bring you back to the squadron. Pack a bag for three or four days.' We packed and later gathered in the ready-room.

"There to greet us and give us a little pep talk was Rear Admiral P.N.L. Bellinger."

'Gentlemen! This is your chance. God Bless you!'

"We were all looking at each other and asking 'How the hell can we get out of here?' We didn't know what was going on, but at the time, ordnancemen were hanging torpedoes from the wings of our aircraft.

"Now, Massey Hughes, our skipper, was an old fighter pilot and wasn't adept at flying the PBYs. In his southern drawl, he said, 'Gentlemen, we will take off in one hour in inverse order of rank.' This was what we used to do in peacetime. And the takeoff was a mass of confusion. Everyone was trying to get the PBYs launched off of Ford Island, into the water and into the air. Finally, they told us we were going to Midway — that's all, Midway.

"The skipper, forgetting he was leading a squadron of PBYs, took off and headed straight for Midway. Well, a Catalina can catch another Catalina in about 500 miles, if the lead plane isn't going too fast. I think we finally caught him at about the French Frigate Shoals; we were straining the planes for all they were worth with those big torpedoes hanging on the wings — must have been doing 90 knots.

"They took the torpedoes off at Midway and gave them to Torpedo Eight. After all the big preparation, we were just carting them out — 18 planes and 36 torpedoes.

"In the bunker that night, the Chief of Staff told us everything that was going to happen."

Jack Coley: The Midway Goony Birds

Jack Coley, who described December 7th at Kaneohe, Hawaii, earlier, was among VP11 pilots assigned to patrol the sea areas west of Kauai during the Midway battle. He continues his story:

"Before the battle began, we were detached to Barking Sands, Kauai, with orders to search for elements of the Japanese attack force.

"During the attack, a B-17 — short of fuel — landed on return from a massive high-level bombing attack on Japanese transports and escort vessels. The pilots had glowing reports of what they had done, but they turned out to be 100 percent erroneous. They never even had a near-miss. But then, it was early in our learning stage as to bombing capabilities and a maneuvering target simply dodged the bombs as they came down.

"The Battle of Midway reminds me of Midway's trademark, at least during the war years: The Goony Bird, a Northern Pacific variety of the migratory Albatross.

"Except for the Midway battle, and an occasional Japanese submarine venting its frustration by shelling the island, anything that resembled excitement was non-existent. But Midway had the Goony Bird and its weird behavior provided good-natured sport for many bored American servicemen.

"They were there in great numbers just before the war and, although we never hurt them, we made a game of altering their flight patterns in landing and takeoffs. When a Goony Bird has been to sea for a long period of time, he loses his depth perception, or something, because coming in to land during his first few days is an absolute disaster.

"We found that if we chased them down-wind, they could never get up enough speed to fly. They would start to run and stretch their wings a little bit, then further and further, really leaning into it, trying to get off the ground. With their necks stretched out and giving it everything they had, they just couldn't quite get airborne. Also, chasing them cross-wind and staying just a little ahead so they couldn't turn up-wind, they would try to drag a wingtip, but their span was so wide, they dragged the up-wind wing and couldn't get enough slippage angle to hold their direction. Their feet would go sideways, kicking sand. Finally, they would make it.

"The Goony Bird laid its eggs in the sand, and once hatched, the chick never wandered from its nest until it was time to begin flying. The chick's instincts told it that once its parent found the nest empty, it would never return again. If we dragged the little chicks out a little ways, they went right back.

"The most intriguing custom of the Goony Bird is the mating dance. Their motions and movements during the mating ritual caused many PBY pilot and crewman to copy, or mimic them. And later, in the states or at a more advanced base — usually helped along by available 'spirits' — these men became the center of attention, demonstrating the 'Goony Bird Dance'.

"The Goony Bird pranced around for a while, then paired off with its potential mate; each stretched its neck and moved it back in a herky-jerky motion. About then, one would stick his neck under one wing — we called it 'getting a nip of passion juice' — then he went back to dancing.

"When the Goony Bird is out to sea, or landing in the water near the beach, there couldn't be a more graceful sight. They soar, seemingly without wing movement, dipping and climbing as if magnetically suspended in flight. But when first attempting to land on the beach after a long absence, they put their feet down like hydro-skis, expecting the sand to offer the same smooth landing surface as the water. The friction of the sand causes them to roll up on their noses, then crumple in a squawking heap of feathers and wounded dignity. In a short while, however, they wise up and come in like a sea gull, backing off with their wings and reducing their velocity just before setting down."

4

The Deadly Aleutians

Unaware that the United States had broken their secret code, the Japanese plotted to divert American attention from Midway, their primary target, by mounting an attack on Dutch Harbor in the Aleutian Island chain. And, on June 3, 1942, the same day Ensign Reid made the initial contact with Japanese forces west of Midway, an Army B-17 spotted a Japanese carrier south of the Aleutians; thus began one of the most difficult campaigns of war in history.

Whether the crushing defeat at Midway prompted the Japanese to take face-saving measures by capturing Kiska and Attu is unclear. But one fact is clear: Of all the theaters of war in which the gallant U.S. Navy served, few proved more devastating from a standpoint of non-enemy elements to men and machines than the Aleutians.

Under the command of then–Captain Leslie E. Gehres, U.S. Navy, Patrol-Wing-Four PBY squadrons flew when all other aircraft were grounded. They patrolled when visibility was limited to the bow gun position from the cockpit and to a blurred rudder assembly from the side blister compartments.

In June of 1942, some PBY Catalinas were equipped with the primitive and often unreliable ASE "Easy" radar. All planes flew without the benefit of radio homing beacons, or mechanical-electrical devices introduced a few months further into craft compasses.

Mountains, jagged and grotesque in their few moments of visibility, rose from sea level to 5000 feet and more. Gale winds sprang up from nowhere, sometimes driving freezing rain horizontally at rates up to 80 knots. The sea was rarely calm and, when so, might change to angry, chopping waves before a PBY could lift off.

But the most treacherous problem of flying the Aleutians waters came from a combination of the ever-present fog and a completely unreliable altimeter. Rapid changes, high and low, of atmosphere pressure could, on a long flight, cause the aircraft altimeter to record as much as 1500–foot altitude when the plane was but a few feet from the water. And to add further interference with normal flight, the island of Bogoslof, north of Umnak, had heavy metal deposits, creating magnetic disturbances on ship and aircraft compasses.

One of the most thorough descriptions of Catalina problems during the Aleutian campaign is presented in Samuel E. Morison's "History of U.S. Naval Operations in World War II;" Volume Seven, pages 15 and 16:

"Blow high, blow low, thick weather or clear, they had to fly. This meant warming up the engines with blow torches, scraping snow and melting ice off the wings, loading heavy bombs or torpedoes with numbed hands, taking off in the dark, sometimes down-wind with an overloaded plane, and, if the plane were water based, with frozen spray obscuring the windshield. . . .

PBY-5A landing on mat on Aleutian Island in typical weather. (courtesy National Archives.)

"Any plane forced down in the wild, open sea was doomed, and unless rescued promptly, the survivors died of exposure. On the flight home, there was always the danger of being dashed to bits against a mountain while the plane 'hung on the props' over the field, waiting for a hole to open in the overcast. Once safe ashore, the crew had to help overhaul their Catalina. In the early days of the campaign, the PBY ground crews lived a sort of gypsy existence, begging tools, clothes, food and even shelter from the Army or any Naval vessel that happened along."

Patwing Four: Maintain Enemy Contact Until Relieved

As if the better and more equipped enemy, together with the conditions defined by Admiral Morison, were not enough facing the men of Patwing Four, their standing orders read: "If contact is made with the enemy: contact will be maintained until the patrol plane is out of fuel, is shot down, or is relieved."

But the men of Naval Patrol-Wing-Four took the PBY Catalina and, together, carved out of the jagged cliffs, impossible weather and freezing sea, an epic tale of bravery and dedication to duty that reads like fiction, but is true. The PBY pilots and crewmen took an airplane that, a short while before hostilities began, was said by some critics to be outdated, and they pressed the war against the Japanese so thoroughly, and with such consistency, that the enemy could not consolidate or expand his foothold on American soil, then helped drive him from that soil.

They paid a tragic price for their accomplishments, however, both in men and machines. PBY Catalina squadrons VP41 and VP43 on 10 June, passing through Kodiak and reporting aboard the tender, AVP-12 Casco, anchored in Nazan Bay, Atka Island. By mid-June, a six – plane detachment of VP51 arrived in Kodiak; VP61 and VP62 joined the Wing in August.

On the morning of June 3, 1942, Japanese Admiral Kakuta, with an occupation and strike force led by the carriers Ryujo and Junyo, steamed toward his first objective, Dutch Harbor. Protecting the two carriers and the invasion group were three cruisers and many destroyers.

A patrolling Army Air corps B-17 spotted the armada through a break in the overcast but was shot down before getting off a radio contact report of the group's position, course and speed.

Fully aware of the Japanese plan to attack Dutch Harbor by air strikes but unaware of the time or from which direction, Captain Gehres had all of his PBYs on patrol that morning; each sought to locate and report the enemy attack force.

Either the enemy or the weather, in the form of fog and snow, caused the loss of Lieutenant (jg) Gene Stockstill of VP42, flying out of Cold Bay. His plane simply disappeared. Lieutenant (jg) Jean Cusick of VP41, flying from Dutch Harbor also went down and, with his entire crew, was lost.

PBY pilot Lieutenant (jg) Lucius Campbell, flying south of the Aleutian chain, spotted the enemy force and began sending radio messages but they were received garbled and incomplete. Coming under attack by Japanese fighters who were flying cover for the convoy, Campbell dodged in and out of clouds, warding off wave after wave of Zero passes, absorbing armor piercing 30 caliber and cannon fire. His rudder control was shot away, as was the forward starboard strut; one aileron was damaged. A fire was started in the tunnel compartment, his radio was rendered inoperable, and one gasoline tank was punctured. Yet, Lieutenant Campbell and his gutty crew continued to shadow the enemy fleet, making four more visual contacts before climbing above the clouds and limping toward Umnak Island.

The Cat ran out of fuel 15 miles short of its destination, and Lieutenant Campbell set it down on the water in a dead-stick landing. Desperately, the crew began bailing water and plugging leaks with pieces of clothing and anything else available. The radioman repaired the radio enough to send off a position report and a corrected version of the PBY's contact. Their luck hadn't yet run out as a nearby Coast Guard Cutter arrived to lift them from the battered seaplane.

Too damaged to salvage, and posing a danger to the cutter, the PBY was set on fire and sunk with machine gunfire. But at this point, cooperation between the two branches of the Navy broke down. Lieutenant Campbell, fearing his contact message may not have been received by command radio, requested the Coast guard vessel repeat the message by radio. The cutter's skipper flatly refused to break radio silence, citing his orders, then continued his patrol.

A Scrappy Aircraft Tender Mothers Its Cats

A short while later, as the first wave of some 20 high-level Japanese bombers from Admiral Kakuta's strike force approached Dutch Harbor, Japanese luck, or timing, came through again. The cloud cover opened up. The bombers scored hits on Fort Mears, and inflicted heavy damage on harbor installations and crew quarters.

As the attack progressed, Ensign Jack Litsey of VP41 began taxiing his PBY for take off. At that moment Japanese Zeros appeared and began strafing everything in sight. One attacked Litsey's plane as it was about to lift off. On the Zero's first pass, two of the crew were killed and a third was wounded. However, when the Zero turned to finish off the Cat, he was met by withering fire from the tender Gillis and was driven off.

With little resistance, the Japanese carrier bombers and fighters attacked Dutch Harbor installations, quarters and aircraft, but the scrappy aircraft tender put up such a battle that few enemy pilots chose to sink that ship at a possible cost of dying for their Emperor. Fighting like a cornered hound, the tender gathered in the PBYs as they came in for fuel and provisions, then completed the dangerous fueling, and sent them back to their assigned patrols. The tender's effort continued, even as the battle raged around it, with many of the ship's complement at battle stations. Each man knew that one small incendiary bomb, or a spark form shrapnel, could explode the gasoline sending them all up in a fiery inferno.

Jack Litsey wasn't alone in his almost contemptuous disregard of the dozens of enemy fighters swarming in, out and over Dutch Harbor on June third. Several didn't make it. All PBYs in the vicinity sustained damage, and some crewmen were killed or injured; but the Cats came into the harbor under fire and lifted off again, still under fire.

By the end of the day, Admiral Kakuta most likely could have landed forces at Dutch Harbor with minimal resistance. His efforts would have been costly, but the long term results of capturing the only armed United States base west of Kodiak, with facilities to mount a strong counter attack, may have been rewarding. With Dutch Harbor in their hands, the Japanese would have effectively blocked all shipping in the Northern Pacific. With submarines and aircraft based at Dutch Harbor, they could have controlled all sea routes into Alaska and to Siberia.

But the wily enemy may have been lulled into believing he could capture any base when the time best suited him. This was still June 3rd. The devastating losses inflicted by the U.S. fleet at Midway had not yet taken place. Admiral Yamamoto's plan was perfect. There could be no failure.

On June 4, the Japanese hit Dutch Harbor with a second air attack. They bombed a hangar housing a PBY, destroying both, and made a direct hit on the transport Northwestern. Their bombing and strafing started fires and blew two fuel tanks. As with the day before, the weather favored the attackers by opening up the cloud cover over the harbor. But for all their weather luck, and all their obvious superiority, there was little lasting damage and, more importantly, a relatively small casualty list.

The PBYs of VP41 and VP42 were flying continuous patrols throughout the two days following the original contact, still desperately searching for contact with the carrier force. Around 0600 on June 4, Lieutenant (jg) Marshall Freerks, of VP42, spotted one of the carriers and its escorts. Low on fuel, but determined to lock in on the attack group, Lieutenant Freerks shadowed the carrier until he was certain all data had been properly radioed. Then, for good measure, he attempted a bombing run on the carrier. He was rewarded with a wall of anti-aircraft fire, knocking out an engine and making his return to base a nail-biter for all hands.

Two PBYs patrolling near Umnak, each with a torpedo under the starboard wing, picked up Lieutenant Freerk's report and decided to try their luck as torpedo attack planes. Lieutenant Commander Cy Perkins found the carrier, and after exhausting most of his fuel, put the slow, lumbering Cat into a long torpedo run. The lone PBY bearing down on the carrier drew the combined fire of the carrier and its escorts, almost blasting it out of the sky. Though he dropped his torpedo, his hopes of directing it to the target had been quite effectively altered.

The PBY held together. But not all patrolling Catalinas enjoyed the same luck as those piloted by Lieutenant Freerk and Lieutenant commander Perkins. On June 5, Ensign Albert Mitchell of VP42, while patrolling off Unalaska, came under simultaneous attack by nine Zeros. Although he maneuvered skillfully, and his crew fought back as best they could, they went down. Evidence discovered later indicated that some of the crew survived the crash, and made it to the life raft, only to be machine-gunned into the freezing arctic water.

Day and night, the Cats patrolled the fog-bound waters and islands of the Aleutian chain, sometimes making what they thought were sure contacts, but never actually spotting the elusive enemy task force. Fatigue became a factor, requiring immediate action by Captain Gehres. Sending out an urgent appeal for relief in the form of additional PBYs, Captain Gehres stressed the requirement as "immediate." Admiral Nimitz answered with an expedite order to Squadron VP43 based in San Diego, California and VP51 at Tongue Point, Oregon.

From VP43 came two units; one headed by Lieutenant Commander C. B. Jones and the other by Lieutenant Commander H. I. Ray. A detachment of PBYs from VP51 was led by Lieutenant Commander D. T. Day.

Beginning June 6, the Catalinas departed their stateside bases in groups of three, flying with bombs hanging from their wings and landing only to refuel and lift off again. All 18 PBYs were on patrol in Aleutian waters by June 10. With few exceptions, none of the pilots or crewmen had ever served in a war zone, let alone the likes of the frigid Aleutians.

While reinforcements were on their way from the states, the Army and Navy forces searching for the Japanese fleet in the northern waters were enduring fits of frustration. On June 5, attacking bombers and fighters of Admiral Kakuta's carriers struck Dutch Harbor for the third day in a row, inflicting some damage. Then the enemy seemed to disappear. Army B-26s and B-17s reported sightings over the next three days but the Cats simply didn't find a sign of the enemy. It was almost as if they had been swallowed up by the avenging northern sea; or, maybe as some suspected, they had given up and returned to Japan.

Japanese Capture Kiska And Attu

Tokyo Radio soon put an end to speculation about their location and fanned the weary flame of hatred and determination in the hearts of PBY people and all America. On June 7, Admiral Kakuta landed troops on, and took possession of, the United States' islands of Kiska and Attu.

News of the Japanese conquest of American territory was received with mixed feelings by PBY airmen of Patwing Four. Maybe now they could get some rest after searching thousands of miles of arctic waters for days

Aleutian Island Chain.

without let – up. Of course, there would be patrols to establish the enemy strength, and they would be called on to bomb and harass the invaders, but everyone knew that Kiska and Attu were worthless to the Americans.

Well, the men of the Cat squadrons hadn't reckoned with a furious homefront, one that demanded immediate action to recover the two pieces of American terrain. Within 24 hours after learning of the Japanese move, Admiral Nimitz ordered the PBY squadrons of the Wing to begin an around-the-clock bombardment of Kiska and Attu until the enemy was driven out.

But first it would be necessary to prove the presence and size of the Japanese garrisons, and Captain Gehres picked Lieutenant (jg) Milton Dahl of VP43 to check out the enemy claim. Lieutenant Dahl's orders were to fly his PBY to Kiska, get down low enough to count ships, garrisions and whatever moved, then do the same at Attu.

Captain Gehres selected the right man, as Lieutenant Dahl not only flew low enough to verify the presence of warships in Kiska Harbor but to count and identify them, to hang around long enough to reconnoiter the enemy troops, then journey over Attu way for more of the same. Here, he encountered a Japanese fighter and had to do a graceful job of dodging to clear out and head for home.

With confirmation of the loss of Kiska and Attu, the order to drive the enemy out by constant bombing became almost idealistic. All available aircraft carriers were busy at Midway and in the South Pacific; we had no airstrip within effective range for use by Army bombers. The almost continuous cloud and fog cover over the target areas meant that effective bombing would necessitate a very low altitude. So, although the PBY Catalina was designed and developed as a long-range patrol, search and rescue aircraft, every flyable PBY from VP41 and VP42, together with the new arrivals from VP43 and VP51, shouldered one more impossible task: Bomb the enemy out of Kiska and Attu. Do it around the clock!

Beginning on June 11, the Catalinas began almost continuous bombing of Kiska, operating from the aircraft tenders Gillis and Casco, both anchored in Nazan Bay, Atka Island. For over 48 hours, they bombed through breaks in the fog and overcast; when there were no openings, they dropped their bombs and hoped for good results.

Because there was little evidence their attacks were accomplishing even limited success, Lieutenant Commander Carroll Jones, skipper of VP43, devised a method unheard of to that time with a PBY. Flying on approach to Kiska Harbor, Lt. Cdr. Jones watched for slight breaks in the clouds. Finding one large enough for fairly good vision, he kicked the lumbering flying boat over into a dive, seeking a target to bomb as he broke through the cover. Spotting a target, he corrected course to drop his bombs, then pulled out of the dive a few hundred feet from the water.

At some point in most Naval fighter-pilot training during World War II, the trainee was introduced to dive bombing. The carrier pilot, flying early SBD dive bombers, became quite proficient in the art and contributed tremendously to carrier aircraft successes. A case in point: It was generally conceded that dive bombers from the Yorktown and Enterprise sank the four Japanese aircraft carriers at Midway.

PBY: The Dive Bomber

To take a slow, 104 – foot – wing-span patrol plane — the PBY Catalina — load it with 2000 pounds of bombs or torpedoes, fill its innards with nine American Navy airmen and, from 2000 feet, kick it into a 75 – to 80 – degree, 240 knot, rivet-popping, screaming dive, had to be an act more self-destructive than Russian Roulette. That is what Lieutenant Commander Jones started, and that is what dozens of other PBY pilots continued in the Aleutians and elsewhere.

For a time, over Kiska, the dive bombing tactics were quite successful; but the enemy soon diagnosed the concept and, when hearing the PBYs in the fog and clouds, trained their anti-aircraft weapons on openings in that cover. When the Cat came flashing down, it was met by a wall of fire. Against an aircraft the size of the PBY, accuracy of gunfire wasn't necessary. The Japanese only had to aim in the direction of the plane to riddle it with bullets.

Ensign James Clark and Machinist Leland Davis piloted two PBYs which were caught in concentrated machine gun fire while dive bombing through the overcast at Kiska. Ensign Clark lost his plane captain and a radioman was critically wounded. His port engine was destroyed, and bullet holes pock-marked the entire aircraft, but he pulled out of the dive and took his dead and wounded back to the tender. Machinist Davis brought his Cat back with so many holes that it sank before the tender Casco could pull it from the water. A few days later, Machinist Davis, at the yoke of another PBY, dove through the clouds over Kiska again and never pulled out. He was awarded the Navy Cross posthumously.

The Catalinas were not successful in driving the enemy from Kiska and Attu, or to bomb him into submission. They were successful in pinning the invader down, keeping him ever alert to their attacks, and exacting an appreciable toll in shipping, as well as sinking several large seaplanes caught moored in the harbors.

Though the continuous bombing effort ended after four days, the PBYs harassed the Japanese on Kiska and Attu throughout the year and well into 1943. The pilots and watch-crewmen suffered continuously from eye strain. Their every waking duty-moment was absorbed in searching for the enemy below, for the enemy in the form of a fighter, or for a mountain popping up out of nowhere.

Four PBY-5s in formation flight over Alaskan Glacier. (courtesy National Archives.)

Gordon Ebbe: "All The Stuff We Dreamed Of"

Lieutenant Gordon Ebbe, Colorado Springs, Colorado, the same Lieutenant Ebbe who participated in the desperate days of defeat and retreat from the Philippines to the shores of Australia, felt he had earned a 30 – day leave in the states. He felt, too, that maybe some stateside duty, training new pilots or the like, should be coming his way after what he had been through during the first five months of the war. He had served his country well and had never flinched from the call of duty. Now someone else could take a turn at the never-ending flights, the constant eye strain, and the ever present danger of being caught too high in the air by the pesky, but deadly Zero.

Gordon Ebbe tells what happened when he was relieved of duty in the South Pacific:

"My relief was supposedly on his way. Another two weeks and I would be rotated back to the states — a long leave — all the stuff we dreamed of. Then it happened. I was transferred to VP41. After two and a half years without a day's leave, away from the states, they gave me two weeks and said, 'Report to Astoria, Oregon, for re-assignment to VP41 and further duty.' I don't have to tell you, I was emotionally down.

"But I reported as ordered, finding Paul Foley as the skipper. He had us flying submarine patrols out of Astoria in what we thought was terrible weather. Little did we know.

"We had some of the first radar. The PBY-5A looked like a Christmas tree because of antennas hanging under the wings; there were wires all down the side of the fuselage. It was crude looking and quite limited but we had it and the Japs didn't — not then, anyway.

"In early May, we were ordered to Kodiak, Alaska, then on to our main base at Dutch Harbor. From years of flying in good weather, except for the monsoons in the tropics, to where we couldn't see a thing, the change was unbelievable. The fog was there all the time.

"After the Japs hit Dutch Harbor in early June, we started flying patrols out of Umnak, a secret base with a landing field. Since we were flying the PBY-5A amphibians, a landing strip was much preferred to those arctic waters.

"We did a lot of flying, and lost an enormous number of people and aircraft to the weather, but I was fortunate. I had a radioman who knew that radar and could see things on it that saved our necks time and time again. Once we almost flew into a vertical cliff, but he started yelling, and I had that PBY on a wingtip coming around. We were close enough to see the color of the rock by my window.

"To stay alive, a bunch of us made up rules on how to fly the Aleutians. It wasn't like any other place in the world. The altimeter was the most important instrument in the plane when we were flying blind in the foggy jet-black nights and heavy weather. But that thing would sometimes read 1500 feet while we were actually only a few feet from the water. Storms moved through rapidly, with high winds, driving snow and rain and still the fog wouldn't dissipate. The relatively warm Japanese current was just south of the island chain. Add that to the cold winds from the north and you get constant fog and a real weather mess.

"One night we flew out of Kodiak because they had such a shortage of Cats and crews. This was a 12-hour patrol in the usual soup. I tried to climb over the top but after a couple thousand feet we still couldn't see a thing. We were heavily loaded, and couldn't accomplish anything at that altitude, so I dropped her down to just above the water.

"Everything was strict radio silence, radar was limited, and Kodiak didn't have a radio range station, so we were really flying it blind. But, in spite of the fog and altitude, we developed a submarine contact on the radar — caught one on the surface.

"I ordered preparations to attack, but we were so close we just couldn't get ready before passing over our target. Our contact was gone by the time we made our second run, probably heard us going over the first time. Though disappointing, it was a definite break in the maddening boredom of the flight.

"Now we were completely disoriented. We had been out too long— and the sub thing—we had no idea where we were or our altitude. I had the radioman slowly run his trailing wire antenna out, like a fishing line trolling behind a boat. He sat there, letting it out–100 feet, 150 feet, until he felt the 'fish' hit the water, then he yelled.

"Darkness was slowly turning to day, and with knowledge of our altitude, we waited for a radar blip that would indicate an island mass. finally it came but what was it? Where were we?

"I put the PBY as close to the jagged shoreline as I dared and we peered through weary, worried eyes for some identifiable outcropping; from time to time I looked at a rapidly shrinking gasoline supply. Well, it must not have been our time, because we spotted a fishing boat and smooth, though oily, water. I landed, taxied up near the boat and asked, 'Which way is Kodiak?'

"They gave us a weird look but said, 'You're pretty close—maybe five miles just over the headland there.'

"Twelve hours of flying, most of it blind, several hours totally lost, and we flew within five miles of our base before finding our way.

Ebbe: An Emergency Off Bogoslof Island

"Just north of Umnak are the Bogoslof Islands. They're weirdlike, with a constant smoky haze around them, and the top of a volcano appearing and disappearing in the smoke and fog.

"One day the skipper called me and said, 'We have an emergency off Bogoslof. The skipper of a submarine is badly wounded and not expected to live. A shell exploded near the conning tower, tearing the guy up. His crew got him as far as Bogoslof and the Navy wants him picked up.'

"I said, 'Okay, but I'm going to strip down my Cat and take a skeleton crew.'

"We were only 80 miles from the sub, so we stripped the PBY of everything removable and loaded a minimum of gasoline. I took my plane captain, a radioman and a corpsman. Finding the sub was no problem but I almost aborted the whole thing when I saw the enormous waves boiling around below us; there was no quiet water in sight.

"I hung her on the props and let her in. The last time I looked at the air speed indicator it was registering 40 knots. Then we hit and without blowing a rivet. We sent the corpsman over to the sub in our rubber life raft with instructions to use his own judgment as to whether he could fix up the sub's skipper enough to survive, and if he could, to bring him back in the raft.

"They strapped the skipper to a Stokes-stretcher and sent him back through that wild sea on our dinky little raft with only the corpsman to keep it from pitching the guy into certain death in the arctic sea. Somehow, they made it.

"But now the fun began. Landing in that 38-degree water had been one thing; taking off from it promised to be something else. The wind was whipping up big waves and the Cat bobbed around in danger of swamping; at slow speed she weather-cocked. So I opened her up and boomed through the waves. I had to get her up on the crest of the waves to stand a chance of lifting off. We went through the first three, and by the fourth one, the cockpit windows just cleared the water. By the fifth and sixth, still hanging on the props, we were hitting the tops and finally cleared.

"The submarine skipper, a commander Williamson, survived but the PBY was mess. At Dutch Harbor, though, they replaced both propellers, patched holes and replaced rivets, and she was ready to fly again.

"How we survived up there doing the things we did, I'll never know. The Aleutians were a special kind of hell, and nothing short of the dream of going home kept the thousands of Navy and Army personnel who served there from going out of their minds. We fought a treacherous, cunning enemy in the Japanese but he was nothing to what we fought in the elements and geography."

Roger Brown: Fog Take Off—Watch The White Line

Roger Brown, a Newport Beach, California, realtor, was a "Buck Ensign" when he arrived in Amchitka, Alaska, as one of the replacements "for the dead of VP42". It was December, 1942; Ensign Brown had just turned 21.

"The squadron had four out of 12 PBYs left and their four-month tour of duty would be three-fourths completed at Christmas. Captain Si Perkins was Commanding Officer, and he had just been decorated with the Navy Cross for dropping torpedoes on a Japanese carrier at Dutch Harbor. Perkins was a reformed drinking man, holding prayer meetings every morning.

"The Captain sent a Lieutenant named 'Mac' McGlothlin to Kodiak to pick up nine enlisted men coming into the squadron as replacements. McGlothlin loaded the Cat with Christmas beer in Kodiak, and when the captain came to greet the new men he found a truck backed up to the PBY unloading beer. Captain Perkins asked, 'Where are my men.'

"McGlothlin, in complete innocence, said, 'But Captain, there wasn't room for the men.' Mac was severely punished, but we had plenty of beer for Christmas.

"Early in 1943, I went back to Whidby Island and went through Operational Training Unit, then back to the Aleutians on Commodore Gehres staff, reporting to Peter Boyle who was an academy graduate. I flew a mixture of anti-submarine warfare and logistics.

"When you flew for Gehres, you never cancelled a flight due to weather. Many times I was led to the end of the runway by a tractor, then I poured on the power and watched the white line. With two torpedoes or four depth charges, there was no single-engine capability. If one engine failed, you'd had it.

"A lot of people don't believe me when I tell them I took off with zero visibility. If you looked carefully you could see that white line right down the nose of airplane. With full power on, you watched the line and your airspeed, holding the Cat on the line until you got her up to 80 knots; then you reached down and pulled. That was the last time you saw land until later in the day when the ceiling would lift somewhat, if you were lucky.

"I had a friend named Stichfield, signed on as my co-pilot when I was at Whidby Island. After we had been in the Aleutians for a month or two, we were sent to Nome to pick up some civilians who had drifted up to an island, then drifted out to sea again. We never found them, though we made two trips and stayed overnight. While we were there, we got into a fight with a bunch of Russian pilots who were flying B-26s through Nome. We managed to get thrown out of all the best bars.

"On the way back, we ran into horrible weather. The water looked like an egg beater was working it. I was at the yoke and guess I just ran out of gas or something, because I got sick, dizzy and disoriented. Must have had vertigo. Before Stichfield knew it, I had caved in over the yoke and the PBY was in a steep dive.

"He took over and calmly pulled us out of the dive and into a normal flight mode. He was a funny man. He couldn't fly instruments for more than five minutes before coming unglued, but he saved my life and the lives of everyone aboard that day by keeping his head. That was his last flight. He transferred to Adak and served the balance of his tour on the beach.

"That was some aircraft, the PBY, and there was a tremendous amount of mutual respect in a Catalina crew. Each guy had a job to do and he did it. The team took the airplane out, did what was expected of them, then brought her back. We shared booze, too. The officers were usually able to get a quart of whiskey or gin, maybe wine or champagne, even with the strict 'no liquor' orders. Sworn to secrecy all around, the crewmen had a little nip or two waiting for them back at the barracks after each flight."

Douglas Birdsall: P-40 Pilot Down In Icy Sea

Douglas Birdsall of Upland, California, was one of the many PBY Catalina pilots who served in two totally opposite war zones: the Southwest Pacific and the Aleutians. After completing his first tour of duty with VP11, piloting PBYs during the Guadalcanal campaign and other South Pacific activities, Douglas found himself en route to Whidby Island and training as a Patrol Plane Commander in Lockheed PV-1 aircraft.

Doug Birdsall tells his story of a dramatic arctic open-sea rescue.

"Prior to deployment in the Aleutians, we flew to Alameda, California, and on to Lockheed aircraft to have the PVs converted to the latest configuration. Then they carted us to Amchitka. There I was assigned an enlisted crew and a PBY-5A. and between PV patrols my designated PBY duty was rescue. Other pilots shared this duty when they weren't scheduled for regular patrols.

"On December 8, 1943, I was preparing to take my brother back to Kiska after he had wangled a one–day visit. The crew was already warming the engines when the operations officer came barrelling down the road in an open command car.

"He said, 'Hurry up, Doug, we've got a P–40 pilot down off the island and you've got to rescue him!'

"I said, 'Ed, I've never made an open–sea landing in my life, haven't even ridden through one.' But he said there wasn't time to round up another crew, so I went out — trying to run through my mind all the things I had been told about open sea landings. One thing I remembered was to try to touch down right at the crest of one swell, and if you bounced off that, by the time you fell into the crest of the next one, you would be all out of speed and would ride down through the trough between swells and be on the water.

"We had a Navy doctor aboard. In part, here is how he saw it:

'On Wednesday, December 8, 1943, the visibility was unrestricted, the sky broken at 2500 feet by stratocumulus clouds; the air temperature was 30 degrees F. and the wind was northeast at 15 knots.

'During strafing practice, the propeller of the P–40 airplane went into maximum high pitch. Just moments later the engine failed. Having insufficient altitude to jump, the pilot rode the plane down, making a full-stall landing three miles west of Bird Cape, off the western tip of Amchitka Island. He was somewhat hasty, however, and released his safety belt just an instant before he hit. As a result, he was thrown forward and received a small laceration on the head. He had sufficient time to get out of the plane before it sank, but unfortunately, he had no life raft with him.

'Luckily, his wing-man knew this condition and called to a nearby Ventura to drop a raft while he was preparing to drop his own. The one from the Ventura inflated in midair and landed well out of reach but the P–40 wing-man dropped his raft within 50 feet of the stranded pilot. With his life belt inflated, the pilot swam to the raft, pulled the toggle that inflated it, and within 15 minutes from the time he landed in the water, was in the raft, though chilled and numb all over. He later stated that he had no feeling after he had been in the water about 10 minutes.

'Just 19 minutes after the first call was received at the operations office of Fleet Air Wing Four on Amchitka, the PBY-5A, piloted by Lieutenant (jg) D. M. Birdsall and NAP N. E. Yenter, a crew of three and Lieutenant O. H. Beahrs, started down the runway. The plane was in the air one–third of the way down the bomber strip, immediately banking to the left.

'Another P-40 pilot directed Lieutenant Birdsall to the scene of the crash; a third P-40 and a Ventura were flying overhead. Two small, single-man yellow rafts were easily spotted. The first was empty, but in the second, two arms were waving frantically. Lieutenant Birdsall lowered the wingtip floats and circled for the approach.

'We braced for the landing. I could see that the swells were high but not until after we landed did I realize they were 15-to 20-feet high. The PBY settled to the water, then there was a crash and the ship trembled like a leaf as the water covered the plane. We had landed in a trough and plowed through a swell. One of the pilots flying overhead said later that it appeared the PBY had gone right through the water.

'One pass was made at the raft but it was quickly carried away from us as we went up on a swell while it went down into the trough. The wind was blowing at a steady 15 knots from the northeast. A line was made ready while we made the second approach; this time the raft passed midway between the wing-tip float and the fuselage. But the swell carried the raft away from us, and took up the slack in the line. The frantic pilot, then, with the energy of an hysterical man, started to pull himself towards us, wrapping the rope around his wrists as he did so.

'Another swell came and his raft submerged. We called to him to give way — we had the other end of the line and no slack — but he continued to pull and the raft skidded out from under him when he was 20 feet from the Catalina. He was once again in the water. As he came down the trough, we pulled him towards us. It was a hectic moment, our thinking the line might slip; but he held on with a deathlike grip. The loops of line were slipping from his wrists as one of us just reached his hand by leaning all the way out of the blister. The pilot then collapsed, and with some difficulty, we pulled him aboard and closed the blister.

'We started removing his wet clothing but our hands were cold and we couldn't unbutton his shirt. With a knife, we cut his clothing away. Just as we were moving him forward, the word was passed along to stand by for an immediate takeoff. The plane was shipping water in a forward compartment. I leaned over the pilot, holding him to the bunk as the engines began to roar.

'The propellers cut into the water as we went up on a swell, then into the next and the next. The PBY gained speed and we felt ourselves bounced into the air only to have that sinking feeling of having the plane drop out from under us. It seemed like minutes before we hit the water, and when we did, I thought the plane was falling apart. A later examination of the plane revealed that some 400 rivets had given way in the hull. But once more we were in the air, and this time there was that good feeling of buoyancy.

'The P-40 pilot, exposed to the 44-degree sea water and the 30-degree arctic wind, had been in the water and on the raft for 55 minutes when we picked him up. After the takeoff, I wrapped him well in blankets. His extremities were almost frigid, the tissue being white, and he couldn't talk. Respiration was slow; the radial pulse was very weak and irregular. I feel sure the heart rate must have been much faster at this time, but when the survivor first came aboard, I could only detect a radial pulse of 10 beats per minute. All peripheral circulation was markedly decreased, especially in the extremities. I noted a small laceration on the top of his head. I had him take a few whiffs of aromatic spirits of ammonia and gave him two ounces of brandy, slowly.

'Through the blankets I massaged the lower extremities, buttocks and back. Flight jackets were used to help warm his head and feet. His condition improved and he mumbled he was cold. When I told him we were five minutes away from base, he said he couldn't stand it any longer. But as we landed, some 15 to 20 minutes after take off, his radial pulse was not so weak and was beating at a rate of 67 beats per minute. His body was still cold but not like ice, as it was when he came out of the water.

'We were back in 44 minutes from the time of our original takeoff. An ambulance was waiting at the far end of the runway where the pilot was transferred to a stretcher and removed from the PBY. In just 80 minutes from the time he landed in the water, he was in the hospital where adequate care and treatment could be applied.

'At the hospital he was put into a warm bed and later, into an electric heating suit; when I saw him a few hours later he was quite comfortable and talking again. Sensation had not totally returned to his extremities but there was considerable tingling. Twenty-four hours later, he was sitting up and eating. After 48 hours, there was still some numbness of the fingers. For five or six days he was quite weak and tired but a week after that he felt well; all body tissues appeared to be healthy.'

Doug Birdsall, his crew and the doctor, Lieutenant O. H. Beahrs, performed heroically as a seasoned team — specifically trained for just such emergencies — but not a single man aboard had ever witnessed an open-sea rescue, let alone participated in one. There is little question but what the underlying respect and confidence in the PBY's ability to hold up under such devastating destructive force helped calm the fears and apprehensions of all aboard, not to mention the man they snatched from the icy jaws of death.

Gilbert Mays: Fog Patrols — Attu, Kiska

By April of 1944, then Lieutenant (jg) G. I. Mays, who now resides in Sparks, Nevada, had already served a tour of duty in the Atlantic with VP53. Piloting Catalinas for VP61, Mays believed that he and his crew, as well as the crews of many U.S. aircraft survived the rugged duty in the Aleutians in part because of the Navy's Loran Navigational System. Loran wasn't developed in time for the early months of the far-north encounter, but it became standard equipment by early 1943.

Gil Mays begins his story in late 1943 with the battle for recovery of the American island of Attu in the Aleutian chain.

"Visibility was an almost forgotten word in the Aleutians. It was nothing to take off with a 50 – foot ceiling, a quarter – mile visibility, and the wind blowing a gale. When flying out of Attu, we got off, pulled the gear up, and flew into the soup. After 14 hours we returned, made a letdown on Murder Point Range in the same crap, and never saw a thing. Our squadron flew in that weather for almost a year. Five hundred hours of actual IFR (Instrument Flight Rules) was not a novelty among VP61 pilots.

"In late 1943 the U.S. Army fought a little – remembered battle with the Japanese over possession of the island of Attu, the most westerly island of the Aleutian chain. After securing the island, attention of the armed forces was then focused on Kiska, located approximately 400 miles to the east. Fortunately, and much to the relief of everyone concerned, the Japanese had evacuated their troops under the cover of fog sometime prior to the arrival of United States landing forces.

"To guard against a possible Japanese attempt to reoccupy the Aleutian chain, VP61 began blanketing patrols to westward.

"Our area of responsibility was divided into eight sectors. The southernmost and longest took from 11 to 14 hours flying time, depending on the wind. Flying sector-eight to the northwest was like getting a day off as flying time for this trip was approximately eight hours. These northwest sectors were favored by the crew, not only for their brevity, but because we came within sight of Kamchatka Peninsula of the USSR. Our alternate landing strip in case we lost an engine, incidentally, was Petropavlousk, situated on the peninsula. We weren't exactly thrilled over the prospect of such a landing in that Russian internment awaited us.

"On the return trip, when favorable weather conditions prevailed, we often flew in the proximity of Komandorskie Islands, though we gave them wide berth because some of our aircraft had drawn Russian anti-aircraft fire when venturing too close.

"I first became aware of the Loran Navigational System in April of 1944. The PBY-5As we had picked up in San Diego and ferried to Ault Field on Whidby Island were equipped with a highly secret black box situated on a corner of the navigator's table. We were instructed not to remove the black cover until we reached Adak, a stop on our flight to Attu. Upon arriving at Adak in mid-April, the pilots were given a one week indoctrination course on the use of this amazing piece of navigation gear.

"Considering the fact we were flying in Aleutian weather with nothing more than primitive radar, low frequency radio, and ADF (Automatic Direction Finder), Loran was most certainly instrumental in saving the lives of many, if not all, of our aircraft crews. With Loran we were able to navigate to within one mile of the actual position of the aircraft.

"The approach to the runway on Attu was always the same, almost directly north on the southern leg of Murder Point radio range station. After passing the low cone, we began a letdown to a minimum altitude of 50 feet. On most letdowns the visibility was such that we depended on the radio altimeter set at 50 feet for purpose of wave-offs. If we didn't have visual contact at 50 feet, we initiated an emergency wave-off for another approach or fly to the only alternate field available on Shimya Island, 100 miles or so to the east. More often than not, if the sea was calm, we would try to find an open spot to the south of the island and land, then bird-dog in on the ADF and taxi up a ramp.

"On one such approach, we came upon the 50–foot minimum as indicated by the red light on our instrument panel. It was raining so hard that the windshield wipers were completely ineffective. We initiated the emergency wave-off which consisted of a sharp climbing turn to the right. But the pilot in the left seat that day, perhaps influenced by vertigo, started a turn to the left and toward a steep mountain. There was no time for explanations. I relieved him of the controls by physically overpowering him and made the correct turn.

"It is not surprising that he took umbrage to my action; for the pressure of flying under those conditions and with the primitive equipment we were using was at times almost unbearable. Tempers were short and flared often.

"The Air Wing Commander on Attu in 1944 was one Commodore Leslie Gehres, USN. He was commonly referred to as the 'Big Ensign,' obviously alluding to the two-inch stripe on his sleeve.

"Perhaps some who were present on Attu at the time may recall the steam–heated barn that housed a cow and chickens which the Commodore had brought in to supply his staff with dairy products. The fact that critical space was taken on the weekly mailplane to import feed for the livestock was not well received. The resident rooster was greatly admired, however, for in the strictly masculine community that existed on Attu, he was the only male getting any action."

Most naval aviators will readily agree that the toughest part of wartime flying is losing a friend and fellow pilot.

Ensign Norman Hill: The Deadly Call — Stormy Night Rescue

"Ensign Norman Hill, a young man of perhaps 22, as we all were, roomed with four other officers and myself in a Quonset hut on Attu. Because our flights were staggered, some pilots were flying, some had standby duty, while others had the day off.

"One particularly windy, blustery night around 2300, we received word that a PV-1 was down in the open sea. Ensign Hill was a member of the duty crew and thus was awakened by a messenger when the rescue call came in.

"I was seated in a part of the Quonset that we used as a lounge. As he brushed past me, he stopped and put his foot on the armrest of the couch I was occupying. He said nothing as he adjusted the oversized foul-weather boots which were part of our flight gear. I looked up from the book I was reading and said, 'I'll see you tomorrow, Norman.'

"He turned and sadly answered, 'Yeah, maybe!'

"I never saw Norman again. The following day we found some debris belonging to his aircraft a few miles off shore. No trace of the PV-1 crew was ever found and they were joined by the 10 men in Norman's crew. For many years I wondered who made the idiotic decision to send a crew out on that miserable night.

"Another incident, this time one from VP43, involved a friend of mine and a PBY5-A. For reasons I no longer recall, they had ditched their aircraft approximately 80 miles south of Attu, near the island of Agattu.

"There were heavy seas and a blinding snow squall that day, but the crew managed to inflate and board the two ten-men life rafts that were standard equipment on all aircraft flying those waters. Shortly after they went down, they were spotted by a PBY crew from VP62 and the pilot circled the Catalina around the downed crew until darkness forced him to abandon the rafts. But before leaving the area, he reported that the crew appeared alive and well.

"A destroyer had been dispatched from Admiral Fletcher's North Pacific Force to effect a rescue but arrived at the crew's last known position after dark and therefore could not locate them.

"To the best of my memory, the rafts were spotted again the next afternoon by a PV-1 crew from VP139 but when the destroyer reached them the next day all hands had died of exposure.

"The only justification for flying in that God-forsaken part of the world was, of course, to investigate ship movements we had detected visually or by radar. Contacts were almost exclusively made by our very excellent radarmen. Upon making radar contact we initiated a letdown. If we were in solid IFR conditions, which was 90 percent of the time, we were 'homed' in by radar. We set the altimeter at about 150 feet to ensure clearing all masts. If visual contact was made, we were directed to challenge via blinker and request identification.

"One particular day, socked in by the usual zero-visibility fog, we detected a ship by radar and commenced our letdown procedure. Evidently, he had picked us up as well for when we passed over him he was ready and fired some device. We heard an explosion and felt a thump somewhere out on the port wing. The control function and maneuverability of the aircraft were unimpaired, however, so we completed the flight without further incident.

"When we landed at Attu and inspected the wing, we found a hole about six inches in diameter. Most fortunately, the damage occurred in a non-critical part of the wing."

Perhaps the last major planned aggressive action by PBY personnel in the Aleutian campaign was the reconnaissance and bombing missions during December of 1943 and January of 1944 on installations in the Paramushiro-Shimushu area of Japan.

Developing their weather, enemy resistance and target areas from assumption, rather than facts, two PBYs from VP43 ventured out from Attu on the night of 22 December 1943. Their journey carried them 665 miles from base, and should have taxed the range and endurance capability of the PBY. But the Cats got there and back, even lingering over the target area for over an hour, photographing enemy installations, before one plane finally dropped its bombs. Three more such missions were carried out by other PBY crews before sufficient information was collected to complete their assignment.

Following is the text of a suggested citation for one of the PBY pilots participating in one of the missions just described: "Suggest Citation for Award of Distinguished Flying Cross to: Lieutenant (jg) Carl O. Riedel, A-V(N), USNR.

CITATION

For heroism and extraordinary achievement in aerial flight, Lt. (jg) Carl O. Riedel, A-V(N), USNR, as commander of a patrol seaplane of Patrol Squadron Forty-Three, made the first flight of an Attu-based U.S. aircraft ever to successfully complete a night reconnaissance bombing mission of the enemy Japanese bases in the Parasmushiro-Shimushu area, Kurile Islands, Japan. This night mission was accomplished at great personal risk, in mid-winter, under extremely hazardous and almost unpredictable weather conditions, with aircraft having no margin of range and speed to insure safe return in case of any error in forecasting or navigation, and with no knowledge of the enemy opposition and defenses to be encountered. It required the utmost piloting ability, courage and devotion to duty. In spite of bad weather conditions over the target, and fire of anti-aircraft batteries, Lt. (jg) Riedel remained in the target area for an hour and 15 minutes, until his position was certain and a clearing of the weather occurred, whereupon he proceeded with his photographic and bombing runs. In addition to possible damage inflicted on the enemy by bombs dropped, valuable information was obtained concerning new enemy installations from photographs made on this mission. Lt. (jg) Riedel's conduct, courage and devotion to duty and superb piloting skill on this occasion was in keeping with the best traditions of the United States Navy and its Naval Air Service.

The PBY Catalinas of Fleet Air Wing Four helped drive the Japanese from Attu in May of 1943, then were present at the discovery of the Japanese abandonment of Kiska in July. And though the enemy no longer held American territory, they kept a force in the Aleutians until late in the war, in the most part, by submarines and long range recon' bombers. The U.S. military was determined that the area would never again fall prey to the enemy and to assure that end the PBY squadrons remained on duty, patrolling, harassing submarines and performing rescue missions until the war moved to the shores of Japan.

5

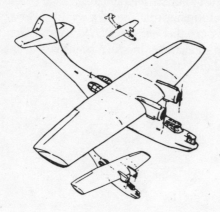

The Neutrality Patrol

On Friday, September 1, 1939, Hitler's ground and air forces invaded Poland. Two days later, Great Britain, France, Australia, and New Zealand declared war on Germany, and World War II had its first declared adversaries. In the months and years to follow, nation after nation became involved until virtually all peoples of the world participated or contributed to one side or both.

The United States, not yet accepting what we considered small appreciation for our role in World War I, declared our complete neutrality. President Franklin Roosevelt announced that the U.S. would abide by the Neutrality Act of 1936 which prohibited the shipment of arms and munitions to belligerent nations; this he did to emphasize our neutral stand.

On Tuesday, September 5th, President Roosevelt ordered the Navy to form a "Neutrality Patrol," its function was to shadow and report on belligerent air and sea craft. This included watching aircraft, submarines and surface vessels venturing near the Atlantic coast or Caribbean zone of American influence.

It was at this time that the PBY, Consolidated Aircraft's patrol bomber, began its illustrious career, a career threatened in those early war days by detractors within the armed forces who considered the aircraft obsolete.

But the "Cat" was not yet ready to quit. The Navy formed five PBY squadrons, each with 12 planes, to fly the Air-Wing of the Neutrality

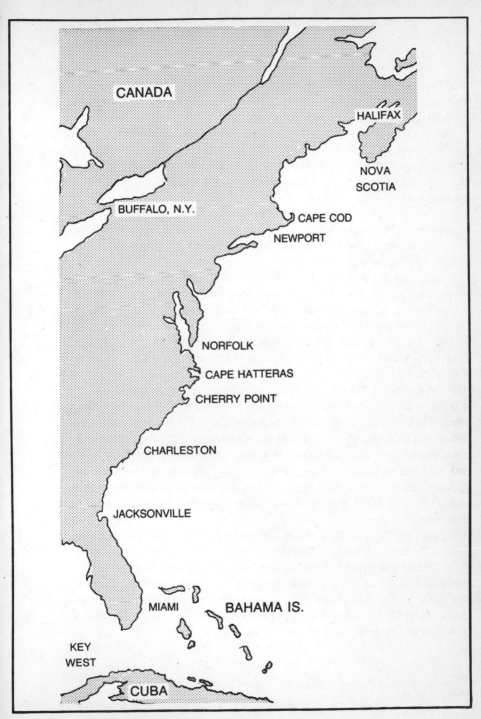

CANADA

HALIFAX

NOVA
SCOTIA

BUFFALO, N.Y.

CAPE COD

NEWPORT

NORFOLK

CAPE HATTERAS

CHERRY POINT

CHARLESTON

JACKSONVILLE

MIAMI

BAHAMA IS.

KEY
WEST

CUBA

United States and Canadian East Coast.

Patrol. The squadrons were designated VP33, VP51, VP52, VP53 and VP54 and they were assigned to sea bases at Norfolk, Virginia, Charleston, South Carolina, Coco Solo, Panama, and Guantanamo Bay, Cuba.

These were the early days of PBY activities. Although the aircraft had been in Navy service for several years, there had been no requirements of a continuing nature to test the ability of the machine or of the men who flew it. Training flights of a specific nature practiced one week often became routine doctrine for months to follow. To assist in developing their skills as bombers, the PBY crews carried water-filled bombs to be dropped on predetermined targets from various altitudes and modes of flight attitude. The beginning patrols were of four – hour duration, usually not more than a couple hundred miles out to sea.

Soon, the careful training and preparations were put to test in long tedious hours of semi-secret convoy coverage of Allied shipping because Germany began flexing its muscles with a weapon most certain to achieve results; the German submarine, more commonly known as the U-Boat.

Although post-war data has revealed that Hitler did not plan the devastating submarine blitz, it proved to be more damaging to Great Britain's battle for survival than either her humiliating losses on the battle fields of Europe or the subsequent saturation bombing of her cities by the German Luftwaffe. Literally hundreds of British and neutral merchant vessels, together with a large percentage of Britain's armed escort ships, were sunk by the U-Boats before the United States entered the war.

But Germany had only 50 submarines available for service when war was declared and production was a mere two-to-four per month. Grand Admiral Eric Raeder, Commander-in-Chief of the German Navy, convinced Hitler to greatly increase submarine output to as many as 25 each month. Thus, under the skillful leadership of Commodore Karl Doenitz, the German land and air blitzes of Europe were nearly upstaged by the lowly-regarded German Navy. This became even more evident after the fall of France; French ports provided much wider operating ranges for the U-Boat fleet.

Hitler had wanted to keep the United States and Great Britain out of the war by whatever means possible, short of halting the blitz, until after the occupation of Europe. Succeeding in that, he then would have attacked Britain in 1944 in an all-out push to bring the island kingdom to its knees in short order. With Europe and Britain under his control, he would sue the United States for peace on his terms. But Great Britain wouldn't play the game his way and declared war just two days after he invaded Poland.

German U-Boat Policy: "Sink At Sight"

On September 4th, the day after war was declared, the British passenger ship Athenia was torpedoed by the German U-Boat U-30 with the loss of 112 civilian lives. With that sinking, the German policy of "sink at sight" began.

The Royal Navy began arming merchant vessels as quickly as its pitifully few gun crews and cannons could be mustered. At the outset of war, arms were available for fewer than one quarter of England's merchant ships. But armed convoys were formed, first at Kingston, then at Halifax, where the Royal Canadian Navy took over escort responsibilities. Armed with four – inch cannons, machine guns and depth charges, and equipped with echo gear, the Corvettes and Frigates provided excellent protection to the limit of their range. No merchant vessels were sunk in the Canadian-escorted Halifax-to-Britain convoys in the early months of the war.

In the first week of the war, in spite of its clearly declared neutrality, the United States was shaken by an attack on the destroyer USS Greer by a German U-Boat. The Greer dodged two torpedoes launched by the U-Boat and responded with depth charges which also missed their mark.

President Roosevelt called the attack an act of piracy and declared: "From now on, if German or Italian vessels of war enter waters, the protection of which is necessary for American defense, they do so at their own risk."

The lines were now clearly drawn and a state of de-facto war existed between the United States and the Axis nations. But resistance remained within the U.S. government to any form of assistance to Great Britain; and Roosevelt, who knew the price America would pay should Hitler succeed in world domination, was put to the strongest test of his political career.

His first success, though hotly contested, was convincing the nations of the Western Hemisphere to make the Neutrality Patrol a "United Policy of the Americas". This was accomplished on October 2nd by the "Act of Panama" and was adopted for the express purpose of keeping the European war out of the Americas. Canada, of course, was not included in the agreement since she was already at war with the Axis nations.

A protective zone, approximately 300 miles wide, was set up from the Atlantic coast of the United States to the southern tip of South America. But its effect, other than to solidify the American nations, would have been negligible had Hitler chosen to challenge it in the early months of the war. The U.S. had the only vessels of war, to speak of, and those had been allowed to deteriorate as a result of the nation's pacifistic policy following the end of World War I.

United States Naval forces in the Atlantic consisted of three old battleships, four heavy cruisers, the aircraft carrier Ranger and a destroyer squadron. The naval air arm consisted almost entirely of the five PBY squadrons, each with 12 planes. This small force of ships and aircraft was charged with the task of patrolling thousands of miles of American coastlines washed by the Atlantic ocean.

When Hitler discovered his efforts to crush Britain were failing, his naval advisors, led by the persistent Commodore Doenitz, chose that time to convince their Fuehrer to allow them to concentrate their growing arsenal of U-Boats on the destruction of Allied supplies while they were still at sea. The plan included the capture of Iceland and the Azores, which would provide further extension of U-Boat operations and create springboard bases for future action against the United States.

But Great Britain anticipated Hitler's intentions in the North Atlantic and took the tiny island nation of Iceland under its protective wing in May of 1940. A few months later, at the request of local governments, the United States occupied Greenland — again, to avoid Hitler's take-over.

With the fall of France came concern in the United States that Vichy might extend the German influence to the French possessions in the Western hemisphere: St. Pierre and Miquelon Islands off Newfoundland, French Guiana, on the South American continent, and Martinique and Guadeloupe in the West Indies. At Martinque, the best harbor in the Lesser Antilles, were the carrier Bearn, cruiser Emile Bertin, a gun boat and six tankers. In negotiations that were backed by threats of U.S. military action, Rear Admiral Robert agreed to freeze the movement of all French military vessels and equipment.

To ensure compliance with this agreement, the U.S. Navy assigned a destroyer squadron and PBY squadron, VP51, under the command of Commander W.J. Mullins, to patrol the French Antilles from bases in San Juan, Puerto Rico. VP51 was joined in early January, 1941, by two more PBY squadrons with bases in San Juan and in Guantanamo, Cuba.

Great Britain, in the first half of 1940, despite tragic reversals and defeat on the European Continent, was holding its own against the German blitz. But the toll taken on their merchant fleet by German U-Boats and escort vessels lost at Dunkirk threatened the nation's survival.

Roosevelt — Churchill: Ships For Bases

President Roosevelt was made aware of this potentially crippling condition of the Royal Navy in September, 1940, during a secret meeting with Prime Minister Winston Churchill. A ships-for-bases deal was worked out between the two leaders which sent Britain 50 U.S. destroyers — some in mothballs since World War I — for a 99-year lease of sites for naval, miliary and air bases in Central and South America.

Fearing German reaction to the ships-for-bases deal, the U.S. Navy began extending the sphere of its air patrol. Three PBYs of VP54 were detached to Bermuda and extensive research got under way toward establishing bases in Greenland. But Hitler was operating in his own way, on his own time-table; so the feared retaliation by U-Boats did not materialize. The long hours of patrol continued with little break in the monotony.

In the early weeks of 1941, the search for suitable bases in Greenland became almost frantic. The U.S. was determined to deny Germany any weather stations or bases for reconnaissance flights in Greenland. In fact,

PBY-5 on water at frigid North Atlantic Naval Base. (courtesy National Archives.)

the need was great for our own weather stations to serve iceberg patrols and for trans-Atlantic flight stopovers. Not to be forgotten was the Danish Cryolite mine at Ivigtut, critically important to the aluminum industry.

Numerous factors prevented simple selection of bases. Temperatures in Greenland drop below freezing by November and remain there until April. Fifty – knot gales whip up without warning as often as once a month and winds to 100 knots plague the west coast. During December and January, there are only six to eight hours of daylight. Ice formation on ships and aircraft adds extreme danger of over-weight. The surface water temperature hovers near 36 degrees in the Labrador Sea, with air temperatures around 20 degrees.

Seaplane anchorages were established at Kungnat Bay, six miles west of Ivigtut in Southwest Greenland and at Gannet Bay on the southern coast. Operations continued from these bases through the early months of 1941, but were highly restricted.

PBYs operated with aircraft tenders USS Goldsborough, Gannet and Lapwing, a credit to the courage and durability of both tender and Catalina personnel. Ice formed on exposed metal and glass. Icebergs haunted every PBY takeoff and landing. Fog closed in without warning and unpredictable winds wreaked havoc. But Greenland was kept secure from enemy use.

In February of 1941, the U.S. Navy commissioned a new base at Argentia, Newfoundland, and VP52 assumed search and patrol duties. More and more the patrols took on the look of convoy cover. Search missions, for the most part, were directed to the suspected locations of German U-Boat packs. Many times the patrols stretched far beyond the U.S. sphere of national sovereignty.

The U.S. Navy formed a support force in March, 1941, that included three destroyer and four aircraft patrol squadrons. The air arm consisted of two PBY and two Martin Mariner squadrons, the PBYs with 12 planes each. Several seaplane tenders supported the squadrons. Rear Admiral Bristol, Jr. headed up the group on the tender Prairie.

This continued U.S. short-of-war policy infuriated the German military leaders and Hitler's admirals pleaded with him to let them dispatch U-Boats into American waters. But Hitler wasn't ready.

On May 24, 1941, all 11 air-ready PBYs of VP52, based at Argentia, were dispatched on a tight umbrella-search of a 500-mile sector southwest of Cape Farewell, Greenland, for the German Battleship Bismarck. She had eluded the British navy after sinking their battleship, HMS Hood. In weather that kept all other aircraft grounded and severely restricted ship activity, the Catalinas searched.

RAF Catalina: Shadow The Bismarck

An RAF Catalina of Squadron 209, dispatched by the British Coastal Command with an American naval officer aboard, spotted the Bismarck on

May 26. It began shadowing the giant battleship and notified the British fleet of its location and course.

Aware of what the presence of a PBY meant to their escape plans, the Bismarck anti-aircraft gunners responded to the Cat's shadowing with a withering barrage of fire. Hit repeatedly, the PBY was repaired in flight by the crew and continued to cover until relieved by another PBY from Squadron 240. British men-of-war converged on the partially crippled "pride of Germany" the following day, some 500 miles west of Land's End. After carrier-based torpedo planes slowed her, heavy guns of the fleet sank her. Once more, the British fleet ruled the North Atlantic.

The Wing Commander aboard USS Albemarle stationed a picket boat at Argentia in mid-May, 1941. Plane moorings were laid, weather conditions studied, and general preparations for seaplane operations were initiated. On May 18, PBYs of VP52 arrived from Quonset Point, Rhode Island, and began patrol flights from Argentia.

July 1st brought changes in Wing and squadron designations for the Newfoundland–based PBYs. The support force became Patrol Wing Seven; Patrol Squadrons VP51, 52 and 53 were redesignated VP71, 72 and 73. Operations continued from Argentia until July, 1943, when most of the Wing was transferred to bases in the United Kingdom.

The German air blitz of England was in full swing when the United States quietly relieved the British of protectorate responsibilities over Iceland in July, 1941. Quickly, the Navy began preparing for PBY and PBM-1 squadrons at Reykjavic. In August, PBY squadron VP73 and PBM-1 squadron VP74 became operational at the base.

Admiral E.J. King, Commander-in-Chief, Atlantic Fleet, expanded the U.S. role in the North Atlantic war further on July 15, 1941 with his "Operational Plan #5" which ordered the Atlantic Fleet to "Support the Defense of Ireland." It further instructed the fleet to: "Capture or destroy vessels engaged in support of sea and air operations directed against Western Hemisphere territory, or United States or Iceland flag shipping."

On July 19, Admiral King issued "Operational Plan #6" which organized Task Force #1. Its primary duty was the defense of Iceland and to: "Escort convoys of United States and Iceland flag shipping, including shipping of any nationality which may join such United States or Iceland flag convoys, between United States ports and bases, and Iceland."

By September, the Atlantic fleet was ready to handle the next move necessary to ensure a sufficient quantity of war machinery and supplies flowing to Britain to stave off Hitler's devastating attacks. And, on September 16, some 50 merchant ships, escorted by Canadian Corvettes and Frigates, sailed out of Halifax harbor, bound for England. On September 17, some 150 miles south of Argentia, a U.S. Navy escort group, consisting of five destroyers, relieved the Canadians and the U.S. was actively escorting Allied shipping.

PBY Catalina squadrons were active in covering Allied shipping out of Argentia and as "eyes" of escort vessels in troubled water areas. Convoys arriving within range of the base at Reykjavik were intercepted and covered by PBY and PBM squadrons through the patrol zones of Iceland. The very presence of these aircraft reduced U-Boat attacks on convoys, as German submarines were operating under instructions to submerge immediately after observing enemy aircraft. Patrol aircraft, spotting submarines, directed escort vessels to their location and often were credited with "assists" when the submarine was sunk.

December 7, 1941: Atlantic Theater

When the United States entered the war in December, 1941, the PBY Catalina constituted almost the entire naval arm of the Atlantic Fleet. A few Martin Mariner patrol planes, Army B – 8 and Hudson bombers, were in service but virtually no other aircraft were available.

Seven patrol wings consisting of four squadrons, each with 12 aircraft, were operating from bases off Central America, Newfoundland, the United States mainland and Iceland; aircraft tenders also moved from area to area as needed. But the near total destruction of our aircraft at Pearl Harbor and Kaneohe Bay on December 7th, coupled with command fears of further attacks on Hawaii and possibly our western states, forced the transfer of most available patrol aircraft to the Pacific theater, specifically, Pearl Harbor.

All but four squadrons were transferred to the Pacific and this paltry group was charged with the task of defending the entire Atlantic theater of war. They were based at Argentia, Norfolk, Jacksonville, Key West, San Juan, Puerto Rico, and Trinidad.

The long – awaited entry of the United States into the war brought with it the feeling that the German U-Boat menace could soon be eliminated. Hardly! finally at war with the U.S., Hitler loosed the strings on Admiral Raeder and Commodore Doenitz, allowing the German Navy to begin its U-Boat blitz of the eastern United States, the Caribbean and waters of the Gulf of Mexico.

Due to Hitler's commitment to the North African campaign, Commodore Doenitz could only spare six submarines for the initial attack on the American sector; six of his best were selected. Their first attack came on January 12, 1942, just over a month after declaring war on the U.S.

The British passenger ship, Cyclops, was sunk off Cape Cod, and within two weeks, 13 vessels and almost 100,000 gross tons of shipping went down between New York and Cape Hatteras. Fifty-eight vessels in all were sunk along the eastern coast of the United States during the month of January. Of this figure, only three were sunk while in convoys.

February saw much the same toll, but now the U-Boats were broadening their range. Sinkings were heavy off Florida and Bermuda and the blitz expanded to the Caribbean and Gulf Coast; the Germans escaped each time almost without loss.

But two years of "practicing war," while maintaining our professed neutrality, proved invaluable in countering the U-Boat blitz of the eastern coast and southern waters. Naval strategists knew what steps were necessary; the problem was in implementing them. In the North Atlantic, when merchant vessels were convoyed with air and sea escorts, losses weren't eliminated, but were drastically reduced. The U.S. and its Allies, fighting for survival in the Atlantic and Pacific oceans, simply didn't have enough escort vessels to protect the thousands of supply ships and merchants vessels loading, unloading, and sailing from Allied docks throughout the world.

The solution didn't come quickly. In fact, it came with a combination of hard-knock programs geared to provide the Allied fleet with patrol bombers, escort vessels and countless new merchant ships. Technology, in the form of more and better radar and sound equipment was expedited. Educational programs were initiated to impress upon merchant seamen, sailors, officials and ordinary citizens not to "loose talk." Closer planning and cooperation were stressed between all branches of the service and Allied nations.

In the early days and weeks of the war, PBY squadrons sighted many submarines but were frustrated by the slow speed of the Catalina when trying to press an attack from five miles or further away. By the time the pilot corrected his course and had dropped sufficient altitude to make an accurate drop, the submarines had time to crash-dive. Although many PBY attacks were successful in damaging U-Boats, and several "probable" kills were registered, the Navy policy of allowing credit for a sinking only when wreckage surfaced after an attack kept the confirmed total relatively low.

During the first nine months of the war in the Atlantic, American PBYs made one confirmed sinking of a German submarine. On August 20, 1942, Lieutenant (jg) R.B. Hopgood, USNR, piloting a PBY for VP73, sank U-464 while covering a convoy south of Iceland.

By now the Catalina pilots were learning to cope with their slow, frustrating speed. Patrolling from two– to 4000–foot altitude, the pilots utilized the traditional PBY practice of keeping every cloud formation, regardless of size, available to them on a moment's notice. When a submarine was spotted, instead of moving in for an immediate attack, the pilot flew his Catalina into the nearest cloud where he planned his course and method of approach. Often, the maneuver caught a submarine off guard long enough for the PBY to arrive on target before the sub could submerge, or while it was yet shallow enough in its dive to sustain damage from the plane's depth charges.

Although the PBYs were having trouble developing a strong anti-submarine attack, they were proving themselves invaluable in other aspects of patrol and rescue. Convoys looked to them to force the U-Boats further out of effective range, to harass them and confound their attack plans. In addition to the many rescues made on their own, the Catalinas spotted, reported, and flew picket-courses around hundreds of survivors from aircraft, military and merchant vessels, the PBY standing by until rescue ships arrived.

PBY Rescue From The Greenland Icecap

Among the many rescues accomplished by PBYs in the Atlantic was one which took place on the Greenland icecap, July 5, 1942. VP93, with PBY-5A amphibians, was operating out of the BW-1 Army base in southern Greenland. Any Army B-17 had been forced down and spotted on the cap with 13 survivors. VP93 sent PBYs out to rescue the crew.

A Catalina commanded by Lieutenant Aram Parunak arrived at the crash scene and found the B-17 crew to be in excellent condition. There was just one problem; they were far too many miles from their base to attempt an overland trek on the rugged and dangerous icecap.

Lieutenant Parunak dropped supplies to the B-17 crew, then searched for several hours to find a way to pick them off the ice. Finally spotting a small body of water which had formed from melting ice, he returned to base and gathered a ground crew to lead the survivors the 12 or so miles from their aircraft to the tiny bubble of water. It took Parunak two trips to lift his

PBY-5a taxiing toward shore, approaching beaching crew, North Atlantic. (courtesy National Archives.)

charges off the ice cap but all were taken back to their base safely, each man with a new appreciation for the slow, lumbering PBY.

Another spectacular rescue was accomplished, this time in the Caribbean, by a Catalina from VP31 which was patrolling between San Juan and Guantanamo.

Navy Ensign Francis Pinter was in command, with two co-pilots and a crew of five. A radio message from another patrol plane described a life raft, with survivors, spotted off Haiti. Ensign Pinter immediately corrected course to intercept the raft and offer aid or rescue.

Arriving over the raft, the PBY crew observed that the survivors were too weak from thirst and exposure to even acknowledge the Catalina's presence. To the men of the PBY, standing by for a rescue ship was out of the question. There were many people in the raft and they needed immediate aid.

The sea was too rough for the open-sea-rescue patrol plane policy of the Navy, but Ensign Pinter sat the Catalina down as close to the raft as possible. With extreme care, the crew began pulling the survivors into the plane through the blister compartment. When all were aboard, the PBY had 17 additional passengers, one of them a woman. The plane's crew of eight men and the survivors of the American merchant ship, Barbara, were safely aboard but not yet airborne.

Ensign Pinter's decision not to jettison his bombs before landing now added considerably to the plane's excessive load. Under the circumstances, according to previous accumulated naval experience and projected capabilities of the PBY, a successful takeoff with that load was considered impossible. But Ensign Pinter turned the throttles over to his co-pilot, Ensign Thompson and began coaxing the lumbering bird into the air.

Riding up one swell, skipping the next, building speed on the top of the waves, the two men worked the PBY into the air. For almost half an hour, the plane hung close to the water before gaining altitude for the flight back to base.

Ensign Pinter's rescue, to that point in PBY history, was the most difficult one successfully brought about, considering weight and sea conditions. It was, however, only the beginning in a long list of "impossible" feats accomplished by the PBY.

Twenty-two United States PBY squadrons served in the Atlantic theater during the two years of neutrality plus the active years from December 7, 1941 through the end of hostilities in April of 1945. Seven Fleet Air Wings governed the PBYs from the eastern seaboard of the United States north to Argentia, Newfoundland, to Greenland, to Iceland, to the Bay of Biscay, to the Mediterranean and Straits of Gibraltar, the African Coast, to the waters off Brazil, the Caribbean and Canal Zone, to the Gulf of Mexico and the thousands of miles of open sea that these areas surrounded.

Although they began the encounter almost alone, the Catalinas were joined in time by a half dozen other types of U.S. patrol aircraft, as well as Free French PBYs, British Lockheed Hudsons and British Sunderlands. They were served in many areas by brave and dedicated men of the aircraft tenders.

Of 103 German U-Boats confirmed as sunk by U.S. Naval forces in the Atlantic during World War II, 18 of them were credited to PBY Catalinas. They shared credit with other U.S. aircraft of the seven FAWs for damaging at least 88 more submarines and were credited with downing three enemy aircraft and damaging 21. They damaged two destroyers, many fishing vessels and trawlers and scared off hundreds of U-Boats, thwarting their attacks on Allied shipping throughout the Atlantic theater.

But of all the successes of the Catalina in the Atlantic theater, the one glorious accomplishment that still lives in the memory of each man involved, was that of saving the lives of 141 men and women who would otherwise have drowned. These were directly credited to "Dumbo" rescues and do not include the hundreds of merchant seamen and military survivors of torpedoed ships and downed aircraft who were saved by rescue ships directed to the scene by the Catalinas and their sister aircraft.

Of the 22 PBY squadrons, many served in a specific base or zone for a relatively short time, moving around from one fleet Air Wing to another. As in all other branches and types of war service, some squadrons encountered the enemy more frequently and with greater impact than others. Some spent their entire tour of duty without seeing the enemy, but all served. All flying personnel spent long, boring hours of diligent searching —sometimes for known objectives, most times not— until their eyes were red and strained, their tempers short and their bodies bone-weary.

6

Patrol Squadron VP84

VP84 was one of the PBY Catalina squadrons serving in several zones of the Atlantic theater. Commissioned October 1, 1941, at N.A.S. Norfolk, Virginia, the squadron moved to San Diego, to Alameda and back to Norfolk before transferring to Argentia, Newfoundland, in June, 1942.

The squadron flew convoy coverage and anti-submarine patrols out of Argentia until October 8, 1942, then moved on to Iceland. Continuing patrols, the Catalinas accounted for three submarines sunk and two more probables in the short year of their assignment at Reykjavik, Iceland.

War diaries and the squadron history of VP84 reveal accounts of enemy encounters and rescue activities while serving in the Iceland area of such frequency and excitement as to give them the flavor of fiction while detailing the stark reality of war.

On December 10, 1942, a PBY, commanded by Lieutenant (jg) L. L. Davis and co-piloted by Ensign Earle B. Abrams, was flying anti-submarine patrol out of Reykjavik. During the patrol, Ensign Abrams sighted a German submarine running on the surface at eight knots, some eight miles distance and 10 degrees off the Catalina's starboard bow.

Apparently the U-Boat crew spotted the Catalina when it was still four miles away and began its dive. The aircraft passed over at 100 yards of the swirl, 27 seconds after the sub's conning tower disappeared. No bombs were dropped.

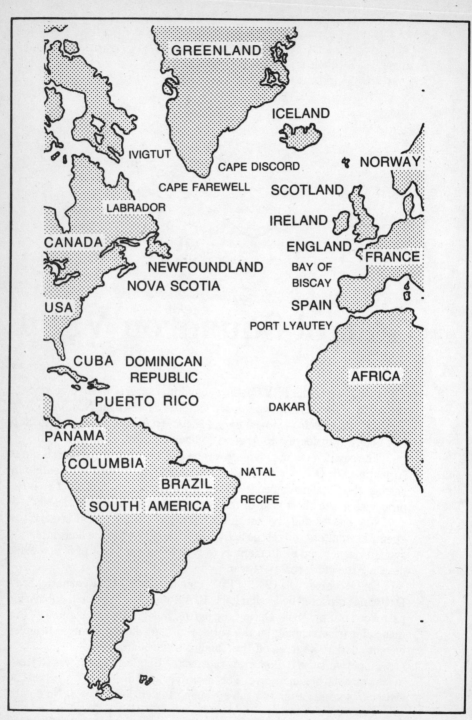

North and South Atlantic Ocean.

At 1226 hours, perhaps the same U-Boat was sighted coming to the surface about 45 degrees on the Cat's port bow, making 10 knots at five miles' distance. Approaching through the clouds, the Catalina began its run at one and a half miles on the starboard beam of the U-Boat. But the U-Boat crew was seen manning their cannon on the carriage bridge, so the Cat broke off the run at 600 yards. Another run began from the U-Boat's port quarter as it started to dive. This time the Catalina crossed over the sub's swirl 11 seconds after the conning tower disappeared. Again, their bombs were not released.

These sight-and-attack encounters continued for almost two hours with the PBY crew spotting the U-Boat on two more occasions, only to arrive too late for an effective attack.

Finally, at 1403, the submarine was spotted at about six miles' distance, 30 degrees on the Cat's starboard bow and riding his vents at 15 knots. Spray was cascading over his bow and he was leaving a good wake. Lieutenant Davis immediately took to a cloud cover at 2200–foot altitude, turning left until the aircraft was abeam of the U-Boat and with the sun at the Catalina's back.

L. L. Davis And Earl B. Abrams

Lieutenant Davis' and Ensign Abrams' debriefing interview picks up as follows; as related by Ensign Abrams:

"When two miles from the U-Boat, we started our run from a point 70 degrees on the U-Boat's starboard bow; the U-Boat had not changed course or speed. We continued on this run and when at 1200 yards distance, the U-Boat opened fire on us with his carriage bridge cannon. We quickly made a right turn and returned fire with our port waist gun. We continued closing on this course until, at about 400 yards dead-ahead, we noticed the U-Boat blowing his tanks, starting to crash dive. Here we made a 120–degree left turn — very steep — about 65 degrees. We held this until we were in a position to go almost down the U-Boat's track. At about 15 degrees on the U-Boats port bow and 30 to 40 yards from the conning tower — elevation 25 to 35 feet — we released our bombs.

"The starboard bomb struck the water 10 feet forward of the conning tower on the starboard side of the U-Boat, three feet from the hull. We had leveled off about three seconds before releasing the bombs and at the time the forward deck was submerged; the deck just forward of the conning tower was awash. The after-deck was plainly visible. At the time of release, the conning tower was about six inches out of the water, just visible; none of the after-deck was now visible.

"The U-Boat was not observed after the explosion. Swirl of the explosion was about 100 feet in diameter; at the same time a man was seen near the outside of the swirl. He was floating, belly up.

"We circled the area and saw oil rising in heavy volume. Two to four minutes later, five floats came to the surface. They were shaped like bed pans, or gas tanks of outboard motor boats, roughly three by two feet in size. Two of these looked aluminum in color and a couple were bluish-gray. One had a board attached, also a line. Two men came up holding on to the floats but only lasted about a minute before sinking into the sea. Oil continued coming up with pieces of wood and other debris. A blue object was seen. It looked like a man at first, then we decided it was a man's jacket.

"When we left the area, the oil slick had spread to about one and two-tenths miles. We returned to base one hour and ten minutes later."

Not all submarine sightings resulted in action as that just described. Most sightings and attempted attacks were a study in frustration for the weary Catalina crews. The following excerpts from the log of one VP84 Catalina quite graphically reflects the normal patrol conditions of North Atlantic PBY flights in those early days of the war. This was a 13–hour patrol. Thirteen hours of engine noise, searching, squinting, cramped necks and butts, cold, red eyes, anger and fatigue.

FAW-5 — Norfolk, Virginia — 20 April 1942.

1900 hours. Plane #7261, Lt. R. G. Touart, PPC; departed base.

1935 hours — Sighted three ships, two tankers, one cargo ship. Position five miles south of Kitty Hawk, N.C.

2255 — Sighted burning ship.

2348 — Sighted second burning ship. Scouted area surrounding each vessel.

0056 — Made bombing run on enemy submarine. Dropped one bomb. Investigation disclosed oil slick. Definite results undetermined.

0800 — Returned to base.

Tragedy was not restricted to military and merchant ships of the North Atlantic. It struck the aircraft of patrol squadrons with far less frequency and with fewer losses of life but was no less heartbreaking to the survivors. In the near-freezing water of the North Atlantic, the few moments life expectancy of an airman was no more or less than that of a sailor. Even in sea-worthy life boats, chances of survival over a few hours were next to nothing. Cutting, freezing winds and salt spray most often froze the men before rescue could be effected.

A Cat Down In The North Atlantic

An example of a Catalina tragedy is covered in the text of the following "Recommendation for Personnel Awards" letter from the Commandant of Fleet Air Wing Seven to the Secretary of the Navy; dated August 25, 1943.

"At 1930, 11 June 1943, a U.S. Navy patrol plane, piloted by Lieutenant (jg) Douglas Selby Vieira, USNR, crashed in the water while making a gallant attempt to rescue the crew of an R.A.F. Fortress, shot down by an enemy submarine. The aircraft was on a search mission for these survivors.

"Lieutenant Vieira and Lieutenant Bodinet made the landing while the rest of the crew manned their assigned positions. The crew of nine abandoned the plane in two life rafts. Lieutenant Vieira and Lieutenant Bodinet swam from the cockpit to the after hatch rather than to risk opening the watertight door and thus hasten the plane's sinking.

"Because the plane seemed to be going down rapidly, all men hastened to leave the ship in spite of rough water and they were unable to take water or flares with them. Under the effects of the cold, sickness, salt water and injuries, one by one, the men died until, on 18 June, Pelletier, Lionel Frederick, ARM1C, was the only man recovered alive.

Pelletier will recover but will not be able to continue on active duty.

"It is recommended that Pelletier, Lionel Frederick, ARM1C, the sole survivor, be awarded the Navy and Marine Corps Medal."

Phillip Bankhardt: "Take The Sub Under Fire"

Philip Bankhardt, who resides in Honolulu, Hawaii, was another of the multiple war zone PBY Catalina pilots. He served first under Patrol Wing Two, operating out of Pearl Harbor, Hawaii, then helping to form VP84 at Norfolk, Virginia, in late 1941. His rather frank recollections of flying experiences in the Atlantic War reveal some of the innovative spirit of the PBY men. It also offers further testimony to the depth of feeling each man had for the aircraft.

"And what about PBY anti-submarine operations in the Atlantic? We were scheduled to get the Martin Mariner PBM seaplanes when they were ready, so all pilots went to Banana River, Florida for check-out. But when we returned we were whisked off to San Diego, California, to pick up new PBY-5A amphibians.

"Our allotment of PBY-5As had the same armament as the old PBY-1s — one 30-caliber machine gun stowed in the bow and two 50-caliber guns, one at each waist hatch. The bow gun still had to be laboriously pushed up into place after the hatch was opened, sending a blast of cold air into the large plexiglass blisters. Pivoted at each end, the blisters rotated inboard, leaving the gunner free to fire at anything abaft the beam.

"To permit countering of submarine fire on an attack run, squadron personnel devised and built a fixed mount in the bow of each plane for a 50-caliber machine gun. The gun was mounted after takeoff, protruding through the hand-hole used to reach out and clean the bombing window. It had been mounted and tested on the ground and worked well. However, Captain Dan Gallery, USN, who was base commander at Reykjavik, directed, in his capacity as senior officer present, that we use 30-caliber guns instead of the 50s. So we had to replace the 50s with 30 caliber guns again and it almost cost my life and the lives of my crew.

"Not many days later, on Easter Sunday, 1943, we were returning from a convoy patrol in a sluggish PBY-5A, flying nose high at a bit over 1000 feet. The plane had been flown in from the states the day before and was put in use before there was time to give it a check. But our ordnance people had installed the fixed gun mount with a 30–caliber in the bow.

"It was about last light, so I had just ordered 'Darken Ship', hoping we might surprise a surfaced submarine. Instead, we were surprised by a sub, on the surface, directly ahead. It was hidden from view of the cockpit because of our nose-high attitude and, presumably, thought we were on an attack run. The first we knew of its presence was when large caliber tracer bullets streaked skyward a few feet in front of us.

"I peeled sharply away to the right to see it and directed the port 50–caliber waist gunner to take the sub under fire. Seconds, minutes passed without our return fire; there were only reports that the gunner was almost ready. I had also directed the bow gunner to mount his 'free' 30–caliber, which was standard on the PBY. I heard and felt a blast of cold air when he opened the hatch, then heard a continuing thrashing about as he struggled in the dark to mount his gun.

"Suddenly, the water around the sub turned white with foam as it flooded its tanks to crash dive. And still there was no fire from our 50–caliber waist gun. I could wait no longer. I had to attack the sub before it disappeared. I swung left and dove toward it and, immediately, the conning tower gun resumed its heavy fire. Tracers streaked all around us. I pulled the Cat's nose up, pressed the firing button on the yoke and watched a fine stream of tracers spurt out from our newly-installed fixed 30, then watched them arch downward to splash harmlessly in the sea, not half-way to the sub. But the splashes were to our advantage as we could tell where our small caliber fire was hitting.

"A 35–knot cross–wind was drifting us as we flew down the bright cone of tracers coming at us from the conning tower. Again I lifted the nose and fired another burst, until the exhilarating moment when our tracers struck and started walking up the sub's deck, then into the conning tower where they bounced crazily around; the sub's gun fell silent.

"As I pointed the nose of the Cat directly at the sub, we drifted way to the left. Correcting, I swung sharply right to cross the sub at an angle and dropped my stick of four depth charges. Then I banked more sharply right to avoid giving them a chance for a no-deflection shot up my rear-end.

"It took almost a 270–degree turn, coming around for another strafing run, before I sighted the submarine again. By then, only its bow protruded at the edge of the massive foamed area left by the depth charge explosion. I fired at the bow with the 30–caliber 'pea-shooter' but it jammed after firing only a few rounds; how thankful I was that it hadn't quit earlier.

"As we circled the scene, the silence on the intercom was suddenly broken by the excited voice of the bow gunner as he announced, 'Bow gun ready to fire, Sir!'

"A later check with the waist gunners revealed that this newly arrived Catalina had a hidden second latch on the blisters which they didn't locate in the darkness. So they couldn't open the blisters to swing their guns into firing position.

"Yes, I wished we had a 50–caliber in our bow that day. I could have silenced the sub's fire much farther out on my run and possibly caused extensive damage. We were lucky. Perhaps the rough sea spoiled their aim long enough for us to get within 30–caliber range; I'll never know.

"In debriefing, I reported it looked like a perplexing miss. But later my crew members told how they saw our depth charges explode directly under the sub, lifting it out of the water and dropping it at the edge of the explosion pattern.

"Sometime later, Captain Gallery was transferred from the naval base and 50–caliber guns replaced the 30s in our PBY-5As. However, even with the lighter guns, that very-heavy-on-the-controls Catalina proved to be an effective and accurate 'fighter' plane when literally kicked around with determination.

"Finally, I know of no evaluation being received on that attack but VP84 got the Presidential Unit Citation for confirmed sinkings of more enemy submarines than any other U.S. Navy squadron to that date."

VP84 Commanding Officer — Poyten C. Staley, Jr.

In an apparent letter of summation, the commander of VP84, Lieutenant Commander Poyten C. Staley, Jr., USN, transmitted a document to the Air Force Commander, U.S. Atlantic Fleet, following termination of the squadron duties in the North Atlantic.

Following is the text of the communication, dated September, 1943:

"Patrol Squadron Eighty-Four settled down in Iceland and went to work. Much has been written of the North Atlantic convoys; little has been said of the planes that covered, or attempted to cover them.

"From November, 1942, until March, 1943, the nights were long and the weather poor. In Iceland, there are two alternate landing fields, both unusable during the winter. The only other alternates are in Scotland and Greenland and these fields are rarely open. Fortunately, the field at Reykjavik is seldom closed completely for a long time. Six hundred feet ceiling and two miles visibility were considered the minimum local conditions; planes frequently returned with half mile visibility and with snow to the water.

"The winter of 1942 was said to be one of the worst in Iceland for 30 years. In the middle of the winter, only four hours of weak daylight were available.

"By agreement between the Royal Air Force Officer in command and the Captain of N.A.S., Iceland, in order to prevent duplication of effort, the R.A.F. Coastal Command exercised operational control of the U.S. Navy aircraft. The radio facilities, experience and equipment of the R.A.F. were largely responsible for our ability to carry on during the winter. The Iceland Fleet Air Group never lost direct control of its aircraft; the R.A.F. being most careful to consult the Group Command about cancellations, additional flights, recalls and other operational details.

"VP84, in spite of an average of 11 aircraft in commission, maintained one-third of the air effort from N.A.S. Iceland with an R.A.F. squadron of Hudsons and one of Liberators maintaining the other two-thirds."

7

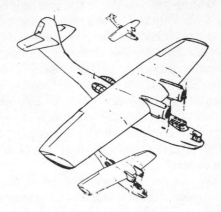

Patrol Squadron VP63

Catalina Squadron VP63 was commissioned at N.A.S. Alemeda, California, on September 19, 1942 under Patrol Wing Seven, with Lieutenant Commander E. O. Wagner, USN, as commanding officer. Despite their relatively "safe" zone for training, the squadron flying personnel found themselves engaged in a cloak and dagger type research of the waters between Hawaii and the Pacific Coast of the United States during the early days of December, 1942. The U.S. suspected the Japanese were planning some kind of attack on the mainland and kept VP63 on constant patrol until the alert was lifted.

Between January 1 and March 1 1943, the squadron took delivery of 15 new PBY-5 seaplanes from the Consolidated Aircraft factory at San Diego, California. Rapid orientation was accomplished during the month of March and the sixth of April found the squadron en route to Quonset Point, Rhode Island, for operations under the Commander of Aircraft anti-Submarine Development Detachment, Atlantic Fleet.

Operations continued from Quonset Point, with detachments flying convoy and anti-submarine patrols from Bermuda, Key West and Jacksonville, Florida, until June 22, 1943. Although there was little success against the U-Boat during that period, the Catalinas of VP63 distinguished themselves in rescue work.

On May 9th, Squadron plane 63-P-6, with Lieutenant Kauffman as patrol commander, was on an anti-submarine sweep 250 miles from Bermuda when flares from a raft were sighted in the distance. As the plane approached, four men waved frantically from the bobbing dot on the sea.

Aware that there were no surface ships in the vicinity, and as the sea was relatively calm, Lieutenant Kauffman decided to make an open–sea landing, despite existing instructions to the contrary. The landing was accomplished smoothly and the four weary, half starved survivors were taken aboard. The rescue became more incredible when the survivors identified themselves as British seamen from the merchant ship Melbourne Star, which had been torpedoed by U-Boats 38 days before.

On May 23, a PB2Y3 patrol plane was lost west of Bermuda but the crew cleared the aircraft in their rubber life rafts. Lieutenant Commander Curtis Hutchings took off from Bermuda at 0400, searched for, and located the survivors. The PBY crew battled a ceiling of only 800 feet and extremely poor visibility, often dropping float lights to spot the rafts, while battling to remain on station.

Patrol Plane Commander, Lieutenant (jg) Spears brought his PBY into the coverage and helped maintain contact with the men on the water. On several occasions, the small rafts slipped from view of the covering aircraft and new search patterns were started. At 1050 surface craft, homing on the Catalina signals, lifted the airmen to safety.

VP63 began transferring Catalina crews and aircraft to Reykjavick, Iceland, via Argentia, Newfoundland, on June 22, 1943 when Commander Wagner led 10 planes on the first leg. Weather conditions delayed their take off for Iceland until the 26th but all 10 aircraft landed safely the following afternoon.

The squadron was based at an R.A.F. station called "Camp Kwitcher-belliakin" and officers of the squadron found the ladies of Iceland to be attractive but rather shy. The enlisted men were confined to the base with no town liberty available.

Operations from Iceland involved convoy escort and further training in the use of M.A.D., the Magnetic Airborne Detection equipment the squadron had been equipped with before leaving the west coast of the U.S. However, the squadron failed to make contact with enemy submarines during its brief assignment at Iceland and didn't put the new equipment to test until the latter part of July, after assignment to Pembroke Dock, South Wales.

VP63 was the first U.S. Navy patrol squadron to be assigned operational duty from the United Kingdom in World War II. Great Britain had been operating PBY Catalinas through the Coastal Command since the first PBY-4, designated Model 28-5, was delivered in March, 1941.

Under operational control of the British 19th Group, Coastal Command, Royal Air Force, the squadron's assignment was to take part in anti-submarine activities in the Bay of Biscay. U.S. policy against deployment of Catalinas in areas where enemy fighters were present was overruled by British insistence that they were using Catalinas in the same area. Although the squadron wasn't credited with sinking a single submarine during the assignment, the Catalina crews of VP63 flew more hours against the enemy than any other squadron attached to the 19th Group.

Hitler capitalized on the excellent ports of Western France by building U-Boat bases at Bordeaux, Brest Le Palais, Lorient and St. Nazaire, all of which bordered on the Bay of Biscay. With free access to these ports, U-Boat crews were able to extend their activities while avoiding the dangerous waters of the Baltic and North Seas en route to German ports.

The R.A.F. sought to make the U-Boats' passage through the Bay of Biscay a major hazard and, hopefully, force them under the surface, reducing their efficiency.

All 15 PBY5s of VP63 were equipped with the M.A.D. detection gear and retro-firing bombs. This unusually heavy equipment, plus full gasoline tanks, created a dangerous takeoff condition. But all flights, even when weather conditions created rough water, were effected without incident.

The first VP63 sighting of German U-Boats in the Bay of Biscay began on July 28, 1943 when a Catalina commanded by Lieutenant (jg) Sam Parker was returning from a lengthy patrol. Crewmen of the plane spotted not one but two U-Boats on the surface and immediately came under fire from their anti-aircraft. Lieutenant Parker, complying with operational instructions, held off making a bombing attack and began homing more aircraft to the scene. He did, however, bring the PBY's machine guns to bear from all available angles, scoring hits on the hull and personnel in the conning tower on one submarine.

When two R.A.F. flying boats arrived, both submarines began to dive. Lieutenant Parker immediately put his Catalina into a power dive, closing the distance to the submarines in seconds and released his bombs just ahead of the swirl of one of them. There was no indication the PBY's bombs found their mark, as a thorough search of the area failed to produce any further sign of either U-Boat.

But action of another sort caught up with one Catalina of VP63 while the squadron was based at Pembroke Dock and that action cost the lives of seven officers and enlisted men of the crew of 10 and loss of the PBY they were flying.

Bill Tanner: Under Attack — Eight German Ju88s

On August 1, 1943, Squadron Plane #10, under the command of Lieutenant William Tanner, Jr., was returning from patrol when his Catalina was attacked by eight German Ju88s.

Lieutenant Tanner was the same PBY pilot who, on the morning of December 7, 1941, reported and attacked a Japanese submarine at Pearl Harbor, over an hour before the Japanese began their sneak attack on Hawaii.

Bill Tanner tells his story of the Ju88 incident with a brief background of his transitional period from the South Pacific to the British Isles.

"Several months after the December 7th attack, we began deploying to the South Pacific, beginning at Suva, then to Efate and on to Espiritu Santo, patrolling toward Guadalcanal. We rotated our planes with Pearl Harbor squadrons until September, 1942, when the Navy ordered some of the more experienced pilots to the war in the Aleutians. I was among a group sent to Alameda, California, to form a new squadron, which was destined, they said, for Aleutian duty. But when we got to Alameda, we were assigned new PBY-5s with some new equipment designated M.A.D., for Magnetic Airborne Detection.

"This equipment was used in submarine search and destroy by alerting the PBY crew to any metalic object on or in the sea within range of its detection limits. We also carried retro-firing bombs which were contact bombs stored in three racks of 15 each. When initial contact was made with a submarine, we were usually able to maintain contact, even after the submarine dived, by means of Sono-Buoys and M.A.D. equipment, followed by an attack with retro-firing bombs.

PBY-5 in flight over mountains. (courtesy General Dynamics.)

"Once an indication was received through the Sono-Buoys that we had located the submarine, we flew a cloverleaf pattern, dropping smoke lights to track his progress. When the submarine's direction was established, we flew down the row of lights in the direction of his movement, controlling the speed of the airplane as we made the attack at the same speed that the retro-bombs were set to fire rearward. This permitted an accurate vertical bomb drop when the M.A.D. equipment indicated the aircraft was directly over the target.

"My squadron, VP63, was re-routed to the North Atlantic, arriving just in time to meet Hitler's new approach to aircraft-submarine encounter. Prior to this time, German subs, upon spotting Allied aircraft, crash-dived to avoid being depth charged. But they were losing too many submarines and the constant under-water slow going was restricting their primary goal of destroying Allied shipping.

"In the summer of 1943, Hitler ordered his submarines transiting the Bay of Biscay to cruise on the surface and engage enemy aircraft with anti-aircraft fire rather than diving when attacked. His submarine personnel proved worthy fighters with deck guns and they fought their way out of many scraps against Allied aircraft.

"We had to concentrate all the anti-sub effort we had in that area and it became a key point in the air-sea war of the Atlantic. We frequently sighted submarines leaving French ports and beginning their race through the Bay of Biscay toward the Atlantic Ocean. We lost a lot of airplanes but the Germans lost a significant number of submarines.

"There was a concentrated joint British-American effort to break the back of Hitler's submarine war at about this time. The British provided Sunderland bombers while the U.S. Navy furnished PB4Y and PBY squadrons. The PB4Ys were the fastest and best armed, so they flew out of Land's End, England, along the French Coast almost to Spain, then directly back. A little further out flew the British Sunderland bombers, then VP63 with our slow, lumbering PBY Catalinas even further out. Theoretically, we were flying far enough away from the French Coast to avoid being caught by German fighter-bombers.

"On my third flight under this plan, in a PBY-5, we had made our turn and were heading back, cruising at about 5000 feet altitude through the tops of scattered clouds, some 600 miles from England and 300 miles off the French Coast.

"Flying into the open, the lookout in the waist reported enemy aircraft about five miles abaft the starboard quarter. This occurred at 3:30 in the afternoon. The crew immediately assumed battle stations and I headed with full power for the nearest cloud layer. However, we were not able to reach the cloud-cover before we were attacked by eight German Junker 88s.

"The first few passes made by the enemy were individual runs from forward of the beam and very slightly above. On these runs, the enemy did not close the range to any less than 200 to 300 yards and comparatively few hits were made on our aircraft. During these attacks, as an evasive measure, I turned our plane toward the attacking aircraft in order to decrease the length of time their guns would bear on us. At the same time, I lost and gained altitude in an effort to make their gunnery more difficult.

"All this time I was attempting to get into the nearest clouds and was successful at times. However, it was impossible to get away from the German aircraft because the clouds did not afford adequate cover. The enemy then started runs from both sides simultaneously, making it more difficult for us to evade their gunfire. They also began to close their range, coming at times as close as 50 to 100 yards.

"Seeing that escape into the clouds was impossible, I jettisoned the bombs. It was now quite evident that we were being severely hit by the aircraft attacking from the starboard side, which were offered a target of our side and bottom as I turned toward the planes attacking from the port side.

"During our evasive actions, we had reached an altitude of about 1000 feet when the rudder cables were shot away. Looking back, it was evident that both fuel tanks were burning and the trailing edges of both wings were aflame. The starboard engine had also failed.

"We didn't last much longer. I lost control of everything in the plane except the elevators. The ailerons and rudder were gone so I couldn't turn. Now my wife has always said she was doing a lot of praying in those days, and I gotta' believe, because as that happened, we were right down on the deck and had about a 35 – knot headwind. I had no power, but with the elevators I was able to get the nose of the Cat in the air and we pancaked into the water with very little forward speed.

"We knew we had one definite kill and we learned later that another one didn't make it back. So we got two for one. However, we lost everybody in the plane except the copilot, the waist gunner and me.

"The copilot, Lieutenant Bob Bedell, hadn't been hurt. I was shot through the elbow and the right flank but the bullet lodged against my backbone. I found out later that it was a 30 – caliber or equivalent. It really didn't give me much discomfort. The waist gunner, Douglas Paterson, wasn't hit by gunfire, but when the plane crashed he was slammed into something and suffered an ugly head injury. His forehead just peeled open. As terrible as he looked, he wasn't badly hurt.

"The plane had water-looped about 45 degrees to starboard when it hit the water and split in the vicinity of the waist hatches. It immediately began settling into the water. The bow remained afloat long enough for the copilot and me to abandon the plane. The copilot exited through the overhead hatch and I escaped through the port pilot's window. I believe that Doug Paterson was thrown out of the port blister of the aircraft along with a life raft, which we subsequently found floating nearby.

"Lieutenant Bedell swam over and inflated the life raft, climbed aboard and assisted Paterson and me inside. While swimming to the raft, I had come upon one of our men who was floating face down in the water. As was the case with six other members of the crew, he was probably dead by the time the PBY hit the water.

"The Germans were still there when we got into the raft, but they didn't shoot at us and dipped their wings as they turned toward France. I guess they figured they had done their job and, unless we were very lucky, the sea would do the rest. In that regard, our troubles were far from over.

"Here we were in a rubber raft. I was hurt but not badly. Paterson looked terrible but Bedell didn't have a scratch. The raft had bullet holes in it but they were controllable with wooden plugs provided for that purpose.

"Bedell got the pump out and started pumping. Then we noticed the raft was getting lower in the water. We discovered the valve in the pump was assembled wrong, actually sucking the air out instead of putting it into the raft. So Bedell sat there and managed to keep us afloat, though low in the water, by blowing air into the raft. This went on all night.

"The final chapter in our story came the next morning when, with the raft near sinking, we were almost run down by a British frigate out on an anti-submarine patrol. They picked us up and I got another scare before the day was over. They didn't have a doctor aboard and their enthusiastic chief medical corpsman decided he was going to perform surgery at sea to remove the bullet from my back. Fortunately, their home base ordered them to transport us immediately to Plymouth, England. So they knocked off their little cutting party.

"At Plymouth, they took us first to a Royal Navy hospital, then to one of our U.S. Army hospitals where they removed the bullet. All went well and I was transferred back to San Diego while the squadron went on to the Straits of Gibraltar. There they did a great job with the magnetic detector equipment. In a confined area like the Straits, they just saturated everything."

Douglas Paterson: One Of Three Survivors

The three survivors of the preceding incident were called upon to describe, in detail, their views of the action. The following vivid description of the engagement was taken from VP63 war diaries and is the actual quotation, in part, by Douglas C. Paterson, ACM3c, the enlisted man who was waist gunner on the ill-fated flight:

"Mr. Tanner gave the order for battle stations. I broke out the starboard waist gun. Rude (Werdin O. Rude, ARM2c) was on watch at the port blister and he manned the port waist gun. Mr. Robertson (Lieutenant (jg) Billy E. Robertson) came into the after-station to direct gunfire.

"The enemy planes came in off the starboard bow to the starboard stern and opened fire. I returned fire at each plane as it came in. Most of them passed to the tail of our plane, slightly above us, and a couple of them passed directly over the blister. I know I made hits on some of them. One of them wavered in the air, then fell off below our plane. I'm sure this was the result of direct hits.

"As I was following one of the planes overhead with gunfire, I noticed Carmack (David R. Carmack, AMM2c) standing in the hatchway. His face was streaked with blood. He didn't speak and appeared dazed. I did not see him after that.

"I dropped my fire for a second early in the battle when I had a stinging sensation in the legs. I learned later that it was caused by fragments of shrapnel from a hit which burst behind me. I rubbed my leg for a moment and returned to my gun. This happened just after I had heard a thud and noticed that Mr. Robertson had fallen into the compartment ahead. His feet lay sideways across the hatchway and he did not move.

"I saw fire in the starboard wing, which was evidently caused by shrapnel that had ignited the gasoline tanks. The bombs had been jettisoned before this.

"After the fire started, we descended rapidly. I felt a violent wrench in my left shoulder, which was up against the gun; at the same time the gun ceased firing. I charged it, then noticed the cover latch was open. The gun must have been sprung by a hit. I hit the cover latch several times with all my might but it would not stay down and I couldn't get the gun back into action. Rude was still firing the port waist gun.

"We continued downward and I noticed that both wings were ablaze. I heard Law (Robert B. Law, AMM2c) call me. He was lying in the walkway in the next compartment, with the door to the after-station closing against his head. His head was very bloody. I pulled him through to the after-station. One of his flying boots caught in the door; I released it and pulled his leg up so that he was free.

"That was the last I remember until I found myself under water.

"I came to the surface in burning oil. I managed to get a breath and went under again and came up again in burning oil. I managed to swim past it. Both times when I emerged, I saw someone floating face down. I don't know whether it was the same person I saw twice or two different men.

"I saw the plane sink. I looked around for some floating object and saw Mr. Bedell (Lieutenant (jg) Robert I. Bedell) in the life raft some distance behind me.

"I swam to the raft and caught onto the rope on the side. I had a terrific pain in my side and could not lift myself up and asked Mr. Bedell to help me. Mr. Tanner was hanging onto the other side of the raft and Mr. Bedell told him there was someone on the other side. Mr. Tanner came around and told Mr. Bedell to get me in first. Mr. Bedell helped me in and then helped Mr. Tanner onto the raft. By the time Mr. Tanner was on the raft, everything was silent; we did not hear anyone calling for help.

"The sea was very rough and during the night the waves broke over the raft and drenched us. The pump in the raft didn't work. There were some leaks in the raft and Mr. Bedell and Mr. Tanner plugged them. I was unable to help them. Mr. Bedell kept us afloat by blowing air into the valve with his own lung power.

"The next day, a Sunderland flying boat passed over us but didn't see us. Then, in the afternoon, we sighted two ships. They passed by and hope diminished as the raft wasn't holding up well. Then one of the ships turned around and came toward us again. It was in the direct rays of the mirror we had on the raft and I flashed it toward the ship. They came alongside and picked us up. Needless to say, our gratitude was beyond expression.

"The ship's corpsman sprinkled sulfa powder into the wound on my head and applied a first aid bandage. He also strapped my back and side.

"We were transferred to another ship a few hours later and arrived in port on August 4th. Mr. Tanner and I were removed to a United States hospital after a brief stay in one in England."

The near miraculous survival of Lieutenant Tanner and two members of his crew defied the laws of probability, but fate wasn't finished with the survivors. On October 15, 1944, Lieutenant Bedell, still with VP63, perished in the crash of a PBY which went down during a routine training mission operating out of Port Lyautey, French Morocco. Following is the text of the log entry relating to the incident:

"Plane No. 20 (Bureau No. 34013) and its entire crew were lost on 15 October in the course of a training flight. Only an oil slick and small pieces of the plane were found off shore in the Atlantic, 24 miles from Port Lyautey. The Patrol Plane Commander was Lieutenant Robert Irving Bedell, the sole survivor, still with the squadron, of the encounter with Ju88s in the Bay of Biscay. A patrol was maintained on the beach for many days after the crash but no bodies were recovered.

"Memorial services were held in the station chapel on 20 October and following the services a plane was flown to the area of the crash where a wreath was dropped on the water."

8

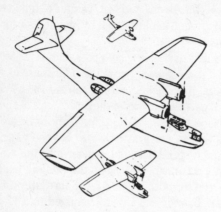

The Straits Of Gibraltar

The commanding officer of Fleet Air Wing Seven, on December 2, 1943, requested permission from the Commander-in-Chief of the U.S. Atlantic Fleet to transfer VP63 from Pembroke Dock, South Wales, to a more suitable area of operations. Citing the squadron's outstanding patrol record against extremely adverse weather conditions, the commander stated his contention that VP63, with the special M.A.D. equipment and extensive training in its use, could better serve the anti-submarine effort where that equipment could be employed.

Orders were received by the squadron on December 13 directing them to proceed at once to Port Lyautey, French Morocco to serve under the commander of Fleet Air Wing 15.

Nestled some 80 miles north of Casablanca, the U.S. Naval Air Station of Port Lyautey straddled the Oued Sebou river 80 miles from where it opened into the Atlantic Ocean. Its location about halfway between Casablanca and the Straits of Gibraltar, plus the excellent seaplane facilities, made the station quite convenient for the patrol planes covering the eastern end of the convoy route, including the approaches to the Straits.

Since the beginning of the war, German U-Boats had passed through the Straits of Gibraltar and into the Mediterranean to harass and destroy Allied shipping and operations. Their journeys, most often at night, were rarely challenged and more rarely interrupted. But upon the arrival of VP63 with its M.A.D. equipment, a detailed plan was formulated to seal off

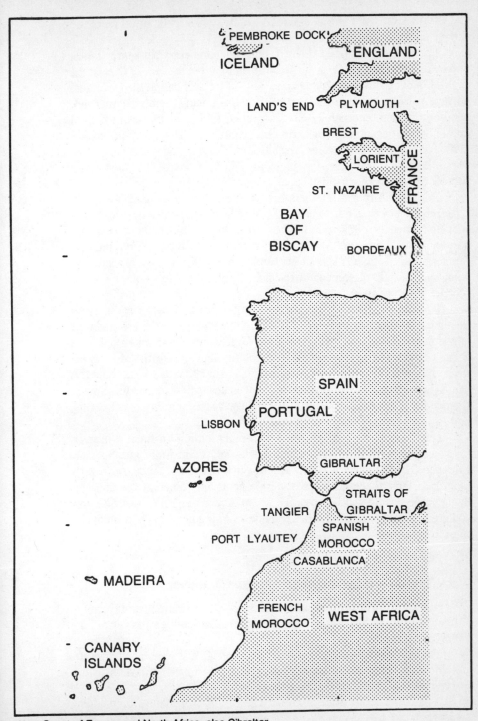

West Coast of Europe and North Africa, also Gibraltar.

the Straits from the passage of enemy traffic of any kind, any time of the day or night.

The British, equipped their Wellington bombers with searchlights, and by scouring the Strait, prevented the uninhibited passage of U-Boats at night. Coupling this with day patrols, they effectively halted the Germans' surface passage through the Straits. But the enemy simply submerged, slipping through on carefully plotted routes, taking advantage of helpful currents that permitted their extra quiet running. With their motor speed almost at full-stop, submarines virtually eliminated the danger from hydrophone detection and echo-ranging was almost as unreliable; destroyer patrols were severely handicapped.

Magnetic Airborne Detection equipment was designed, not as an initial contact device, nor to be used over a large expanse of water. It was more effective as a follow-up locater, after submarines had been sighted and forced to submerge. As explained earlier, M.A.D. equipment builds a fence around the enemy submarine rapidly and with exceptional accuracy, then by strategic placement of the float lights, the sub's course can be plotted from the aircraft.

To build an effective barrier across the Straits, it was necessary to develop a thorough knowledge of the shape and length of the area, as well as the depth of waters flowing through. Approximately 35 miles long, the Straits narrow toward the middle to about eight miles near the Mediterranean end and its channel depth, which is less than 100 fathoms, is about the same throughout. The U-Boat corridor was suspected to remain as near the middle of this deeper water as possible so as to minimize maneuvering and to avoid contact with the channel walls.

The "fence" plan called for a two-plane circuit to form a barrier between points off Point Caraminal, Spain, and Point Malabata, Spanish Morocco. The Catalinas would fly a course in the shape of a race track, with four – mile legs, three-quarters of a mile apart and joined at the ends by flying three-needle-width turns. To complement the PBY coverage and add greater fire-power, the Allies provided varying numbers of destroyers to patrol the zone.

Track The U-Boat By Magnetic Airborne Detection

Following is a description of one such coordinated attack on a German U-Boat by PBYs of VP63 and destroyers of the British Fleet, as related by VP63 historians.

"On the 15th of May the effectiveness of M.A.D. – equipped aircraft was demonstrated when a submarine attempted to make a daylight, submerged passage through the Straits.

"That afternoon, plane number 12 with Patrol Plane Commander Lieutenant (jg) M.J. Vopatek and plane number one with patrol plane commander Lieutenant H. L. Worrel, were flying the 'fence' in the Straits north of Point Malabata.

"While on a northerly heading, plane number 12 obtained a M.A.D. signal. Plane number one, on a southerly heading, immediately crossed over and also obtained contact. The planes then proceeded with cloverleaf tracking which resulted in a line of float lights showing the submarine to be on an east-north-easterly course of 075 degrees.

"Lieutenant (jg) Vopatek called British surface vessels in the area by voice and requested them to close the position. Plane number 12 then launched a sono-buoy but did not have reception from it, although plane number one tuned in on it and heard definite propeller noises.

"The planes continued to track and the line of floats showed the submarine to be continuing on the same course at a speed of four to five knots. At 1530, plane number 12 made a bombing run and fired 30 retro-bombs in three ripples of 10 each on a good M.A.D. signal. The position of the attack was one and one-fourth miles east of the initial contact. But neither plane was able to receive on the sono-buoy at the time and the explosions were not heard. However, there was a subsequent report from the captain of the HMS Blackfly that several officers who were in the wardroom of the ship, which is below the water line, heard explosions but could not provide details as the ship was several miles away.

"Following the attack by plane number 12, crews of both planes observed a number of pieces of splintered wood floating in the water at the position of the attack. No oil was observed.

"The planes continued cloverleaf tracking and the signals obtained showed that the submarine was still underway on about the same course. Plane number 12 then launched three additional sono-buoys but could not pick up submarine sounds. The first radioman of plane number one, however, again reported picking up screw noises from the buoys. This was before the arrival of any surface craft.

"At 1550, the first surface vessel was approaching from the east and Lieutenant Worrel in plane number one proceeded to attack while the area remained clear. At 1552, he fired 24 retro-bombs, in three ripples of eight, on good M.A.D. contact. One sizeable piece of wood and the appearance of new lumber was sighted on the surface following the attack. No other results were observed.

"British escort craft, HMS, Kilmarnock and HMS Blackfly, of Gibraltar, and HMS Aubriettia, Corvette of the Flower Group, joined in the search and attack. The Patrol Plane Commanders continued with cloverleaf tracking and instructed the ships by voice communication to make attacks ahead of the easterly end of the line of float lights.

"At 1630, the Blackfly made an attack with depth charges, which was followed a few minutes later by an attack by the Kilmarnock. The Blackfly then attacked again but these attacks were all inaccurate and no results were observed from them. The attacks were all astern of the submarine, which indicated they had been directed at 'submarine bubble targets' launched by the U-Boat. The aircraft continued to track and to mark, accurately, the successive positions of the submerged submarine so that the surface vessels could attack at the correct position. The pilots requested the ships to make their attacks at the position marked by the float lights rather than at Asdic targets, then coached them as to the correct location.

"M.A.D. tracking was continued until the Kilmarnock hoisted a pennant warning of an imminent hedgehog attack. The aircraft withdrew to avoid being hit by the hedgehogs which rise to a considerable height in their trajectory.

"The final M.A.D. contact with the submarine, obtained by plane number one at 1648, appeared to be stronger than any previous, indicating that the submarine was probably coming to the surface. At 1651, the Kilmarnock fired its hedgehog bombs at a position immediately ahead of the line of float lights, the exact point where the submarine should have been at the time. Within two minutes after the attack, the crews of both planes observed underwater explosions and saw two great bubbles of air rise to the surface.

"The planes made additional cloverleaf passes in the area but no further contacts were obtained. A modified spiral search was then carried out, with results. While flying the spiral, the crews of both planes observed pieces of wood floating in the area where the attacks had been made.

"Planes number eight and three arrived at 1707 and 1741 and a new interception patrol was commenced further east in the Straits to cover the remote possibility that the U-Boat escaped the attacks and was still proceeding to the east. This patrol was continued until darkness.

"At 1815, plane number three observed an oil slick in the water in the area where the final attack was made. The slick was stationary and continued to increase in size during the evening until it was more than a mile in length and about 200 yards wide. By the next day it had spread over a distance of 12 miles in the Straits."

Lt. Cmd. Curtis Hutchings: "U-Boats Have Always Avoided Us"

A squadron memorandum issued on June 9, 1944, by then— Commanding Officer, Lieutenant Commander Curtis Hutchings U.S.N., sums up the accomplishments and reflects the pride of VP63 during its service in the Bay of Biscay and at Port Lyautey, French Morocco. The memorandum read in part:

"Patrol Squadron Sixty-Three has always been an outstanding squadron. We have always done the job we set out to do. There has never been a ship sunk by enemy submarines within operational range of our aircraft.

"The most submarines any squadron has sunk were three. Two other squadrons accomplished this feat; each squadron securing approximately

PBY-5 in flight over lake. (courtesy General Dynamics.)

75 sightings and 50 attacks. This squadron has sunk three U-Boats without seeing them. Probably several more have been sunk but the nature of our equipment precluded the possibility of obtaining conclusive evidence in some cases. This command has been informed on numerous occasions that such a feat was impossible. It was not impossible for the personnel of VP63.

"Unfortunately, U-Boats have always avoided us and, consequently, we have never been in a 'hot spot' area.

"We flew more hours than any squadron operating in the Bay of Biscay and more than doubled the time of most squadrons. Our coordinated patrol principles were adopted in the Bay of Biscay and the French U-Boat bases were effectively bottled up. Shipping losses in the Atlantic immediately dropped from nearly 10 ships per month to less than six monthly.

"Upon arriving at Port Lyautey, U-Boats were passing through the Straits of Gibraltar at will. Shipping losses in the Mediterranean were exceedingly high, and as a result, the offensive in Italy was suffering considerably. Patrol Squadron 63, on its own initiative, designed the patrols and tactics to cut off the Straits and put these plans into operation. These tactics did deny the Straits to the U-Boats, assisting greatly in the establishment of the Anzio Beachhead, the present successful offensive in Italy, and the invasion of Western France.

"As a result of our outstanding effort here, the expression 'Sixty-Three' is known around the world. This command is exceedingly proud of the squadron and its officers and men. All hands can well be proud of our squadron and our accomplishments."

By January of 1943, the combined operations of aircraft and ships brought U-Boat activities in the Mediterranean almost to a complete halt. The Allies invaded Southern France, employing hundreds of vessels in the action and the ports of Marseilles and Toulon were captured without the loss of a single ship by submarine. Only three or four submarines remained in the Mediterranean after these ports were captured and at least one of the subs was known to have been scuttled by its crew.

Stoughton Atwood: "Real Navy Flying"

Stoughton Atwood, who resides in Topsham, Maine, was an Ensign —junior officer, he called himself—when the PBY entered his career. Beginning as an Aviation Cadet at NAS Jacksonville, Florida, Atwood completed 1200 hours in the Catalinas. After his PBY days, he flew PB4Ys until retiring from active duty in November, 1945. He remained in the active reserve, attaining the rank of Commander before full retirement in 1980. His affection for the PBY is undisguised in the story he tells.

"I first became acquainted with the PBY on March 6, 1942 when I was assigned to the flying boat training squadron at Jacksonville, Florida. We were awed by the big boats with retractable wingtip floats and thought, 'This is real Navy flying'. It was different—with all the increased numbers of personnel necessary to conduct operation—compared to the smaller aircraft we had flown. As time went on, I became quite familiar with the Catalina and upon completion of training was assigned to VP53, which was forming-up in Norfolk, Virginia, under fleet Air Wing Five.

"Continuing our training with the PBY-5 seaplane, we served short stints in Norfolk and Key West before assignment to Port of Spain, Trinidad. During a year of anti-sub patrols and convoy coverage, we junior pilots moved up to first pilot and eventually to Patrol Plane Commanders.

"Flights out of Trinidad didn't differentiate between day and night and we flew patrols almost around the clock, Sea-sweeps were mostly eastward in the interest of protecting shipping. Many convoys were made up in the Gulf of Paria and it became our lot to escort them as far across the Atlantic Ocean as our range would permit.

"Far more often than not these patrols were boring, sometimes unbelievably so. But there were periods when we came into contact with the enemy and our squadron planes received credit for a number of submarine kills in the resulting encounters. In my own case, I was involved in a number of sightings but no confirmed kills; although we did drop depth charges several times.

"The Navy had an advance base on Essequibo River, just upstream from Georgetown, British Guiana. After a long patrol, we would often lay over there instead of flying on to Trinidad. Landing at that base was an experience within itself as the river leading into it was smooth as glass and always quiet, nothing like the choppy water at Trinidad. The glassy surface of the water was so deceptive we developed quite proficient landing techniques, using power landings since we were never quite sure of our exact height above water. Many pilots, approaching the Essequibo River, were surprised at the moment of touchdown, believing they were still in the air.

"The PBY was a constant source of surprise with its flexibility, durability and forgiveness. It seems it could always do a little more than was expected of it. I recall flying 32 people out of Guiana to Port of Spain, an evacuation of some kind. We loaded them all aboard — stacked like sardines — and took off with ease.

"A pilot, senior to me, and I were transporting a naval inspector to the island of Martinique to examine a communication facility. Martinique had no harbor, so it was necessary to land in rather full swells and taxi. But when it came time to take off, the plane commander demonstrated a quality of the PBY that surprised even a believer like me.

"We taxied out to sea, which was down-wind from the island, for a couple of miles in order to get a long enough takeoff run up-wind. But then we were faced with the problem of following large swells. The water was anything but horizontal. Our pilot literally followed the contour of the surface, a series of very large swells, to the point where we were tossed into the air on the peak of one of them. Without sufficient flying speed to remain aloft, we nosed over and followed the trough up the cap of the next swell, gaining a little more flying speed, catapulting ourselves into the air, skipping the next trough, coming down the hill side of the next swell and repeating this until sufficient flying speed was obtained to stay in the air.

"Most of us felt, after experiencing many different conditions in take-off and landings in the PBY, that we really were Naval Aviators and that until one became proficient in a flying boat, he really didn't have a claim to being a true Naval Aviator.

"Long night patrols, though boring from the standpoint of enemy contact frequency, were filled with navigational duties for at least one of the officers aboard. We were kept busy laying out our course on the chart and keeping track of the wind with frequent wind bearings and drift sights. On many nights, after flight plotting a course change, I approached the cockpit to find the airplane on auto-pilot and both pilots sound asleep. The PBY auto-pilot was so dependable, falling asleep on a calm, dark night seemed almost forgivable. Of course, the proper procedure called for one of the three pilots to catch an hour's nap in one of the three bunks that was standard equipment on the Catalina; each man could then be more alert to sit his position.

"On one such occasion, as I tried to catch a short snooze, our mission took us through an angry thunderhead. Suddenly, we were caught in a powerful downdraft and I was thrust up against the overhead, unable to get back down to the bunk. I made my way back to the cockpit, strictly hand-over-hand on the overhead, and just as I arrived, the PBY bottomed out, crashing me in a heap to the bilge below. Fortunately, no one was hurt but we had lost over 2000 feet with the plane completely in the control of the downdraft.

"Communications between PBYs covering convoys and the escort leader became one of the more difficult tasks to master for the flying boat crews. We often circled the escort leader while one of the pilots or a radioman exchanged signals with a signalman on the ship—both using Aldis lamps. Then of course there were always the signal flags. Radio communications was a no-no, as the convoy positions were kept secret, hopefully, from roving enemy submarines.

Keep The Nose Down Till It's Time

"There was a period of time in which as junior pilots we spent many hours practicing landings and takeoffs under the watchful and sometimes horrified eye of our senior pilot. Now, it so happened that one of the senior pilots, for reasons of his own, simply would not let his junior pilot, an Ensign named Pappy Squires, practice handling the plane during these critical moments of flying. This drew the ire of most of the pilots in the squadron and each of us 'juniors' vowed to make it up to the guy when we graduated to Patrol Plane Commanders. Well, it came to pass that I was the first to keep the pledge.

"I drew Pappy Squires as a temporary co-pilot shortly after I got my promotion. I was delighted with the prospect of helping Pappy progress but was, frankly, more excited about having a chance to put his former senior pilot to shame.

"The flight was to be a night patrol and we were preparing to take off at dusk. As usual, the cut in the bay from which our operations commenced was reasonably well protected from the higher waves in the open bay. But with a heavy load and a long run, we normally went well past the break-water and encountered some pretty good chops. The trick was to raise the nose of the aircraft just the right height so that the plane continued to accelerate without taking to the air. It was a neat trick to keep that nose down so the waves didn't throw you into the air before you could maintain flying speed, and yet not plow to a point where you weren't accelerating.

"I had explained all of this to Pappy, confidently sitting him in the first pilot seat, while I climbed into the co-pilot's to man the throttles and coach him. We made a good start and got up on the step; my left hand held the throttles forward. Should I let go, the clutch wasn't tight enough to hold the power on. The vibrations would gradually shake the throttles loose and the power would fade off. So it was absolutely necessary to hold forth on those throttle handles.

"I noticed we were, in fact, plowing and not gaining speed. With my right hand, I motioned for Pappy to raise the nose just slightly. He misunderstood my signal, thinking I meant him to horse it into the air and pulled the nose too high. Without sufficient air speed to hold us in the air, we began to porpoise. Then, at one point, I determined that with the right amount of hold on the yoke, we could get airborne. I let go of the throttles to help. As I did so, the power faded off and we stalled back into the waves with an awful wallop.

"The impact opened the bottom of the hull like a can of sardines and I'll never forget the sound of rushing water behind the pilot's seat — like Niagara Falls in reverse. We experienced what a carrier pilot goes through when he catches the wire; our run was abruptly halted and water rapidly began filling the compartment behind us. Fortunately, the water-tight door was closed into the pilot's compartment so that no water reached us.

"As we headed for the beach, gingerly picking our way amongst fishing boats, the crew pulled the radio gear and our navigational documents and stowed them as high as possible. Somehow we reached shoal water and bottomed so that we didn't sink too deeply into the bay.

"We thought we were going to get quite a ribbing when we got back to base because it was common practice for all non-flying pilots to watch the night takeoffs from the top of the hill. As it happened, they watched the beginning, thought we were well on our way and never saw the accident.

"A typical example of the 'Navy Way' involved the paint scheme on the Catalinas in the Trinidad area. Somewhere along the line, we got a report that our aircraft was much better camouflaged from below when they were painted white. To test it ourselves, we painted one plane white and made some flights that demonstrated to the satisfaction of our squadron command that the plane was much less visible from below and it seems this white airplane had 80 percent more submarine sightings than the ones painted Navy blue.

"Our skipper got into some trouble, in spite of the results, because he had never obtained clearance to do the plane in white. The order was countermanded and the plane restored to its original color. Then, before the repaint had dried, an order came down to paint all planes white. So, so like the Navy.

"There was a rather bizarre incident in our squadron that involved some of the enlisted Aviation Pilots. One of them, named Steel, I believe, lost his finger one day as a result of guiding the pilot to the buoy. It was common practice to open up the hatch over the navigator's table and, while the pilot approached the buoy, have someone stand there and point to it as an aid in making a good approach. Of course, it was a dangerous position because it was right in front of the propeller. Steel simply ran his finger right into the prop and got it cut off.

"But in telling the story, and explaining to his replacement the danger of the operation, another AP stood in the same position. This time, the plane was on the ramp, on its beaching gear, with engines revved up. He reached around and pointed to show how not to do it and stuck his own finger into the prop, cutting it off."

Gilbert Mays: Navigator—Take A Bearing

Lieutenant Commander G. I. Mays, who later served a tour of duty in the Aleutian Islands, graduated from flight school at Corpus Christi, Texas, on March 17, 1943. His first duty station was NAS Norfolk, Virginia. He tells his story of Atlantic theater duty.

"After spending a couple of weeks at the Breezy Point BOQ (Bachelor Officer's Quarters), I received word one evening to report to operations for a flight to NAS Opa Loca, Florida, just outside of Miami. The flight in a DC-3 was rough, unpleasant and bumpy and was completed mostly in solid IFR (Instrument Flight Rules) conditions.

"Following a short stay in the Miami area and some visits to the infamous 'Seven Seas' night spot, I boarded an old Sikorsky four–engine flying boat flown by Pan American for the flight to Trinidad, British West Indies, via Guantanamo Bay and San Juan, Puerto Rico. Upon arrival I was assigned as the junior member of a PBY–5 crew.

"The squadron mission was to fly anti-submarine cover for convoys departing New Orleans en route to the African theater. We departed Trinidad each evening just at sunset and armed with the convoy's position, course and speed, intercepted the string of ships just south of the Dominican Republic. Throughout the night we flew a preplanned pattern over the convoy, then were relieved at daylight by other patrol aircraft.

"For a junior birdman just out of flight school, the intercepts required by these flights presented navigational problems of monumental proportions.

"The majority of the plane commanders were very senior Lieutenants, trained in the mid-thirties and all seemed to be ten feet tall to us 'Boot' Ensigns. The particular Patrol Plane Commander I broke in with had me believing that the success or failure of the flight was completely dependent on the accuracy of my navigation. It seemed to me that he was always lost, and considering the fact I was never too certain of my whereabouts, the flights were arduous marathons that became all the more dismal because I was airsick a good deal of the time.

"It wasn't until a couple of years later when I became a plane commander and started playing the same games with my junior Ensign navigators that it came to me that rascal had been putting me on. How the hell can one get lost in the Caribbean Sea?

"These flights, as with most patrol flights, were long, grueling and unrewarding, without much to show for our efforts. However, we were compensated one night for our perseverance with an unusual opportunity. We quite suddenly came upon what appeared to be a surfaced submarine. We dropped our stick of four torpex depth charges but were unable to verify a hit. My part was relatively minor, consisting of setting up the mechanism in the bow to insure the depth charges fell at proper intervals.

"Regardless of the results, whether we did or did not sink the sub, the incident served to break the monotony and was certainly a powerful morale booster."

Convairiety: Busy Cats Off Brazil

PBY contributions to U-Boat resistance off South America were no less spectacular than any zone of the Atlantic theater.

"Convairiety," Consolidated-Vultee's house organ, offers a brief synopsis in their Installment #48, "History of Convair."

"A South American PBY patrol was established in the opening days of the war. Six PBY-5s of Patron 52 arrived December 11 at Natal, Brazil, eventual headquarters of Fleet Air Wing Six. Cats patrolled the entire rim of Brazil.

"The PBYs saw plenty of action after the Nazis opened a U-Boat blitz off Brazil in the summer of 1943. By then the subs had adopted the tactics of staying on the surface and dueling the planes.

"Lt. (jg) Frank F. Jare, piloting a Patron 94 Catalina, was killed in such a fight with U-590 but a sister Cat flown by Lt. (jg) S.E. Auslander, found the sub two hours later and sank it with bombs.

"On July 21 Auslander had an indecisive hour-long battle with U-662 while escorting an 18-ship convoy. The next day the sub was sunk by a Cat piloted by Lt. (jg) R. H. Howland. On July 24, three planes attacked the U-199 and the kill was credited to a PBY of the Brazilian Navy."

"The war in Europe and the Pacific exploded with Allied invasions and massive naval attacks during June, 1944. On June 6, the long–awaited allied invasion of Europe began with landings on the beaches of Normandy, France. In the Pacific, U.S. Naval forces bombed and shelled Japanese installations on Saipan, Tinian, Guam, Rota, and Pagan Islands in the Mariannas. Over 300 Japanese aircraft and their carriers Shokaku and Taiho were shot down or sunk in the Battle of the Philippine Seas on June 19–20. Throughout the month, furious battles raged in both theaters. Definitely, the war was heating to a climax.

Ercell Hart: Great Ragged Island Experience

There was little doubt, therefore, that Lieutenant Commander Ercell Hart, who reports his Pacific experiences in other segments, had other matters on his mind when the call came to lead a salvage expedition to recover a PBY–5, stranded on a coral reef of Great Ragged Island in the Bahamas. Nonetheless, he gathered his crew and set out to perform his duty.

He prefaces his story with the Island's discovery by Columbus in 1492 and reconstructs the situation leading to the PBY's grounding.

"Columbus sighted it first back in 1492, an insignificant little island no more than four miles long with a hill at its south end less than 100 feet high. There was nothing about it or its string of neighboring islets that invited more than a cursory visual inspection as the Santa Maria and her accompanying caravels Nina and Pinta coasted southward along the eastern fringe of the Great Bahama Bank that Friday afternoon of 26 October. It had been a fortnight since the cry of 'Tierra! Tierra!' had been shouted from the Pinta's forecastle deck by lookout Rodrigo de Triana, tearing away forever the murky veil that separated the Old World from the New.

"To Lieutenant Constantine Economou in June, 1944, Great Ragged Island, with its sand beach and quiet water in a cove on its eastern shore, looked like a great place to set her down. 'Her' was his PBY-5 with the starboard engine dead and the port engine beginning to overheat. Returning to Guantanamo Bay with the laboring engine was out of the question.

Caribbean and northern nations of South America.

PBY-5 in flight off Naval Air Station, Jacksonville, Florida. (courtesy Ercell Hart file.)

He doubted if he could even make it to the little advance base at Great Exuma Island, some 75 miles ahead. Economou and his crew, on a navigation training flight from the PBY operational training base at Jacksonville, Florida, had almost finished their training course. The flight to Guantanamo, Cuba and return would be part of the final phase.

'Floats down,' signalled Economou. "He and the other two pilots in the crew had practiced simulated single-engine landings in the coffee-colored water of the St. John's River in Jacksonville but now it was the real thing with no chance to try it over again if he didn't do it right. Making an approach on one engine meant trim tabs cranked all the way over to help rudder control with the asymmetrical power, then cranking the rudder tab back toward neutral as power was reduced and finally cut just before touching down. His left leg was already cramped from keeping on course against the thrust of the port engine, trying to balance its power with the two needs — maintaining altitude and directional control.

"The offshore channel water was choppy but along the sandy beach was a swath of quiet water with some shoals or a reef between it and deep

119

water. Economou aimed for the smooth water paralleling the shore, even though it wasn't right into the wind, hoping he wouldn't end up in a water loop because of the cross–wind and the single-engine approach. Kerswish! Not bad. Now to taxi in behind that bit of a point at the end of the beach and anchor in the slight lee it would afford. Power up on that port engine for some directional control—wow! 'Round she goes, headed for the beach. Throttle back, idle it. Now she wants to weather-cock into the wind. No good, we'll be out in the channel if we don't turn her. Power up again! Not too much right rudder! She won't turn cross–wind. Come on, dammit, more power. Ker-unch!

"The PBY rammed onto the coral shelf that extended out from the point at the cusp of the beach, punching holes through the dur-aluminum skin of her bottom and popping rivets along the seams. The choppy seas skewed her around and she came firmly aground on parallel ridges of coral. With rocks showing through the bottom and water knee–deep in the bilges, it looked like she was there to stay. A rubber boat trip to the beach, a hike across the island led by local residents, and a telegraphed message from the government station at the settlement resulted in an eventual return of the crew to Jacksonville.

"Defiantly Perched There, Her Wings Stiffly Spread"

"Then began phase two of the incident. As Chief Flight Instructor of the operational training unit to which the plane belonged, I also had the assignment of Crash and Salvage Officer of the squadron. With a small crew of mechanics and a radioman, a supply of tools, rations and gear for establishing a short-term camp at the wreck site, I flew to the small U.S. base on Great Exuma Island. There we embarked on a boat for the trip to Great Ragged. I was to determine whether it would be feasible to make repairs that would enable the plane to be salvaged intact. If not, my orders were to salvage those parts that were practical to bring back, destroy some other specified items, and to burn the plane. It was still wartime and zealous officials didn't want the enemy, wherever he might pop up, to get at that dependable old Catalina.

"We examined the wreck, determined that it would not be feasible or economical to get her flying again, nor to get any more of her back to base than we could disassemble and haul back on the utility patrol boat available from the Great Exuma station. We set up camp ashore and began removal of the components selected to be salvaged.

"Our activities, our camp and our personnel, were the object of rather continuous but very courteous observation by the residents of the island, who we found to be industrious, self sufficient and generous. Although most of these present–day inhabitants had Africa as their original homeland and traced no ancestry back to the 'Indians' found by Columbus, I couldn't help but recall, as we made efforts to repay them for their kindness

Lt. Cmdr. Ercell Hart with island friends at base camp on Great Ragged Island, Bahamas.

and assistance to us, the words of Columbus. 'In order that we might win good friendship, I gave to them red caps and to some glass beads.' We hadn't brought any glass beads, but a few Navy white hats got exchanged and canned corned beef seemed to be welcome.

"The day came when we had gleaned all practical items of salvage, had packed them on the patrol boat, had struck our camp and were ready for the cremation. The Catalina's fuel and oil tanks remained with the same quantities aboard as the day she fetched up on the reef. We intended to merely open up the tanks, fluff up some gasoline-soaked tinder around the filler necks, break a few lines in the cabane section, stand off a safe distance and fire a Very pistol signal flare into her and run like hell. Now anyone associated with aviation activities has an extremely respectful attitude toward gasoline, oil and fire. The consequences of an accidental fire are too horrible to contemplate. We prepared her funeral pyre with extreme care.

"When all was ready, we stood on the bank within flareshot, hesitating, reluctant I think, to do the dirty deed. Okay, let 'er go. Good-bye old girl! Pop! The Very's red flare bounded along the top of the wing and plopped into the water. Fire Two! A clean miss. Didn't figure the cross-wind right. Put a little Kentucky windage in the next one. Pop! Right into the tinder pile. Don't get in my way when I leave! What in tarnation . . .? Nothing's happening. More flares. Still nothing.

"We put the rubber boat back in the water, paddled out to the wreck again, approaching a little gingerly, not knowing whether there might be a smoldering wick somewhere that might flare up with a big whoosh. No sign of even any scorching. This time we made sure our wicks and tinder in the fuel tank necks were wet with gasoline and reaching the fuel below. We stuffed more tinder into the mechanic's station in the cabane section, opened up more fuel lines, wet everything down with gas and oil, then rowed off to where we figured we could, just with good luck, place a shot into the cabane window and still be able to beat a retreat to safety. This time our 'bird-nest' of tinder ignited, smoke and flames made an ominous display, and we got that rubber boat up on the step as we made for shore.

"Some 15 minutes later we lay offshore in the patrol boat, watching the dismal sight as black smoke and rather desultory flames issued from the hulk. She seemed to be defiantly perched there, her wings stiffly spread for takeoff, no crumbling, no boom, no fireball, no theatrics. Somehow my mind spun back to a time when as a boy I was given the disagreeable task of drowning a litter of kittens and I cried as I watched small bubbles rise from the sack, unable to wrench my eyes away from the sight. When the patrol boat's engines revved up into a roar, no one looked back."

9

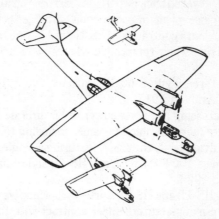

The Flying Boat

Naval patrol aircraft, so long denied a respectable place in the brief annals of aviation, surged to the forefront in fame and glory during the war years of 1940 to 1945, then faded into obscurity, almost before the guns were silenced. Their contribution to the Allied victory over the Axis powers in World War II may never be thoroughly documented. There is little doubt, however, that their activities, patrolling as "eyes of the fleet," attacking enemy submarines and shipping, hauling personnel and equipment to and from remote areas of the world and rescuing thousands of survivors from would-be watery graves, effectively shortened the war and reduced the grisly count of casualties on both sides.

The Consolidated PBY Catalinas became the backbone of Allied seaplane and amphibian patrol craft. The final design, though slow and lumbering, proved more universally adaptable to any climate, as well as to Allied needs of a patrol aircraft.

Events leading to the development of the PBY Catalina, and to that of other patrol aircraft, began shortly after man first ascended into the air in motorized flight.

The first powered seaplane to make a successful flight was the Hydravion by French designer Henri Fabre. Powered by one Gnome seven-cylinder rotary engine, the Hydravion was flown by Fabre, making his first flight ever, on March 28, 1910. He extended his flights from the original 1000 feet to almost four miles in the first two days of flying.

On January 26, 1911, Glenn Curtiss flew the first practical seaplane. A Golden Flyer type, modified and mounted on a single central float; it had small stabilizing skid floats under the lower wingtips.

He landed his aircraft alongside the USS Pennsylvania, was hoisted aboard by a winch, lowered back into the sea and took off again, proving the feasibility of using a seaplane in conjunction with fleet activities.

His effort won him a contract for U.S. Navy Aircraft Number One, and was nicknamed Triad when retractable wheels were added to the main float.

Curtiss sold three Type-E-60 HP-biplanes and a Triad single-float plane to the U.S. Army in 1911.

Gradually increasing the horsepower of his aircraft engines, Curtiss continued to create more durable seaplanes, including the 100 HP Model F-Pusher Engine flying boat, the HS-1, featuring a single 375 HP Liberty engine that became a 400 HP HS-1L and HS-2L and remained in the U.S. Navy service until 1926.

Almost 1000 HS-1L and HS-2L Curtiss seaplanes were manufactured by Curtiss and five manufacturers under contract with the Curtiss Aeroplane and Motor Company.

With the coming of World War I, and with German submarine attacks on Allied shipping creating havoc, Curtiss and competitors for Navy contracts began a concentrated effort to create a seaplane capable of stalking and bombing the U-Boat, or at the very least, hound his every move — keeping him under water and limiting his maneuverability.

The British Royal Navy took delivery of two Curtiss H-4 seaplanes in November, 1914 and five more during 1915. The two 90 – horsepower Curtiss OX-5 engines proved insufficient to power the aircraft with any degree of efficiency. As a result, 100 HP engines were used on 50 more H-4 seaplanes ordered by the British in 1915. Called the "Small Americas," beginning in July, 1916, these aircraft were replaced by a larger Curtiss H-8 seaplane called the "Large Americas."

Featuring two 160 – HP Curtiss engines, the H-8 once again proved under-powered and their engines were soon replaced with 275 HP Rolls-Royce Eagles; at this point, the aircraft became the H-12.

A British Curtiss H-12 sent a German Zeppelin down in flames on May 14, 1917, becoming the first American-made airplane to shoot down an enemy aircraft. Then, in less than a week, another Curtiss H-12 attacked a German U-Boat.

The First Trans-Atlantic Flight

Perhaps the most famous Curtiss seaplanes of the early days of aviation were the four Navy-Curtiss Flying Boats employed to bridge the Atlantic for the first time by air.

Spawned as an idea in 1917 to create a long range, rugged patrol plane to combat the German U-Boat menace, long delays in manufacturing and the end of the war, found the plane unnecessary. However, the challenge of making the first flight across the Atlantic stimulated the Navy into creating a special NC Plane Division, designated Number One; it was placed under the command of Commander John H. Towers, USN. The aircraft were numbered: NC-1 through NC-4.

Preparations for the historic flight in training of flight and support personnel, logistics, communications, weather forecasting and locating rescue ships at intervals along the route took several months.

Progress was hampered by storm damage to NC-1 and NC-4, relegating NC-2 to the role of parts supply for its three sister aircraft, yielding to their cannibalizing of parts, a wing and tail sections to meet the scheduled flight date.

But on May 8, 1919, the three seaplanes took off from the Naval Air Station at Rockaway, Long Island, with a planned route to Halifax, Nova Scotia, then to Trepassey, Newfoundland, to the Azores, to Lisbon and on to Plymouth, England.

Along the way, NC-4 developed engine trouble, landed at sea, and taxied almost 100 miles to Chatham, Massachusetts, where it was repaired and flew on to meet NC-1 and NC-3 in Trepassey.

On May 16, the three aircraft took off for the Azores, but only NC-4 made it, arriving in Horta, Azores at noon the following day. NC-1 and NC-3 landed at sea in thick fog and battered by a heavy sea, NC-1 sank when towing attempts failed. The crew was rescued by a Greek steamship and proceeded on to Horta. NC-3 taxied over 300 miles under her own power, arriving at Ponta Delgada on May 19 but was damaged too much to fly.

NC-4 continued the flight on May 20, arriving in Plymouth on May 30. After receiving the British Cross of Gallantry, the crew boarded a Navy transport for its victorious journey home.

Curtiss was not the only aircraft manufacturer vying for a piece of the new seaplane flying boat, patrol aircraft market spreading throughout the world during the four decades that followed Glenn Curtiss' 1911 flight. Boeing, Martin, Douglas, Keystone, Sikorsky, Hall, Consolidated and the Naval Aircraft Factory in Philadelphia, as well as many foreign designers and aircraft manufacturers, accepted the challenge to compete in the market.

Boeing: The Flying Dreadnaught

In 1918, Boeing landed a U.S. Navy contract to construct 50 Curtiss HS-2L flying boats as trainers; they delivered only 25 but established the firm as a major producer of large flying boats. In 1925, the U.S. Navy gave

Boeing an order to create a long range flying boat with the capability of flying non-stop from the U.S. mainland to Hawaii.

Called the "Flying Dreadnaught," and designated PB-1, Boeing's biplane was powered by two Packard 800 – HP back-to-back engines, between the hull and upper wing, turning Hamilton four-bladed birch propellers that rotated in opposite directions to reduce torque. The plane had a maximum speed of 112 miles per hour with a 9000 – foot service ceiling, a fuel capacity of 1700 gallons and a 2500 – mile range. In 1928, the Navy replaced the PB-1's Packard engines with Pratt-Whitney R-1690 air-cooled engines developing 475 HP each.

The Navy ordered 25 Douglas PD-1 flying boats in January of 1928. The Douglas offer was a biplane with two Wright R-1750, 525 HP air-cooled engines, a wing span of 72 feet, 10 inches and a top speed of 121 miles per hour. Its service ceiling was 11,600 feet and it had a maximum range of 1465 miles.

Martin Aircraft landed orders in 1929 for 30 Martin PM-1s. This aircraft was equipped with 575 – HP Wright Cyclone engines developing a top speed of 118 miles per hour and a service ceiling of 8500 feet. Deliveries of the PM-1 began in June of 1930 and Martin received an order for 25 PM-2s which were equipped with twin rudders, replacing the single rudder of the PM-1s. The change slightly increased the Martin craft's range and added 1000 feet to its service ceiling. Martin's experience in the PM series was later reflected in the highly successful U.S. Navy patrol bomber, PBM.

Various manufacturers contributed to the evolution of the flying boat in the late twenties and early thirties. Keystone's PK-1, while sticking with the biplane concept, incorporated the ring cowling, slightly increasing the aircraft's speed and service ceiling. Hall Aluminum Company developed the PH-1, featuring a new single rudder tail, enclosed cockpits and Wright R-1820-86 Cyclone engines.

But the U.S. Navy wanted longer range, more rugged seaplanes that could fly safely from the United States to Alaska, Hawaii, or the Canal Zone. Engineers from the Bureau of Aeronautics commissioned Consolidated Aircraft of Buffalo, New York, to build the prototype of a 100 – foot-plus wing span monoplane with such goals in mind.

Consolidated Aircraft: Reuben Fleet

Consolidated Aircraft, under the guidance of the colorful, aggressive American patriot, Major Reuben Fleet, became the world leader in manufacturing seaplanes, dominating that segment of aircraft for well over a decade. And, perhaps the single – most important ingredient, besides Reuben Fleet himself, in the Consolidated success story was the hiring of I.M. "Mac" Laddon as manager of Design and Research Engineering.

Laddon's staff began designing Consolidated's entry into the long – range bomber competition, teaming with Sikorsky Manufacturing, but

Consolidated Commodore, civilian airline model of the military version Admiral, flying over Statue of Liberty. (courtesy General Dynamics.)

were unsuccessful in the venture. The Consolidated-Sikorsky offering came in third in a field of four; the winner was Curtiss with its B-2 Condor bomber.

However, Major Fleet was unbowed by the setback, moving his team, under Laddon's direction, to the Consolidated headquarters in Buffalo,

New York, where they immediately began work on the design of a long-range flying boat-patrol bomber. And, on February 29, 1928, the Consolidated team won the design contract and an order from the Navy for a Prototype airplane.

The first Consolidated experimental patrol aircraft was officially designated the XPY-1; Major Fleet named it the "Admiral" honoring Admiral Moffett in appreciation for his efforts in putting the contract together.

With a 100-foot wing span, two 450-HP Pratt-Whitney "Wasp" engines, standing 17 feet, four inches high and 61 feet, nine inches long, the XPY-1 was designed for 118 miles per hour maximum speed with a 15,000 foot service ceiling. Its most interesting feature from the Navy's viewpoint was its expected 2600 mile maximum range.

By late 1928 the XPY-1 Consolidated patrol plane was ready for its maiden test flight. But ice on the waters of the Niagara River and Lake Erie prohibited a water takeoff and the romance between Reuben Fleet and the City of Buffalo, New York, began to wane.

Partially disassembled and loaded on railroad flat cars, the untested new aircraft was transported to Washington where it was reassembled and flown for the first time on January 10, 1929. "Mac" Laddon was a passenger on the craft's first flight to observe the fruits of his handiwork.

That flight and subsequent flights the following day brought an enthusiastic endorsement from the Navy and the first official demonstration for the Navy Test Board was scheduled for January 22, 1929. Although quite successful and praised by Assistant Secretary of Navy-Air, Edward Warner, who rode as a passenger, the XPY-1 was not accepted until a third Wasp engine was installed on top of the wing between the two original engines. Secretary Warner insisted the aircraft obtain a speed of 135 miles per hour.

But the contract prize of nine XPY-1 Admirals eluded Reuben Fleet and his Consolidated Company as the Navy put the design out to bid. Glenn L. Martin Company landed the contract with a no-engineering-cost lower quotation.

Undaunted, Fleet converted the XPY-1 Admiral patrol plane into a long-range commercial aircraft and introduced it as the "Commodore." Shrewd business maneuvers by Fleet and a knack for knowing when to make a move, perhaps, supplied the basis for his partial underwriting of a new airline in South America called the New York, Rio and Buenos Aires Line, Incorporated. The Commodore became the aircraft used in this venture and the line prospered through airmail transport contracts with Argentina, Uruguay and Brazil.

Reuben Fleet and "Mac" Laddon were still smarting from the loss of the Navy contract on the XPY-1 and research was begun following a merger of the NYRBA Lines with Pan-Am to create an improved patrol plane from their Admiral design.

Consolidated XPBY prototype of PBY, 1936. (courtesy General Dynamics.)

Consolidated: P2Y-1 "Ranger"

Consolidated apparently found the right combination of innovations with the introduction of the XP2Y-1. The new aircraft featured two 575 "Hornet" engines, cleaner lines, with fewer struts and wires, but added strength to the horizontal structure supporting the floats. Before the prototype of the XP2Y-1 was flown, the Navy ordered 23 for production under the name of P2Y-1 "Ranger," requiring the planes to be of the three-engine concept. However, the Navy saw the error of the design in time and the order was filled with two-engine aircraft.

With "Mac" Laddon continuing to improve the design as the order progressed, the final P2Y-1 was equipped with two 750–HP Wright Cyclone engines mounted, for the first time, in the leading edge of the wing. Also, the engine cowling was streamlined into the wing, making a smooth, unbroken contour. This innovation was designed by Frederic E. Weick, of the National Advisory Committee for Aeronautics. Called the NACA Cowling, it shielded the cylinders while directing air circulation around them.

On September 7, 1933, a six–plane detachment of P2Y-1 Ranger patrol planes, flown by pilots and crewmen of Navy Squadron VP-5, took off from Norfolk, Virginia, on a non-stop flight to Coco Solo, Panama. The

Consolidated PBY-1. First production of PBY beginning in September, 1936. (courtesy National Archives.)

25–hour, 19–minute flight of 2059 miles broke the previous longest multiple aircraft flight record and marked the beginning of one of the most incredible lists of "first" in aviation history.

Hardly had the record flight been made when the recipients of the six Consolidated Rangers, VP10, based at Coco Solo, began preparations to fly them to Pearl Harbor, Hawaii. With the seaplane tender USS Wright stationed at Acapulco, Mexico, to service planes, the six P2Y-1 Rangers, under the command of Lieutenant Commander Kneffler McGinnis, departed Coco Solo on October 7, 1933 and landed at Acapulco 14 hours later.

Failure of one Ranger to take off in the windless bay at Acapulco the next day reduced the flight to five planes, but did not diminish the accomplishment, as the planes landed in San Diego just 19 hours after takeoff.

The six P2Y-1s were flown to San Francisco in early January of 1934 where they waited for the signal to take off for Hawaii. Finally, on January 10th, again under the command of Lieutenant Commander McGinnis, the six Rangers flew out of San Francisco Bay en route to Pearl Harbor, Hawaii, 24 and one-half hours, and 2400 miles to the west.

In the spring of 1935, Consolidated delivered a prototype of the XP3Y-1 long–range patrol plane and, in so doing, brought the final PBY design one giant step closer to reality. Many new innovations were incorporated into the design.

"Mac" Laddon included the Fleetster concept of making the fuel cell an integral part of the wing. This application was the first successful use of gas-tight wing tanks. In addition, new wing struts were supported by the fuselage. There were no external braces on the tail assembly. The horizontal structure supporting the floats was eliminated and new retractable floats folded into the ends of the wing, making smooth outer wingtips that were hydraulically lowered when landing. Two Twin Wasp 825–HP engines were mounted in the leading edge of the wing which now was supported above the fuselage by a pedestal arrangement that housed the engineer's compartment. Exhaust gases were used in a thermal de-icing system diverting heat through internal ducts to the leading edge of the wing and stabilizer tail assembly.

PBY: "P" For Patrol, "B" For Bomber, "Y" For Consolidated

In June, 1935, the Navy ordered 60 of the new XP3Y-1s and promptly redesignated them PBY-1. The "P" for patrol, "B" for bomber, "Y" for Consolidated, which was the Consolidated Aircraft Manufacturing identification letter assigned by the Navy. "C" had previously been assigned to Curtiss Aircraft.

Proving the advanced design of the PBY-1, Lieutenant Commander McGinnis once more piloted a Consolidated aircraft to a new record. Flying non-stop, on October 14, 1935, from Coco Solo, Canal Zone to San Francisco, he covered a distance of 3443 miles in under 34 hours. This was a new world distance record for seaplanes.

Consolidated moved the bulk of its manufacturing from Buffalo to San Diego in 1935, dedicating the new plant at Lindberg Field on October 20th. The new XP3Y-1 was flown in from San Francisco to highlight the ceremonies.

With Reuben Fleet providing the initiative for which he became famous, the Consolidated company continued to upgrade the PBY and the Navy continued buying it. An order for 50 improved PBY-2s was placed in

Consolidated PBY-1 on takeoff, San Diego, California, 1936. (courtesy Leon Freeman file.)

Consolidated PBY-1. Head-on view in flight, 1936. (courtesy National Archives.)

July of 1936; then 66 PBY-3s, with 1000 – HP Twin Wasp engines were ordered, almost before the ink was dry on the PBY-2 contract.

The first U.S. Navy squadron to take delivery of PBYs was VP11, which formed in July, 1936, when transfer orders were received to Trans-Pac to Pearl Harbor from San Diego. Under the capable leadership of Lieutenant Commander Laverne Pope, the 12 PBYs of VP11 were air-

Consolidated PBY-2 on step for takeoff. Production model of second PBY design beginning May, 1937. (courtesy National Archives.)

Consolidated PBY-1. PBY Squadron VP6 at San Diego Naval Air Station, 1936. (courtesy Leon Freeman file.)

borne and formed-up in a little over one-half hour from the moment the first plane lifted off the step and into the air.

From this beginning, PBY squadrons began to deploy in greater numbers to Hawaii, the Canal Zone and Norfolk, Virginia. With each new movement of squadrons, old seaplane records fell, new speed records were set and mass flights grew larger.

During the phenomenal growth period of the PBY, two civilian model #28's were manufactured for Dr. Richard Archibold who was research associate of the American Museum of Natural History. Dr. Archibold originally ordered one of the patrol planes, dubbed, "Guba," for research into the wilds of New Guinea but sold the aircraft to Russia for use in an attempt to locate and rescue a famous Russian flyer, Sigismund Levanevsky. The Russian and his crew were lost on a trans-polar flight to Fairbanks, Alaska.

Though the rescue attempt was a failure, the Guba excelled operationally, proving its capabilities in extremely cold weather. In another "first," the Guba made the first coast-to-coast, non-stop flying boat flight.

The second Guba, designated Model #28-3, was delivered to Dr. Archibold on December 3, 1937 and, after several test flights, the doctor and his party flew the aircraft to New Guinea. Here again, the design proved outstanding as the plane responded faultlessly in the high altitude and heat of the tropic island.

Consolidated Model 28-2 with Cyclone engines; made for Dr. Archibold, sold to Russia. (courtesy General Dynamics.)

The Guba's maneuverability in close areas and its positive response enabled the doctor to follow the contour of the land masses in New Guinea and to land on remote lakes and water far from mapped and charted portions of the island.

In a little less than a year, Dr. Archibold's expedition made 168 flights in the New Guinea area, carried over a half million pounds of food and

Consolidated PBY-2 in flight. First production model of second series of PBYs, 1937. (courtesy General Dynamics.)

Model 28-5, Canadian "Canso;" one of 14 amphibious PBYs. (courtesy General Dynamics.)

equipment to remote areas and discovered a new tribe of natives along the Balim River. The Guba was required to frequently land and take off from Lake Habbema, which was over two miles above sea level.

Its return home was a spectacular event in itself, as the doctor, complying with a request by the British government to survey a new aerial route across the Indian Ocean, took the long way home, flying the globe at its greatest diameter. Two more "firsts" were added to the growing list accomplished by the Consolidated PBY. One was the longest flight over water by any aircraft as the Guba flew from Dakar, West Africa, to St. Thomas in the West Indies, a distance of 3200 miles. The other was the first seaplane to fly around the world.

R-1830-72 Wasp engines, delivering 1050-HP at takeoff, were featured in the early version of the PBY-4, which was first tested in May, 1938. This aircraft still had sliding hatches in the fuselage. The final four featured new waist blisters that enclosed the rear observation positions and provided a wide viewing angle for eye-balling on long search missions. Additionally, the blisters could be lifted back to provide near-free mobility for gunners manning 50-caliber machine guns mounted in each compartment.

135

With the addition of blisters, more powerful engines, and later strengthening of the aft-hull to prevent cave-in on water landings, the PBY entered its final stages of modification.

Before those changes were accomplished, Reuben Fleet agreed to provide design and manufacturing technology to Russia to build a PBY plant at Taganrog.

A purchase agreement for three Model 28-2 freight-type seaplanes along the design of the PBY-1 was reached in February of 1937. The exact number of PBYs manufactured by Russia is not known but believed to be slightly less than 200.

With the outbreak of war in Europe, the PBY evolved into the PBY-5 series with Pratt-Whitney R-1830-82, 1200–HP engines and became popular with Great Britain who ordered 50; Canada ordered 50 and Australia, 18. In 1940, the Dutch, operating from the East Indies, purchased 36.

A PBY-4 was used to create the XPBY-5A, converting it into an amphibian aircraft. The landing gear retracted into wheelwells in the sides of the hull. A nose wheel, located in the bow, retracted into the hull and automatic hatches closed it in. One central hydraulic power unit controlled the landing gear but was backed by a manual override.

Consolidated PBY-6A. Final configuration of PBY series. First delivery, January, 1945. Manufactured in New Orleans, Louisiana. (courtesy General Dynamics.)

First test flown in 1939, the new model amphibian design was incorporated into the last 33 of the 200 PBY order which had been placed by the U.S. Navy shortly after the war broke out in Europe.

Though there were calls and plans for faster, better armed patrol planes, and several manufacturers, including Consolidated, had new models ready for testing, the PBY Catalina was already in production. The need was immediate for hundreds of patrol bombers, without the normal delays involved in tooling and personnel training.

Reuben Fleet proved his strength and cunning as an organizer and manager in providing PBY-5s to equip 16 U.S. Navy squadrons by January of 1942. And, the Navy continued to place orders during 1942: 586 PBY-5s, 627 PBY-5As, and 225 PBY-5B Catalinas to Great Britian through lend-lease.

In 1941, Canadian Vickers of Montreal began production of an order for Catalinas that would result in 230 Model OA-10As for the U.S. Army, and 139 Canso-A Models for the Royal Canadian Air Force. Meanwhile, Boeing of Canada at Vancouver was building 240 PB2B-1s for the U.S. Navy and Great Britain, and 67 PB2B-2s for the RCAF. During this same period, the Naval Aircraft factory at Philadelphia was producing the PBN-1 "Nomad" version, most of the 156 constructed going to Russia under lend-lease.

In July of 1943, the Consolidated Aircraft Company, by then known as Convair, after merging with Vultee, began manufacturing PBYs in New Orleans, Louisiana. It was in this new facility that the final PBY Catalina design was produced and would be designated PBY-6A.

10

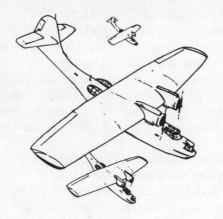

The Learning Years

Long before World War II broke out, PBY pilots and crewmen were learning to respect the PBY for its reliability and endurance. Crewmen particularly sought duty in the PBY squadrons, and once assigned, protected their "bird" with the pride of new fathers. Service in the seaplane squadrons was considered some of the best duty in the Navy.

The first Navy squadron to be officially designated "PBY" was VP11. Formed in 1936, under the command of Lieutenant Commander L. A. Pope, USN, the squadron actually began with only one PBY—the XPBY-1. The remainder of the squadron was made up of XP3D-2s and PBM-1s.

George Davis: The First PBY Squadrons

George Davis retired as Captain, USN, but began his PBY career as a seaman first class in December, 1936. Captain Davis offers insight into the rather confusing changes in squadron designation which have led to numerous heated discussions as to just which squadron did which in the early days.

"I joined VP11 at NAS North Island, California, on 12 December 1936 as a seaman first class, almost directly from Class B AMM school, NAS Norfolk, Virginia, which was a six–month course. About the time I joined, VP6 flight personnel had set up shop at NAS North Island and had been issued 12 production model PBY-1s; they were in training for a Trans-Pac to NAS Ford Island, Pearl Harbor. So, although VP11 was credited as being the first PBY squadron, it was only on the basis of their sole XPBY-1; VP6 drew their full bag of PBY-1s, trained and Trans-Pacing before VP11 had all of their new aircraft. I was quite aware of this because as of 13 December 1936 I was a member of the beach crew handling both squadrons.

"The beach crew consisted of a beachmaster, four to six side mount men and two tail men. After we learned how much water to add to the side mount tires to give them neutral bouyancy, two men could handle a side mount and, on a calm day, one six-footer could handle a side mount alone. Beach-crewing in San Diego in the winter wasn't the most comfortable. Our wader-cuffs and neck always leaked and beaching for two squadrons kept us in the water throughout the working day, or night. If one got into water above his chin, he would be trying to cadge beers from Davy Jones.

"VP11, after outfitting and training, went on the 1937 maneuvers Trans-Pacing to Pearl Harbor. By then I was an AMM3/c in the engineering gang and we went along to support the planes, riding the old USS Langley, a CV-1 class seaplane tender. For those games, the Langley anchored just south of French Frigate Shoals. We laid mooring buoys inside the reef and pumped gas from hand pump bowsers out of 50 – foot motor-sailors. We also got to stretch our sea-legs with the Goony Birds while we were digging latrines on the down-wind side of the island.

When the maneuvers ended, VP11 exchanged their 12 PBY-1s for VP8's PH-1s and took them back to the states. Eleven of us from VP11 were transferred to VP8 with the planes to provide a 'trained' nucleus. I spent over a year in the engineering gang, chafing to become a permanent plane crew member — very impatiently.

"I learned to pull every engine and airframe check, change engines and props, control adjustment, fuel and oil system and paint fabric. I flew a lot, without flight pay, as did many other youngsters.

"We had to learn aircraft operations, mooring and vice-versa, emergency repairs and machine guns and gunnery. We had to field strip the 30 – and 50 – caliber guns; the mechs' fired the '50s from the waist hatch, the radioman fired the 30 from the tunnel and the pilots manned the bow 30 – caliber.

"Manning the waist guns was interesting. The PBY-1 didn't have the blister waist-hatch but rather a sliding hatch, which was contoured to blend into the hull shape and for gunnery we rolled the waist-hatch all the way forward, then cranked up a bracket which lifted the rear of the hatch about 18 inches, making a windshield for the gunner. Shooting a target at level or above, we stood on the gunner's step, well down in the hull. However, if the target was below our level, we had to sit on the top hatch rail with our feet on the bottom, or outboard rail. Then, as the target passed under, we pulled ourselves erect on the bottom rail, aiming and firing all the while and eventually standing erect, looking down three to 4000 feet, just hanging on to the gun.

"The gunner had a safety belt attached to the inside top of the hull, but the belt toggle buckle often was knocked open by our elbow and we were doing this drill less safety belt or parachute. Amazingly, I never heard of anyone being lost that way.

"I participated in many gunnery hops, bombing and scouting missions, refueling from submarines, scrubbed millions of acres of bilges and enjoyed advance-base operations at French Frigate Shoals, Johnston Island and Midway."

Laverne Pope: Report As Commanding Officer, NAS Wake Island

The Commanding Officer of VP11, Lieutenant Commander Laverne Pope, mentioned by Captain Davis, had his own observations of the first PBY's capabilities.

"At the time the PBY came out, we didn't know what a straightforward airplane it really was and we were making flat speed landings, thinking we couldn't do stall-landings. Now that was incredible, that a plane as responsive as the PBY could have been tricky in landing.

"We were flying the XPY-1 for two or three months before the test pilot of Consolidated got hold of it and several of us started doing stall-landings. Meanwhile, the first squadron to get the PBYs was out in Honolulu still doing speed landings. If we had stuck to the original concept of speed landing, the PBY could never have been used in rough water and it simply would have faded out of use.

"I took command of VP11 when it was first commissioned in 1936 and was assigned to San Diego, California. At the time, there were two other patrol plane squadrons flying out of the base: VP3 and VP7. The three were joined into a patrol wing under Admiral Ernest J. King, who was in charge of the scouting forces of Pacific Fleet. Later, a full Commander named Buckmaster became Patrol Wing Commander, but not until Admiral King was convinced he could handle the job.

"After two years under Buckmaster, I became Operations Officer for Kenneth Whiting, Commander of Patrol Wing Two at Pearl. That was also a two–year tour and when I got there they said, 'See that cane field that has just been planted? That's your field. Your tour of duty will last until it is harvested; that's when you will go home.'

"I became thoroughly at ease with patrol planes. In spite of the fact that carrier and fighter aircraft seemed to be the thing for a career in aviation, I liked the Catalinas.

"Just before the war, I had been serving on the tender Albermarle and was given orders which were unsatisfactory to me. I was ordered to report as Commanding Officer Naval Air Station, Wake Island and I knew nothing about Wake. I protested that to send me to Wake Island with no knowledge of their plans simply didn't make sense, so they sent me to the Bureau of Ships. I spent a week going over plans for Wake, then was given a leave to begin on December 7, 1941.

"I was on leave, traveling as the prospective Commander of Wake Island, when the Japs hit Pearl Harbor. Immediately, I returned to the West Coast but the transportation system was so messed up, I sat cooling my heels waiting for a ship or airplane to take me to my command. I never got there. The Japs took Wake in the first three weeks and Cunningham was taken prisoner of war. I took his scheduled command at Johnston Island."

Philip Bankhardt: "A Cup Of Coffee, Or A Steaming Steak"

Philip Bankhardt, Honolulu, Hawaii, told of his experiences flying the PBY with VP84 during his tour of duty in the Atlantic theater but his service days with the Catalina began in 1939 when the PBY-1 was the plane of the day.

"The PBY-1 was a bit underpowered and understabilized for some pilots. When fully loaded, it just couldn't break free on takeoff from slick, smooth water. In fact, it was sometimes necessary to employ a motor launch to generate waves. Many pilots will remember grinding along for miles before giving up and taxiing back for another try.

"In 1939, on one of those frustrating tries, down West-Loch, off Pearl Harbor, the sugar cane fields were just too close ahead. But before chopping the throttle, I figured, 'Why not try for an extra tug by using a bigger bite on the props?' With the propellers spinning at maximum permissible RPM, 2450, I reached up and pulled the pitch controls to give them that bigger bite at a higher pitch. There came a quick tug and we leaped free, into the air. The inertia of the spinning props was enough to deliver a moment of added thrust before the RPM dropped from the higher pitch setting. By this time we were free of the surface drag and remained airborne at reduced thrust. Perhaps the thrust bearing or cylinder heads took an extra strain, but it worked.

"One day during fleet problems, we were assigned to fly simulated bombing runs at 10,000 feet over the 'battle line.' This would give the anti-aircraft gunners good practice by training their guns on us. Carrier pilots also made easy passes at us 'sitting ducks.' But then, the fighter pilots pulled alongside to ridicule our plight. That was when some of our pilots raised a cup of coffee or a steaming steak dinner to show how good we had it. Those fighter pilots dove hurriedly away with second thoughts, no doubt, on P-Boat duty.

"Almost three years later, in August and September of 1941, while we were seriously flying twice-a-day search patrols to detect any possible approaching Japanese attack, orders trickled in for most of the now-seasoned Patrol Plane Commanders to return to the United States mainland to form new squadrons; the Navy was expanding its patrol bomber fleet.

"Admiral P.N.L. Bellinger was commander of Patrol Wing Two at the time and responsible for scouting to detect any approaching enemy fleet. He impounded the transfer orders, protesting by letter to the Bureau of Navigation that his was the hottest spot in the Navy, therefore, he needed operationally qualified pilots, not fresh graduates just out of flight school. However, Washington came back with a letter directing Admiral Bellinger to comply with the transfer orders. He took them out of his safe, released his essential plane commanders, and put the Washington letter in the safe.

"In Norfolk, Virginia, on December 7th, when I heard the radio report of the Pearl Harbor attack, my instant question was, 'Where were those PBY patrols?' Many months later, I learned that all of the twice-a-day patrols had been discontinued while the new pilots were being trained to do their job.

"After the Japanese surrender in 1945, the Pearl Harbor investigation pointed to Admiral Bellinger for letting the enemy sneak in. I was told that he produced that 'obey orders' letter he had placed in his safe when he released the transfer orders for all those PBY Patrol Plane Commanders."

The problems of flying a PBY seaplane during its brief presence in the world of aviation were many and occasionally complex. If the water wasn't too rough, it was too smooth; if the plane was pampered on takeoff, it porpoised and the only successful way to land at sea was in a stall-mode. These, among a number of other features, made the PBY a special aircraft —almost too simple to handle under the command of a knowledgeable pilot but deadly to a novice. Its early days were loaded with minor problems inflicted upon it by careless or incompetent personnel. One such incident involved salt water spray and its removal from the windshield.

Ercell Hart: "Like Flying Into Red Glue"

Ercell Hart, who contributed to the Atlantic section, tells of a mix-up in the use of windshield anti-icing solution.

"When a PBY taxied for takeoff, spray was whipped up by the propellers and the bow wave, and was deposited on the windshield and side windows of the cockpit, limiting the pilot's view until it was swept away by the windstream or wiped by wipers. If the temperature was freezing, the spray froze in place and remained as an obstruction to view until removed. If the takeoff was from salt water, the spray dried on the windshield as an opaque frost. Safety of flight, as well as the PBY's usual mission of search, called for clear vision.

"No windshield washing or wiping provisions were designed into the first PBYs and after a takeoff from salt water or in freezing weather, something had to be done to remove the obstruction to vision. One solution available to flight crews was for one of the crew to spray fresh water or anti-icing solution onto the windshield from a position in the nose turret. This called for some improvisation with squirters devised by members of the crew and for a 'volunteer' to brave the 100–mph windstorm in the nose of the turret while squirting the fluid.

"Engineers at Consolidated remedied the situation in later modifications by installing a windshield de-icing system. The anti-icing fluid was colored red for identification and, of course, it had a specific coded identity labeled on its storage tank.

"After a number of choppy water takeoffs and use of the new push-button window washer for clearing off dried salt, the containers needed refilling. It was at this point, when our squadron, VP10, was stationed at Pearl Harbor, having just received new PBYs equipped with these new devices, that we were put to the test of Murphy's Law: The unexpected was to be expected.

"Some benighted mech, assigned to refilling the tank, and seeing the remaining dregs of red fluid in the tank, 'identified' it as the familiar red hydraulic oil used elsewhere in the aircraft's system. He topped off the little tank with hydraulic oil, secured the rig, neat and proper, ready to do whatever it was supposed to do. Just what that was, obviously, he wasn't sure.

"On the next takeoff in the choppy channel, the usual salt spray splattered the windshield and I believe it was Ensign Lew Drill who confidently toggled the windshield washer to flush it off. But suddenly a gloriously rosy flow came from the spray nozzles and a glutinous mixture of hydraulic oil and salt bathed the glass in front of each pilot, obscuring all forward view.

'It was like flying into red glue,' Lew reported later.

"Some frantic snatching to open the side cockpit windows, and swabbing at the oily mess with handkerchiefs and rags, opened up enough smeary peepholes to make a landing and taxi back to the ramp. There they cleaned off the gluey gunk, flushed out the system, and made a new start."

Stories of the PBY making incredible landings at sea, on snow packs in Greenland and Manchuria, taking off with weight-loads far above the maximum load limit and generally defying the manufacturer's design limitations, could hardly top that of a VP14 Catalina landing on, and taking off from, a mud pond in Texas.

Bill Tanner: PBY Mud Landing

Bill Tanner, Rossmoor, California, who later served in the Pacific and Atlantic, relates his PBY beginning and tells the story of an overland ferry flight of PBY seaplanes.

"When the war started in Europe, I was really disappointed that the Navy reduced the standard one–year pilot training course at Pensacola, Florida, to six or seven months. Also, they split the classes early in the game, deciding which of us went to carrier aviation and which were to fly the big boats.

"Most of us wanted carrier-type operations, mainly because in carrier aviation the aircraft had but one pilot and a pilot began flying his own aircraft immediately upon joining the fleet. In big boats, there were three pilots; one flew as navigator, one as co-pilot and one as the Patrol Plane Commander. As a result, it took a year or so to qualify as a Patrol Plane Commander.

"When we were split-out during the first week or two, I got the concentrated course leading to big aircraft.

"I received my wings and Ensign's commission in May of 1940 and was very happy with my first assignment: Patrol Squadron Fourteen at San Diego, primarily because I had grown up in San Pedro, California, and had graduated from USC. I was back home. My parents and brothers were still living in San Pedro.

"One very interesting episode occurred while we were at San Diego. We had received the first of the new PBY-5 seaplanes to be delivered to the fleet and after about two or three months were ordered to ferry them to Pensacola, Florida. Ferrying seaplanes across the United States had never been done before. Seaplanes had been flown to the east coast through the Canal Zone and up along the eastern seaboard in several jumps but never across the continent. However, this airplane had larger engines than earlier PBYs and was considered reliable enough, so we headed east — nonstop — for Pensacola.

"I was flying as the fourth pilot and navigator on the Commanding Officer's PBY since we had an excess of pilots. On the way, we ran into some of the worst weather I had ever experienced or have experienced since. Severe thunderstorms tossed us all over the skies of Texas, forcing us to deploy the planes in our regular plan for such emergencies. We separated and each aircraft was on its own.

"The squadron commander, Lieutenant Commander Bill Rassieur, fought the plane and the elements and brought us out of the storm with ice all over the airplane. We got a fix on our location which told us we were over north Texas, so we set a course for Corpus Christi as an alternate to Pensacola. We made it safely, as did several other Catalinas of the group. Others continued on toward Pensacola and arrived safely.

"But an unusual thing happened to one of the PBYs which helped qualify it as a truly incredible aircraft. The weather became so severe that the plane commander ordered his crew to bail-out, intending that he and his co-pilot would follow as soon as the rest were safely clear of the aircraft. Then, with only he and his co-pilot aboard, the plane broke out of the storm into relatively clear skies.

"With their navigational gear inoperative, voice radio unreliable because of the static in the air, without the assistance of the blister men and engineer, and with darkness coming on, the two pilots began a desperate search for a body of water on which to land. The first 'lake' they spotted happened to be on the King Ranch in Texas and it really wasn't a lake but a big puddle of mud with a thin covering of water. By the time they were close enough for a good look, it was too late to abort the landing. However, they put the plane down without damage.

"After their initial relief at being on terra-firma, how to get the PBY out of the mud and airborne again became their primary goal and two days passed before they were ready to try their dampened wings. With the assistance of personnel from NAS Corpus Christi, they lightened the plane by removing everything that could be detached and not affect the aircraft's flight worthiness. The PBY was then maneuvered near a tree at the down-wind edge of the mud puddle and a heavy line was attached from the tree to the tail of the plane. The pilot and co-pilot, without a crew, started the engines and, with the line drawn taut, engines at full power, gave the signal to chop the line. The Catalina rumbled and rambled through the mud but got up on the step and was airborne just as it ran out of water and mud.

"The two pilots who engineered that remarkable feat were Lieutenant Murray Hanson and Ensign Bob Clark. Together they flew the plane on into Pensacola with a 20-foot line trailing behind. The PBY was not damaged and remained in service throughout the early years of the war in the Pacific."

Gilbert Mays: Wheels-Up Landing

LCDR Gilbert Mays was a victim of a stateside "landing" after he had served a tour of duty in the Atlantic theater and another in the wilds of the Aleutians. He candidly admits to an embarrassing turn of events.

"Upon returning to the states from the Aleutian tour in December of 1944, we all received a hard-earned 30-day leave. When mine was up, I reported to NAS Oak Harbor on Whidbey Island, Washington, with orders to join in the reforming of VP61 in preparation for a second tour in the Aleutians.

"The R-1830 Pratt and Whitney engines in the PBY-5A's we brought back were very tired. Most were approaching 2000 hours running time. These engines, incidentally, were most reliable. Never once during our nine-month tour did they ever so much as cough or spit.

"We were to be assigned new aircraft and I, along with a co-pilot, a mechanic, a radioman and an observer, were sent to the Consolidated plant in San Diego, California, to pick up and ferry a new PBY-5A back to Whidbey Island.

"On the return flight, we flew up the central valley of California to the foothills of the Cascade Mountains. At Red Bluff, California, we were informed by the local control tower that there was a cold front between us and our destination. In those days, we were not permitted to file IFR (Instrument Flight Rules) when on ferry orders, so we had no choice but to land at Red Bluff and sweat out the weather.

"I suspect that any pilot who has flown for any length of time has a tale to tell that may seem comical currently, but was most embarrassing at the time of its occurrence.

"On the second day of our stay in Red Bluff, I decided, at the request of my radioman, to fly a short local flight. We had some adjustments to make that could not be made on the ground. Another transient pilot who was ferrying an SNJ Navy trainer asked if he could go along and I agreed. During the course of the flight, he asked if he might try a landing and, seeing no harm in this, I granted his request. This act on my part triggered a sequence of events that I would regret for many years.

"We came in on our final approach in a southerly direction, thus placing the control tower on my left. We discovered later that either by design or error when keying the microphone while it was in the 'Inter-Communication' position, the control tower frequency was cut out.

"As we came in over the fence at the end of the runway, the control tower noticed our landing gear was retracted and immediately called but of course was unable to reach me. Then they tried flares but I was looking to my right and very diligently giving the SNJ pilot landing instructions. I was completely oblivious of the tower's frantic effort to avert the impending disaster. To this day it is difficult to believe that everyone aboard that day had their heads up-and-locked at exactly the same time. But we did!

"We made contact with the asphalt runway but so smoothly that I still failed to recognize my predicament. Had I awakened at that instant, I could have easily applied power and taken a wave-off. But I didn't.

"I was absolutely nauseated and stunned to the point of mental paralysis when finally I became cognizant of the situation. That P-boat looked damned ridiculous sitting on the runway on its keel with the port wing also resting on the surface. If anything positive can be said concerning this fiasco, it would be that we touched down so easily that the keel and the retracted float suffered minimal damage.

"We called out the local 'cherry-picker' and the plane was raised to where I could lower the gear, and after he set me down, I taxied to the parking area.

"Now came the difficult part: initiate a dispatch to Ault Field, informing them of my circumstances. Directly, I received word that Lieutenant Commander Harry Holt was on his way in an SNB Beechcraft to inspect the damage and to advise. Harry Holt was a tough old bird who had begun his naval flying career in the mid-20s as an Aviation Pilot.

"I was distressed and alarmed, probably more like petrified, when I learned that it was ol' Harry who was the investigating officer. He didn't take kindly to 'Jaygees' busting up his airplanes.

"I met him upon arrival and directed him to the aircraft, making certain that I stayed well behind him and to his left. When he got to the plane, he got down on his hands and knees and inspected the keel. Other than to ask directions to the aircraft, Harry hadn't said a word to me, which was surprising. It was completely out of character for Harry to remain calm.

"Finally, he crawled out from under the PBY and serenely said to me, 'Well, kid, don't worry about it too much. I've done this twice myself. Fly it up to Sand Point, Seattle, and sell it to A and R'.

"With that, he made an about face, climbed into his Beechcraft and flew off.

"The next day, the weather cleared and I did indeed fly that Catalina to NAS Sand Point and sold it to A and R."

Philip Storm: Stateside Testing And Rescue

Many of the most spectacular capabilities of the PBY were discovered by pilots who were forced into desperate actions during combat, or while attempting an open-sea rescue. But there were stateside squadrons, flying endless hours of boring coast patrol, spotting downed airmen and swamped fishermen for Coast Guard rescue boats and testing ideas dreamed up by a multitude of planners. Somehow, the Catalina was most always chosen to prove or disprove each new concept from rescue to bombing.

Philip Storm, Westlake Village, California, piloted PBYs off the coast of Southern California and, in so doing, fell heir to much of the testing mentioned.

"I was a First Pilot flying PBYs off the West Coast, and in particular, out of Los Alamitos Naval Air Station, Goleta Marine Corps Base, San Diego, and San Nichols Island off the Southern California coast. Primarily, we were involved in offshore crash and carrier landing activities. We worked closely with Coast Guard crash boats in our rescue program and directed them to the scene of a downed airplane or flyer whenever possible. Our planes carried emergency supplies, rafts and other rescue equipment.

"One experiment involved the dropping of a raft from the wing of a PBY by means of a special parachute. A man named David Swanson and I were selected to act as downed airmen who would accept this 'blessing from the sky,' climb aboard and be effectively 'rescued.' The Navy was so sure of the success of this endeavor they filmed the complete operation for use in training classes.

"The boat was dropped, landing close enough to us and in an upright position, but that was the end of the good points of the plan. We made it to the boat dressed in the normal gear of a flyer down at sea but as strong as we were we had to battle with all of our strength to climb aboard. It seems the freeboard of the boat was made intentionally high to avoid swamping in rough water. It simply presented an obstacle too great for the condition of the average man in the sea. The plan itself was a good one, what with a good supply of rations and a parachute to use as a cover — but to no avail.

"Another subject of Navy training films in which I was a participant proved quite successful. Toward the end of the war, we began testing a Jato-assist concept for rapid acceleration of the Catalina on takeoff. These were large containers resembling CO_2 bottles which were attached to the fuselage of the PBY just aft of the blisters. The idea was to take you right through the step and off of rough ocean water. From a dead stop, we would give the Cat full throttle, then push the Jato bottle button rigged up on the yoke and literally burst into the air. In the first moments of clearing the water, we would mush quite badly and, with an airspeed of 50 to 60 knots, at first had a tendency to lower the nose. But we had to mush along until the aircraft engines took full control of the plane's lift. As the Jato program was modified, better control was accomplished and the concept became well accepted by Catalina pilots.

"I graduated Navy but the Coast Guard came along as well as the Marines, and both were looking for pilots. They had a regular selection board, offering extra enticements such as a couple hundred dollars and steady flying. By that time some Navy pilots were wanting for flight action and I wanted to fly.

"We flew with a small crew: Pilot, Co-Pilot, Crew Chief, Radioman and one guy back in the blister. In addition, we were well stocked with rescue equipment.

"There were frequent routine rescue missions. One Sunday, for example, flying out of Los Alamitos, we were alerted that a pilot was down somewhere off the mainland near San Clemente. It was getting dark but I knew the channel well and we found him right away. We dropped flares and directed a surface vessel over to pick him up. His total time in the water was about 15 minutes.

"Another rescue took place off Goleta. A father and son were losing their sail boat; again, it was getting dark. I flew the PBY right down the middle of the channel, where we found the boat full of water and going down. Whitecaps were strong and everywhere. Fortunately, the Coast Guard had dispatched a crash boat, which was a converted PT boat, and it came a runnin.'

"We picked up a Corsair pilot southwest of San Clemente late one afternoon. It happened that the pilot had his IFF (Identification-Friend-or-Foe) on and working with a good signal, so we had good direction and flew right over his raft. The sea wasn't too rough and the swells were far enough apart to give us a good clean pick-up. But the seaman in the blister, who was standing on a platform rigged for rescue assistance, got the line from the sea drogue wrapped around his leg and it pulled him out of the aircraft, almost squeezing his leg off. We had far more trouble rescuing him and saving his leg than in saving the downed pilot.

"All told I was involved in 17 offshore landings, plus rescues that were effected with other craft. I loved flying the PBY. It was a great bird. Stalling it, bending it around; there was no end to its tolerance."

R. L. Summers: San Francisco Air Raid Alert

A short anecdote is offered by R. L. Summers, Honolulu, Hawaii, regarding an incident in the fog of San Francisco.

"We were flying patrols out of Alameda, California; anti-submarine, they called it. Those were hairy days. The fog could be so thick that we would have to take off on instruments on a compass course not knowing what ships were in the bay, or where.

"One day, after our patrol, coming in toward San Francisco Bay, we met a wall of fog. It was late in the evening and, while all of us had practiced blind landings by radio beams, none of us were really sure of ourselves. Four of the PBYs landed at the entrance to the bay and taxied into Alameda. I, having plenty of gas, throttled back and took us back out to sea, hoping the fog would clear by the time we got back.

"After a couple of aborted attempts and back to sea, we made it in. The next morning I learned that San Francisco was alerted twice for a possible air raid during the night. I'm sure it was my plane they had reported. All of the newspapers had headlines about unidentified planes approaching San Francisco. We, of course, didn't say a word."

Consairways: They Also Served

Physical handicap, in various forms, kept some loyal American flyers from qualifying for military service. Most of these men were anxious to serve their nation but couldn't pass the physicals. Some found a way around their handicap by joining civilian transport groups which ferried everything from critical freight, to personnel, to aircraft they were flying.

One such group was called "Consairways," headquartered at the San Diego facilities of Consolidated Aircraft and deriving most of its members from a pool of trans-Pacific pilots and crewmen who had delivered PBYs to the Netherlands East Indies prior to the war. These men and many more who joined them, performed an heroic service to the United States from their inception in April of 1942 until disbanded in December of 1945. Their records included flying over 300 million passenger miles and freighting over 100 million tons of cargo.

Leo J. Dorney: "A Quart Of Fear-Water"

Leo J. Dorney, La Mesa, California, was one of the pilots in this group. His handicap was tipping the scales at a weight far under the acceptable minimum. But his weight didn't keep him from flying thousands of miles for Consairways.

"In the early part of 1942, Captain Ed Jones and I were waiting return transportation from Elizabeth City, North Carolina, following delivery of two PBYs which were to be picked up by the British. We were approached by a Britisher who claimed there was something wrong with one of the PBYs we had just delivered.

149

"We went to where the aircraft was moored on the water, started the engines and asked the British officer to kindly show us what we had done to establish the problem. He and his crew went through the procedure and started down the waterways for takeoff at a slow rate of speed. It was then we discovered they were dragging the buoy with them, having thrown off the upper cable and leaving the lower one attached.

"One afternoon about four, towards the end of 1942, we left San Diego for Honolulu sporting an engine that was intermittently rough. Progress was slow in that we were somewhat overloaded and the engine continued acting up all night. About three in the morning, Guy Irwin, my flight engineer, who had been watching things in the tower, yelled over the intercom, 'Feather that son-of-a-bitch, feather that son-of-a-bitch!'

"Fortunately, I asked which one and Guy yelled, 'The right one!'

"I feathered it as it was burping badly. The left engine had been the one giving us all the trouble and had I instinctively feathered it, we would surely have gone down. In spite of one engine out and the other running rough, we made it into the bay at Kaneohe without further trouble.

"In early 1943, we were delivering a series of PBYs to Australia and, as usual, were allowed to select the routes we felt were best beyond Honolulu. On this particular occasion, I selected Wallis Island as a refueling stop. But, because of very rough water and a heavier-than-normal aircraft, I couldn't get my beast off the water.

"Following three tries and with cylinder head temperatures 'off the instrument panel,' I decided to make one final attempt before retiring for the day and waiting for smoother water in the morning. The Cat was showing signs of making it up when I realized I had crept up on the reef circling the lagoon we used for takeoffs and landings. Rather than try to stop, and possibly hit the reef, I hoisted the plane into the air, jumped the narrow reef and continued the takeoff in the open ocean.

"After becoming airborne, I took off my Navy flight suit and wrang out what seemed to be about a quart of 'fear-water.' Never in my life had I been in such a predicament."

Herbert Sharp: The Secret Norden Bombsight

Another civilian who served his country working with the PBY Catalinas of Consolidated Aircraft is Herbert Sharp of La Mesa, California. Herb began his career with the Catalina before it was so named and long before World War II.

"As a leadman in final assembly at Consolidated Aircraft, I was part of a small crew which accompanied the first PBY to the Naval Air Station at North Island, San Diego, in 1936. Our assignment was to maintain the plane during Navy Trial Board evaluation. Later, in production, I was final assembly supervisor for the forward section.

"I personally installed the first Norden Bomb Sight in a PBY. Security was so tight on the unit at the time that Mister Norden, a Navy security man and I were isolated in the plane when the Sight was out of its box. When attaching the unit to its mounting base, with the cover off, they were to make sure I looked only down the shank of the screw driver at the head of the mounting screw and not at any of the components between which I had to insert the screw driver!

"Much later, I was in the South Pacific under contract with the U.S. Army Air Forces. My specific moves were under orders by the Far East Air Service Command in support of various B-24 bomber groups. While on this tour, I saw one PBY return to base with bullet holes all over the wing, tail and hull. The PBY crew claimed to have outfought Japanese Zeros on that mission.

"The story they gave us was that five Zeros came at them from out of the sun. The plane commander dove the PBY for the water surface in a screaming, more-than-red-line dive, pulling out at the very water surface. Some of the Zeros following the Catalina down collided with each other and the rest mushed into the sea, unable to pull out of their dive."

11

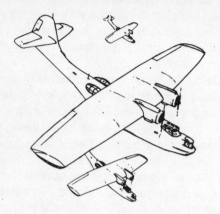

Pearl Harbor
To The Solomons

"We'll drive the Japs back to Tokyo in six weeks" became the battle cry of shocked Americans when word of the Pearl Harbor attack reached the mainland. And most nonmilitary residents, including many uninformed politicians, sincerely thought it possible. But the men who had cried out for years to prepare — to arm — knew it would be a long, desperate struggle and that many of their countrymen would perish before ultimate victory. They believed in the depth of resolve and creative genius of Americans, however, and from this belief drew the necessary strength to continue fighting when the enemy seemed to have the military might, the unbelievable know-how and incredible good luck to sweep through obstacle after obstacle in his path — almost as if they were nonexistent.

Perhaps this strength was wearing a little thin during the bleak days of January through March of 1942. The battered military forces of the United States, Australia, New Zealand, Britain, and the Dutch, fell back from the Philippines, Burma, Malay and the East Indies. The Japanese struck where they wanted, when they wanted, and seemed to suffer virtually no losses while inflicting crippling blows each time they encountered Allied resistance. By the beginning of March, the "Sons of Nippon" had destroyed all resistance between Japan and Australia and were preparing to consolidate New Guinea, the one remaining land mass necessary before conquest, or destruction, of Australia and New Zealand.

But New Guinea would become their first stumbling block, their first defeat and, coupled with the loss of Guadalcanal and Tulagi, would mark a shift in their war effort from offensive to defensive, a change from which they would never recover.

Along the way, however, the combined forces of General Tojo's Imperial Army and Admiral Yamamoto's Imperial Navy captured Wake Island, consolidated their positions in Indonesia, the Philippines and East Indies and overran the northern island groups of New Britain, New Ireland, Marshalls, Gilberts and the Solomons.

On January 6, 1942, Japanese aircraft from Truk Island hit the Australian air base at Rabual, signaling the beginning of their assault on the Bismarck Archipelago. Meeting only token resistance from the depleted ranks of its Australian defenders, landing forces of the Japanese Army attacked Rabaul on January 23, securing the area within days. From the fighter-bomber landing strip on Rabaul, and those developed by the Japanese, the enemy launched aircraft of all descriptions in their quest for control of the skies of the Southwest Pacific.

The New Ireland base at Rabaul was so important to their plan, that the enemy built an armed bastion which withstood two years of Allied air attacks before being bypassed. And, within a few days of their initial landings, the Japanese further secured their position by occupying most of the island groups of New Ireland and New Britain, giving Japan control of the Bismarck Archipelago and bringing the Coral Sea within range.

Meanwhile, on December 20, 1941, Admiral Ernest J. King was appointed Commander-in-Chief United States Fleet and immediately set about the task of building a defense against the onslaught of Japanese forces. He drew an imaginary line between Midway and Brisbane, Australia — linked Fiji and Samoa — and directed that no retreat would be made beyond that line. Communications between Australia and New Zealand could not be interrupted; Hawaii and Midway must be protected, at all cost.

With Japanese submarines shelling Allied island bases throughout the Southwest Pacific, speculation varied as to where the enemy would strike next. Admiral King ordered all Navy patrol bomber groups and Army bomber groups to Fiji and New Caledonia, though he knew it would be of little value should Japan concentrate an invasion force in that area.

More importantly, a strong counter strike was needed to bolster morale and to give the Japanese cause to consider the possibility of having over-extended their supply lines. Rear Admiral Chester W. Nimitz, Commander-in-Chief Pacific Fleet, dispatched the carriers Enterprise and Yorktown to carry out air attacks on islands in the Marshalls and Gilberts. Splitting the two carriers and their escorts into two groups, the Yorktown, under Rear Admiral Frank J. Fletcher, hit Mili, Makin and Jaluit, while the Enterprise, under Admiral Bill Halsey, combined shore bombardment from

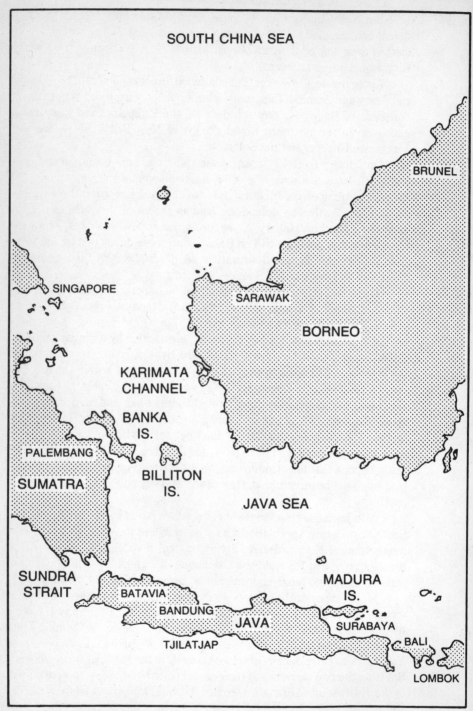

South Central Pacific Islands.

the cruisers Salt Lake City and Northampton with air attacks on Maloelap, Wotje and Kwajalein. The American raids had the desired result with regard to morale but did little to impress the Japanese war strategists.

Throughout February and March, the Japanese kept up their relentless pressure on Allied forces. On February 23, they struck Darwin, Australia with a devastating air raid. Conventional Army troops occupied Rangoon, Burma on March 8 and, on the same day, landed troops at Lae and Salamaua, New Guinea.

During this same period, Admiral Halsey struck a hit and run blow on Wake Island, shelling it first with two heavy cruisers then launching fighters and dive bombers from the carrier Enterprise. Also, Vice Admiral Wilson Brown, leading the carriers Yorktown and Lexington, and seeking a fight, found himself in a position to disrupt the enemy landings at Lae and Salamaua by launching a massive air strike of over 100 fighters and torpedo bombers from off the south shore of Papua. Their success, though limited in enemy vessels sunk, was no less remarkable by the fact that only one plane was lost and they twice crossed the 15,000–foot Owen Stanley mountains. And now, confidence had returned to the Allied forces.

Vice Admiral Nagumo's carrier force had wandered the far reaches of the Pacific, from the attack on Pearl Harbor to Rabaul, the East Indies and Darwin, inflicting crippling blows on Allied vessels and bases. His forces virtually swept the skies clear of Allied aircraft, while sustaining varying losses of aircraft, all without the loss of a single fighting ship. Then, on April 5, he took his fleet of five carriers, four battleships, three cruisers and eight destroyers into the Eastern Indian Ocean in search of the remnants of the British Fleet. The British, forewarned by a patrol plane of the enemy fleet's movements, deployed their fleet of three carriers, five battleships, eight cruisers, and an impressive number of destroyers and submarines. British Admiral Somerville wanted to meet his adversary at sea, not in the port at Colombo or Trincomalee, Ceylon.

The Japanese air attack on Colombo that Easter Sunday destroyed most of the shore installations and sank one destroyer; two dozen R.A.F. fighters were shot down while a like number of the attackers were lost. But the news from the British view would only get worse as two of their heavy cruisers were sunk that afternoon, and their carrier Hermes, with a destroyer escort, was sunk just three days later; most of the carrier's aircraft were also lost. Once more, Admiral Nagumo brought his fighting ships through without a single loss.

Japanese Tide Of Conquest Slows At Coral Sea

But the Admiral's carriers had been losing aircraft — few to compare with his enemy's losses but, nonetheless, he had lost many aircraft. More costly, he had lost many of the veteran pilots who had performed so skillfully at Pearl Harbor and in subsequent battles. Now he must retire to

Japan and replenish the carriers with new planes and replacement pilots. The planes were no problem but the quality of the airmen was to be far inferior to the original group. Also, only two of Nagumo's carriers would remain on station to participate in the Battle of the Coral Sea, one month later.

In Burma, the Japanese Army rolled along against ever-weakening resistance. On May 1, 1942, they overran Mandalay, effectively cutting off China from land or sea access and sealing the anchor of the Burma Road. The stage was now set for the conquest of New Guinea's Papuan Peninsula, New Guinea in general, and Port Moresby and Milne Bay, specifically.

Now, however, the war machinery of the United States was beginning to pop out men and equipment, a small trickle of which was making its way into the hands of General MacArthur and on to Admiral King. So when the now cocky Japanese steamed into the Coral Sea in May, he wasn't fully prepared for the encounter that would turn him back for the first time and mark the beginning of the end to his conquest of the Pacific.

In ships, planes and personnel lost during the Battle of the Coral Sea, there was no standout winner. But in terms of effect on the war itself, the Japanese invasion armada turned back and no invasion of consequence was successful for them during the balance of hostilities.

The first verification that the tide of war was shifting came just one month later when the Japanese suffered a shattering defeat in the Battle of Midway. Speculation by historians had it that if Nagumo hadn't attacked the British Fleet and shore installations at Ceylon ports, resulting in a high price paid in carrier aircraft, and could have kept his five carriers available through the Coral Sea encounter — likewise making them available for the Battle of Midway — the outcome of both battles and perhaps the duration of the war may have been entirely different. On the other hand, had the Allies been blessed with just average timing in several battles of the early days of the war, there may not have been a Coral Sea or Midway battle.

Premier Tojo wanted Port Moresby and all of the Papuan Peninsula. It was critically important to his plan for cutting the life lines of Australia and New Zealand. Control of Papua by the Japanese meant control of the Bismarck, Coral and Solomon Seas. In addition, he was far from convinced that the Allies could put up an appreciable defense against his fighting forces.

By late August, the Japanese Army had accumulated some 10,000 troops in and around the recently occupied base at Buna. From there, they planned to march 100 miles across the near-impassable Owen Stanley mountains, taking Port Moresby with ground forces. But disease, starvation and the incredible Australians stopped them 30 miles short of Port Moresby, then the Aussies drove the remnants back over the Owen Stanleys.

PBY activities in the Southwest Pacific were quite limited during the first months of the war, due primarily to the Japanese destruction of six squadrons on Oahu December 7, 1941 and three squadrons in and around the Philippines during the following three months. The United States transferred several squadrons from East Coast and Atlantic duty to Pearl Harbor and Kaneohe within two weeks after the beginning of hostilities. One of these, VP71, assigned to Kaneohe, along with six Catalinas from VP14, began early flights to Noumea, New Caledonia.

Fleet Air Wings One and Two, headquartered at the Naval Air Stations at Kaneohe and Ford Island, Pearl Harbor, respectively, were charged with the responsibility of establishing air routes and bases in the area of the Southwest Pacific. Noumea, New Caledonia, became one of the first bases, other than those already established in Australia and New Zealand.

The U.S. Catalina squadrons, or segments of them, together with their Australian and New Zealand patrol plane Allies, flew convoy coverage, submarine patrol, personnel transfers, massive equipment transport, fleet and base bombing missions and endless hours of day and night patrols. They battled air-to-air with enemy bombers and fighters and, in between, rescued hundreds of airmen, shipboard survivors and evacuees from islands overrun by the Japanese. They delivered supplies to the courageous coastwatchers who daily risked their lives to report enemy air and sea movements. And when a coastwatcher, with his native associates, came across Allied survivors, most often it was a Catalina that responded to the call for pick-up. By early 1943, other classes of patrol aircraft joined the PBYs in the Pacific, but for the first year, it was all Catalinas, plus a few Moth-Minors flown by U.S. Allies.

Jack Coley, Accidental Bombing — PBY Damage

Jack Coley, Patrol Squadron Eleven, was but one of many frustrated PBY pilots who shared the limited Catalinas with a pool of men from six squadrons in Hawaii that were decimated by the December 7th raid. Replacement aircraft slowly trickled in, but patrols, rescue missions, convoy duty and freight transport kept all patrol aircraft in the air almost every day and night during those trying early months of the war. Sandwiched into this schedule was a rigid training program designed to develop officers and enlisted men into professional airmen and to thoroughly familiarize them with their aircraft. The success of this latter effort was not long in becoming evident over and over again.

Ensign Coley joined VP11 in 1940, flew with the squadron through its first tour, contributing most effectively to the myriad of accomplishments credited to the PBYs.

Ensign Jack Coley's report:

"Before we went south, we were running patrols out of Kaneohe. We flew 700-mile searches with a particular approach pattern that was coded every day as to how to get back in and to make identifying turns and the like. Then we came into the coastal waters and threw out a smoke light — giving the gunners in our crew something to shoot at. For gunnery experience we strafed the smoke light, making a half-dozen passes, then went back and landed at the base.

"At that time, our bombs were released with a Norden Bomb Sight but we also had a manual release which was a 'T' handle with exposed cables running back to a winch line.

"On this particular day, the Aviation Pilot in my crew, a tall lanky guy, was at the bow gun. I made the first pass with the float light on the port side, then came around on the other side for the starboard waist gunner. As the bow was swinging around, the AP put his 'size twelves' across the cables and two 500 – pound bombs on the starboard wing fell off. Their arming wires were more taut than the release wires, so they went armed. Almost immediately, the plane caught a Wham — Wham, double detonation and a hunk of shrapnel as big as two hands went up through the hull, through the food locker, right alongside the guy in the mechanic's station, up through the top of the fuselage and through the wing.

"Shrapnel caused a number of other holes but nobody got hurt. However, there was this big hole in the hull and one in the wing that was spewing fuel and we were kind of young and inexperienced.

"'Better shut down that engine', I thought, 'before the gas ignites from the exhaust.' I shut her down and we flew some 50 miles back to base at an altitude of 100 feet, ready to ditch at the first sign of trouble. We were afraid to light off the radio because of a possible spark from a bare wire. But base got word, somehow, that we were in trouble and cleared our way in. It was under those circumstances I made my first nighttime single-engine landing, bringing the Catalina close in to the ramp. From there, I taxied the Cat to where the beaching crew mounted the beaching gear before the plane could sink.

"It took on a considerable amount of water but without damaging any critical gear. Examination revealed that the torque tube to the starboard aileron had been severed, allowing the wheel to work only the left aileron; somehow, we were still able to fly. Sometime later, when the squadron went south, my crew and I flew that same plane.

"On January 3, 1942, I had night patrol out of Hilo. Our routine was to fly around the island clockwise, then go back around counter-clockwise. We repeated that routine all night long, taking off at about six o'clock and landing about seven the next morning.

"At about 2:30 a.m., we saw a blinking light on the side of a hill — about a half mile up — so we flew over to investigate. Suddenly, the waist gunner said, 'There's a submarine in the moon-streak!'

"We had flown between the sub and the coast. The light came from a car on the island and, at the time, there was a complete blackout of the island. Also, there weren't supposed to be any U.S. subs anywhere near; then, too, there was all the talk about Japs landing spies.

"We made the classic 90/270-degree turn and came back — surprised to see him still on the surface. We dropped some flares to mark the spot and made another turn to come back and attack. Well, naturally, he had pulled the cork by the time we got back; we never saw him again.

"We were just not expecting it and weren't in a bombing mode. Obviously, we should have come back the first time ready to attack instead of confirm."

There is no humor to the kill-or-be-killed aspect of war. To watch one's buddies die, to kill and destroy, is a tragedy enjoyed by no sane human being. But Americans and their down-under Australian and New Zealand Allies found humor in adversity — enjoyment while deprived of all but the basic necessities — and friendships closer than the bonds of blood. The men who flew the PBYs were hardly exceptions to this rule; in fact, they may have set the pattern for making the best of a nasty, deadly situation.

William A. Barker: Dig A Hole — Bury The Dirt

Bill Barker retired as a Chief Aviation Ordnanceman in 1960, but before that he fought the Japanese from a PBY Catalina patrol bomber. Bill was assigned to VP11 in February, 1942 as a seaman second class, while the squadron was based at the Naval Air Station, Kaneohe Bay, Oahu, Hawaii. Directing his efforts toward aircraft ordnance, he entered schools in bombsight, bombardier training and air gunnery, and was assigned to a flight crew just as the Battle of Midway occurred. Along the way, Bill's search for excitement exposed him to a number of embarrassing situations.

The first of several stories by Bill Barker begins at a beer garden at Kaneohe Bay.

"There was a beer garden at the Ship's store building at Kaneohe Bay and every night was party night. As was the custom, every night was also fight night — a pressure-venting encounter between a dozen or so sailors. On one such evening, I decided to stay out of the fight and made my way to the top of a stack of empty beer boxes where, I determined, I would watch the goings-on. But as the battle progressed, I was overcome with the desire to participate; so I began reaching out with an empty beer bottle to rap some staggering swabby on the head as he went by. Then I'd hide on top of the boxes. Boy, what a sport! But someone spotted me and the sport became a catastrophe.

"During air-gunnery training, we practiced air-to-air combat in JRF Grumman float-type aircraft with two student gunners and a pilot. One student waited down in the float area while his buddy manned the 30-caliber machine gun from the rear cockpit, then they swapped places. On this particular day, I was to fire second. When it came my turn, I wiggled my way into the cockpit where I waited for the gunnery run on a sleeve towed by another aircraft. My buddy was to latch the platform under me as he went below but forgot to. I had grasped the gun and was firing at the

159

sleeve when suddenly the platform gave way beneath me. In my fear and excitement, I held onto the grip of the gun and continued firing, cleanly shooting off the plane's antenna before finally letting go and dropping down.

"A Second Class Naval Aviator pilot was flying the aircraft, and after we landed, called me out to the flight line, walked to a little wooden operation shack and got a shovel. He took me out behind the shack and said, 'Dig a hole!'

"So I dug a hole. I went back around and said, 'The hole's dug.'

"He said, 'Okay, now you gotta' bury the dirt.'

"I walked behind the shack and started to shovel the dirt back into the same hole.

"He walked up and said, 'No, No! You can't put the dirt back in that hole. You've got to bury it somewhere else.'

"I asked, 'where can I bury it?'

"So I proceeded to dig another hole, put the dirt from the first hole in the second hole and said, 'Now what do I do with the dirt from this hole?'

"He said, 'You've gotta' bury it.'

"I started putting it back into the first hole and he said, 'No, you can't put it in that hole. Gotta' put it in another hole.'

"Well, I dug about three more holes before he finally turned me loose."

George Poulos: Mission — Find And Cover Two Lost Cats

George Poulos piloted a PBY for VP11 during the early war years but counts his Catalina experiences back to 1940 when the United States Navy was practically on a war footing. The Catalina squadrons were doing everything but dropping bombs in their "Neutrality Patrol" and like activities.

George tells of a specific flight on December 8, 1941.

"The PBY had many characteristics that enabled it to perform far beyond its original expectations. Among these was the exceptionally sturdy structure and, though there was a penalty paid for this in added weight, the high-lift wing could accommodate it. It enabled the Catalina to take off with weight loads considerably greater than the design specifications allowed. Further, these combinations made the PBY the best airplane for open – sea landings by a wide margin.

"Although the high-lift, high drag, wing made the PBY a slow airplane and the butt of many jokes among the glamour aviators, it also made it the safest. Tremendous ground effect of the wing made it almost impossible to fly the PBY into the water. The lower it flew, the more 'tail-up' trim it could tolerate — to the point that at five or 10 feet off the water, an additional 15 knots airspead was realized.

"On December 8, 1941, I flew my first wartime patrol. Takeoff was late in the afternoon with instructions to investigate a reported mystery ship at a specified distance and bearing. The search continued until darkness and no contact was made; the return to Pearl Harbor was in darkness with a totally blacked-out Oahu. After a careful landing to avoid the battleship Nevada, which had been beached right at the seaplane approach to Drydock Channel, as well as debris still in the channel, I made several passes toward the beaching ramp but was flagged away by the beachmaster. Finally, a boat came out and advised that there was no more beaching gear available and that we would have to tie up to a buoy in Pearl City Channel.

"Finding a buoy in a darkened channel with no lighting was not an easy chore and very time consuming. Taxi time from landing to buoy tie-up was three and one-half hours and the engines did not load-up or overheat. No other aircraft I've flown could have tolerated that abuse."

George continues his story with a Christmas lost-plane search.

"During Christmas 1941, I was assigned to work with the tender McFarland, a converted World War I four-stacker anchored in Hilo Bay. At daybreak on Christmas Day, we took off with instructions to circle the big island, Hawaii, clockwise, looking for evidence that the Japanese may have landed troops by submarine during the night before.

"Upon completion of the morning mission, and prior to fueling for the afternoon circuit, I received orders from the tender to proceed to the south point of Hawaii and set up a systematic search for two of Patrol Squadron 51's PBY-5s, the seaplane model. The two aircraft were flying in from San Diego, got off course, ran out of fuel and had to land in the open sea. The vague location, 'South of Hawaii,' was based on a single directional bearing taken when they sent their one and only message to Pearl that they were running out of fuel.

"After setting up a search pattern, I ordered the engines leaned to the minimum flow specified in the manual in view of our low fuel condition. As darkness approached, it appeared our search pattern was not going to produce results so I altered it to proceed directly to an area where we computed the two planes would be if they had mistakenly applied their magnetic variation in reverse. This I considered a possibility because VP51 had been an East Coast squadron where the magnetic variation is opposite from the Pacific. The distance south of Oahu supported this theory.

"Darkness had already come when we located the first PBY — within a few miles of our calculated position. The message to Pearl Harbor headquarters giving latitude and longitude was dispatched simultaneously with Aldis Lamp to the airplane on the water. We learned that the second aircraft had continued on its course rather than join them on the water; 20 miles down-course, we found them.

"With the message to Pearl, we included, 'leaving site to return to Hilo Bay.' Within a minute we received the message, 'Cannot proceed to Hilo Bay since McFarland was dispatched to the area at 1300 hours. Remain on site until McFarland arrives, then return to Pearl.'

"Wow! Pearl Harbor was five hours away. It was now 1900 hours and although the McFarland had been en route for six hours, it was still, according to our calculations, an hour and a half away. We had been flying, except for a few minutes on Hilo Bay between missions, since 0600.

"I reduced power to the minimum required to stay in the air. The PBY hung in the air on that tremendous high-lift wing at about 70 knots as we set our course to keep flying the 20 miles between the two airplanes so as not to lose them in the darkness. A message came from the McFarland, 'Send MO's so we can take a bearing.'

"Our message back, 'Wilco, what is your position and estimated arrival?' Our fears were confirmed — still an hour away and our fuel getting lower and lower.

"I gave the order to reduce the fuel mixture until the engines coughed, then enriched it just to the next cog on the quadrant; carefully, one engine at a time. This significantly reduced our fuel consumption but would the cylinder-head temperatures hold? They started to rise — five degrees, 10 degrees, then held at 12 degrees above normal.

"Finally, a search light was flashing around the horizon — the McFarland's. We took a bearing on it, gave the McFarland a course correction to the nearest plane and advised her of the position of the other one relative to the first. We altered our hover pattern from between the PBYs and started flying between the McFarland and the nearest plane. The engines were still okay, except for an occasional cough, but with no excessive temperature.

"At 2020 hours, the McFarland began conducting Aldis Lamp communications with the first Catalina. We advised them we were heading back to Pearl. Their message back, 'Thanks for your help and good luck.'

"Now we had to change our flight regime from one of maximum endurance to maximum range. At our weight, the graphs showed about 85 knots true airspeed and Pearl Harbor 440 miles away, with normal trade winds from the starboard beam. If it shifted to a head wind, there was no way to reach Pearl, no matter how much we leaned the fuel mixture.

"Upon notifying Pearl of our plight, we were asked to report our position and remaining fuel every half hour. The next three hours were uneventful except that all aboard had anxious moments each time an engine coughed. Suddenly, one of the crew asked, 'When do we eat?' It dawned on everyone that we had not had anything to eat since 0500 hours in the morning on the McFarland. It was now 2300 hours.

"The wind continued to be favorable and we were able to make a land sighting on Lanai right on schedule. The next message from Pearl asked that we advise them when we were 30 miles off Koko Head. This would be an important landfall since security for Oahu required approach to the island only at specific points — Koko Head was one of them.

"When we sent our 30 miles from Koko Head we got a pleasant surprise in the return message. 'Change course, proceed directly to Pearl, advise when five miles from Diamond Head.'

We sent our five – mile report and got an even bigger surprise; flood lights all over the south western part of Hawaii lit up the previously darkened Oahu — a first since December 7th. We were told to make voice contact with Ford Island Tower, an unprecedented concession, for landing instructions.

"Finally, we had Pearl in sight. Our landing instructions were to use Drydock Channel by direct approach. I guided the old faithful PBY right down the entrance to Pearl with plenty of lighting — floats down — a quick turn to the right over the beached Nevada and we were on the water in Drydock Channel.

"A sigh of relief came from the entire crew. The searchlights were extinguished and within seconds I could see the beachmaster's flashlight beckoning me to the beaching ramp. I pushed the starboard throttle forward to turn toward the ramp; the engine sputtered and died. We had run out of gas. Within a minute, the port engine also quit. Immediately, a crash boat came up announcing they had been alerted that we could be in trouble and were ready for any eventuality. All we needed was a tow to the ramp.

"It was 0100 hours, December 26, 1941 when we disembarked from the Catalina at the ramp. We had been aboard for 19 hours. Almost immediately a fueling crew arrived and we advised them we needed only a small fuel load to return to Kaneohe the next day.

"Sorry, Sir,' the chief said, 'Our instructions are that every plane gets the maximum load for an all-out patrol effort in the morning.'

"Chief,' I said, 'you follow your instructions but this airplane goes to VP11 at Kaneohe tomorrow morning, not on patrol.' If we had to make a maximum weight landing in order to get home, so be it.

"A personnel carrier appeared to take us to quarters but some of the crew decided to sleep on the aircraft rather than in the barracks, to ensure that no one got aboard and took off for an all-day patrol with our old faithful 'workhorse.' The PBY had just completed a mission no other aircraft could have accomplished and we felt very much attached to it.

"At the BOQ, all rooms were full and we were given sleeping bags to stretch out in the hallways. At 0400 the early breakfast began and sleep in the hallways was impossible; besides, it was 23 hours since we had a meal. We climbed out of the bags and went to breakfast. By then it seemed ridiculous to delay our return to Kaneohe any longer; if we could round up the crew, we might as well go. We got the next personnel carrier to the ramp area and found the crew waiting. They had found the same conditions in the barracks, sleeping in corridors, and had given up.

"When I arrived in my room in the Kaneohe BOQ, my roommate was still in bed. 'What are you doing here?,' he asked. 'I thought you were on that easy boondoggle, making lazy eights.'

"Yeah, but that's been changed,' I replied.

'You should have been here on Christmas Day,' he continued. 'Did we have a good dinner? It was the best meal they have cooked here since the December 7 attack. What did you have?'

"Not very much,' I replied, 'but I'll tell you about it when I wake up in a couple of days.' "

Wes Hicks: Night Landing Between The Palms

Wes Hicks finished flight training at Corpus Christi, Texas, on August 27, 1942 and was certified as an instrument pilot on October 16, 1942. He began his PBY service with VP71 at Kaneohe Naval Air Station.

At the time, VP71 was one of several Catalina squadrons patrolling the waters around the Hawaiian Islands, as well as Canton Island, Johnston and Midway. A detachment of VP71 Catalinas flying out of Canton was credited with rescuing the crews of four Army Air Force B-24 bombers who became lost and were forced to ditch while on a flight to support Colonel Carlson's Raiders.

Wes was a pilot aboard one of the four PBYs sent in search of the downed Army airmen. He begins his story with the search.

"We were flying out of Canton Island, 15 miles abeam of each other, in an effort to spot the crews of the four B-24s. I think the Colonel was attacking one of the Ellice islands and the B-24s were supposed to soften up the area but they never got there.

"On one night flight, our PBY started losing oil in one of the engines, so we had to feather the propeller and head for Funi Futi Island, a short distance to the southwest. Arriving over the island before daylight, we were faced with the problem of getting down on a tiny landing strip, cut out of the palm trees, which had no lighting for night landings.

"Recognizing our plight, base personnel placed jeeps with their lights on at each end of the runway and we threaded our way between the coconut palms, landing safely though a little frazzled in the nerve department.

"A ground crew repaired the oil leak but we were too late to participate in the rescue of the B-24 crews. As it happened, all personnel from the four planes were picked up safely.

"When Eddie Rickenbacker was rescued by an OS2U pilot, he was taken to Funi Futi where a PBY, piloted by a Lieutenant Wright from VP71, picked him up and returned him to Hawaii."

Ercell Hart: #1120 Salad Oil

Ercell Hart, who contributed to the Atlantic section, was a Lieutenant (jg) USNR at the time of the following situation, a classic example of the flexibility of the incredible Catalina.

"I was a pilot of a PBY-5A, amphibious model, flying a search patrol out of Oahu in early 1942. Not long after a dawn departure, while some distance south of the island, an oil tank filler cover on top of the wing came off and the wind pressure began sucking the oil out of the tank. Our first evidence of the loss was a low oil pressure reading and reduced oil quantity on the starboard engine. Soon it became necessary to shut the engine down and head for home. Because it was early in the patrol, we were heavy with fuel — too heavy to maintain altitude on one engine. We made a reasonably smooth landing, considering the limited maneuverability with one engine, in a moderate sea driven by the usual trade winds.

"I decided to taxi toward Oahu, figuring to reach the lee of the island where assistance from Pearl Harbor could be expected. We had radioed a brief description of our trouble and our location before landing.

"Our course, the direction of the NE trade winds, and the one remaining engine, didn't make a simple combination to taxi on the desired heading. The PBY's big tail makes it weather-cock directly into the wind. With two engines, asymmetrical power permits steering cross wind with assistance from the rudder as necessary. By streaming a sea anchor — a cone-shaped drogue of rope and canvas — from the port waist hatch, we finally achieved a somewhat workable balance of forces and slowly made headway toward Waianae coast.

"After we had been thrashing along for some time, a destroyer came up over the horizon and hove-to nearby. They sent over a boat and we explained our trouble. 'Would you by chance have any aviation lube oil, type 1120?,' I asked. After a conference back at the ship, they assured us they did and brought some over in unlabeled five-gallon cans.

'Are you sure this is 1120 oil?' I questioned. The mech and I had stuck our fingers in the filler holes of the cans. They came out dripping clear, colorless oil, nothing like the lube oil we were familiar with. We smelled it. Nothing distinguishable.

'Yep, that's what is — 1120,' the whaleboat's coxswain assured us.

"The mech and I looked at each other, at the unlabeled oil, at the waiting destroyer and at the increasing sea conditions. We didn't want to louse up the engine with something odd-ball and have it fail during an open-sea takeoff; a second forced landing might not be as good as the first. The plugs and pencils we had wedged into the holes where we'd popped rivets on the first landing wouldn't hold forever. 'Looks more like salad oil than lube oil,' I told the mech.

'Yeh, but it feels about right and they say it's 1120. They must use it in their machinery somewhere. I never had duty on a tin can,' he said.

"Okay, let's go,' I ordered. We hoisted the cans on a hand line from whaleboat to wing top and, after lots of slipping, sliding and spilling, we got the '1120 salad oil' into the tank and topped off.

"Now we could taxi with two-engine control and without resort to the sea anchor. A few more hours of plunging along into the wind-driven chop got us into relatively smooth water. We had tried one takeoff run while the DD stood by, but couldn't make it; seas too rough and plane too heavy. The lee of the land and the approaching twilight decided the next attempt for us. We got off successfully and landed after dark at Pearl Harbor.

The '1120 salad oil' got us home and at each retelling of the story, the salad oil got more authenticated: 'Yep, right out of the galley! Mazola labels right on the cans,' etc.

"I happened to hear the story a few years later. The teller didn't know I was the guy it happened to. It was a pretty good yarn.'

12

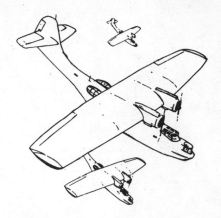

To Hold Australia

The Allied retreat from the Philippines and East Indies in the early months of the war cost U.S. Navy Patrol Squadrons VP101, 102 and 22 all but two of their PBYs. With most of their personnel dead, captured, or scattered throughout the Southwest Pacific, the remnants of these squadrons should have licked their wounds and ended Catalina activities in that war zone for several months or longer. But men who had been trained to fly Catalinas were transferred to Australia before replacement aircraft were available, primarily to form flying crews for the few PBYs that could be gathered together for defense of the West Coast of Australia.

One such man was Ensign Thomas L. Birch who retired after 23 years service as a U.S. Navy Commander and who now resides in Los Altos, California. He reveals the frustration experienced by Catalina pilots and crewmen as they struggled, it seemed, to single-handedly stop the Japanese from invading Australia.

Ensign Thomas L. Birch: Three Cats To Patrol West Australia

"As the war started, Bert Gregg, George Milliken and I were graduating from flight school at Corpus Christi, Texas, with Gold Wings and Ensign commissions. Our orders read: 'to VP101, Fleet Air Wing Ten, Sangley Point, Manila, Philippine Islands.

Australia.

"We didn't make it to the Philippines, as the Japs overran most of the South Pacific before we got there. We joined what was left of the squadron at Perth, Australia, in February, 1942, reporting aboard the seaplane tender, USS Langley.

"One day, not long after I reported aboard, I returned from a flight to learn that the Langley had put all Naval Aviators ashore, with their gear, to make room for a P–47 group which was being transferred to Java in a final attempt to hold back the Japs. There was only one problem: No one had unloaded my uniforms, flight and other personal gear. Bill Hardy, Buzz LeFever and Pete Schmuck had the same problem. We arrived at Perth BOQ with nothing more than our flight suits to prove we were United States Naval Aviators.

'No problem,' the Wing said. The Langley would deliver their load of planes and pilots, return, and we would soon be back on board. But the Langley was sunk out of Surabaja, Java, and with it went all my personal gear.

"In April 1942, VP102, VP21 and VP22 were all decommissioned and their pilots and crewmen were reassigned to VP101. But that was to last for only a short time as the big evacuation was on. Most of the PBY survivors were to be returned to the states for reassignment to new squadrons.

"As my luck would have it, I returned from a flight in an Australian Moth-Minor one day to find I was one of a few PBY pilots who would remain in Australia to protect the coast for a few more weeks. So, with just my flight suit, skivvy shorts, and with a few other Naval Aviators, I watched the USS Mount Vernon sail for the states.

We had three PBYs to protect the West Coast of Australia and one of them was a Dutch aircraft with the altimeter in meters and the airspeed in kilometers. To fly it, we put the RPM where it looked normal and the throttles where the flight engineer said they looked okay. Man, what a way to fly!

"In the beginning we flew one patrol a day, but after a scare that the Japs were sending an invasion fleet to attack the coast, we stepped up our flights to three a day. The only exceptions were when a plane was down for maintenance. Our flights averaged 12 hours each.

"I can't recall the names of all the Naval Aviators who made up that small band of Catalina pilots but a few stand out in my memory.

"Bill Hardy was a former Naval Aviator who was in the Dutch East Indies to teach the Dutch how to fly PBYs in Java. He rejoined the Navy while still in Java and made his way to Australia just ahead of the Jap invasion of the East Indies.

"Pete Schmuck had been shot down in a PBY in the Philippines, was picked up in Manila Bay, and arrived in Perth on board a seaplane tender.

"Buzz Lefever had flown with VP22 and, after losing most of their planes in a Jap air raid, he and many of the squadron survivors made their way to Perth.

"With these guys, Tom Pollock and the rest, we formed the three PBY crews who flew the only long – range flights over the Indian Ocean until the middle of May when Captain George Mundorff brought 12 new PBYs and full flight crews to Perth. At that time, VP101 was reborn.

"Our short effort was ended but we felt then, as those of us who survived feel today, that those three defenseless PBY Catalinas helped stop the Japs from invading Australia during the very critical early months of 1942.

"During two months with our three Catalinas, I had flown hundreds of hours, had been on the alert every day and now was wearing an Australian Flight Lieutenant's clothes that I had won in a poker game at Pierce Airdrome. My gold aviator's wings had been cast from dental gold by an Aussie dentist, costing me a bottle of Scotch and a couple of Aussie pounds. But, at that, I looked as good or better than my rag-tag buddies.

"George Mundorff took one look at my buddies and me and promptly had us restricted to the BOQ forever. However, a couple of my Ensign friends equipped me with the correct uniform and I was free again. Somehow, the 'fearless aviators' had been replaced by a complete squadron and the war was over for us. Or was it?

"We started flying patrols over the whole Indian Ocean, staging from Perth, Geraldton and Exmouth Gulf on the West Coast. As a 'veteran,' I joined the operations team, briefing the new pilots on how to fight the war in Australia.

"Now, the most that had happened to me was when once we were chased by Jap Bettys and had lost part of the left aileron to a 20mm cannon shot; and, of course, there were those hundreds of hours in the air, looking at nothing. But I was a 'vet' and could tell those guys just what they should do — inflating my ego and making me the most disliked Ensign in the squadron. Fortunately, Tom Pollock squared me away and I redeemed myself with the rest of the group.

"Tom was one of the PBY pilots who flew into Corrigedor and rescued a planeload of Navy and Army nurses and high officials just before the island fell to the Japs. He was finally recognized for that accomplishment and later promoted to Captain of one of the seaplane tenders.

"My first officer-of-the-day duty was at Pelican Point, Perth, Australia. As the most junior officer in the squadron, I qualified for OOD and stood my first watch. I qualified, I believe, only to relieve the more senior officers so that they could chase the Aussie girls all over town. The Aussie girls were rather easy to catch at that time because all of the Aussie males of our age were off chasing Germans in North Africa.

"So there I was, OOD, when a PBY landed and taxied over to the ramp. The beaching crew that night had long since taken off after the girls, so I waved the Catalina in and it came to rest on the sandy beach. Carefully, I tied a couple of lines to the plane and proceeded with refueling; the aircraft was scheduled to fly out again at 0500. Well, when the crew arrived to preflight the plane at 0400, they found it high and dry on the beach. The tide had gone out and there was no budging that Cat. By the time the flight finally began at 10 that morning, I had been chewed on by the Commanding Officer and the Commodore of the Wing; he just happened to have come down to watch the day's flight operations.

The Lighthouse Keeper's Daughter

"With a full complement of PBYs, we began sending detachments to advance bases; one of which was the small town of Geraldton, about 300 miles north of Perth. My crew had deployed and we arrived in town for a social visit and dance at the Town Hall. There I met the lighthouse keeper's daughter, a beautiful teenage blonde, who was in town for the dance. Since I had been out of touch with the fairer sex for a number of months, she soon became the most luscious girl in town. I succumbed to her charms and was in 'love' overnight. But our romance was hindered by a frustrating problem.

"Since she lived at the lighthouse across the lagoon, I would come in after flying all day and shower, shave and dress, then go down to the dock where I would take the lighthouse dory and row out to the point. I would pick up Gwendelyn Ann, row her back across the lagoon, and we did our thing for the evening. But she had to be back before the midnight curfew, so I had to row and row again. Alas, the affair was short-lived as I simply could find no way of necking in the dory, particularly when I was always tired.

"At Exmouth Gulf, we were staging off a seaplane tender and I had the plane watch of PBYs moored at the buoys. Once more, the junior officers had the duty while their senior officers were relaxing on the tender. Part of the preflight check was to check the wires of the depth charges slung on the wing. To do this, we removed a cover from the check panel over the navigator's table.

"Well, I pulled on the wires to make sure they were still attached and the depth charge on the right wing fell off, quite closely followed by the one on the left wing. Immediately, the question: Did I pull the arming wire first? It would take three seconds for the answer. I think that was the night my hair started turning grey—at the ripe old age of twenty-three. It goes without saying, the bombs didn't go off but we quickly moved the plane to another anchorage.

"Flying predetermined vectors on regular schedule became routine. We stepped up our patrols, flying further and further north until meeting Jap Betty and Mavis patrol planes became common practice. We would jockey to get the 50-calibers into position and fire like mad with tracer bullets every third round to scare them off. They turned back and we returned to base ready to get them the next day. It was about that time I began to think as a naval officer for the first time. 'We can win this war,' I thought. 'We can chase the Jap over the horizon and defeat him in his own land'."

Russell Enterline: To Stay With A Faithful Friend

Russell Enterline, of Aurora, Colorado, previously told of his activities and escape from the Philippines and Java. After arriving in Perth, Australia, he made his way into VP101 as it was reforming. Enterline was with the squadron when orders came to move up to Morotai to patrol and to harass the Japanese invasion of New Guinea.

"En route from Perth to Morotai, we hopped from Adalaide to Brisbane, to Bowen and Townsville. The tenders Orca, Tangier, Half Moon, San Carlos and San Pablo served our squadron as we moved about from place to place.

"One morning, as we returned from an all-night patrol, we were set upon by three Jap fighters. The pilot said, 'We'll fool those little bastards' and dropped the PBY about 1000 feet in altitude to less than 100 feet where we leveled off and pulled back on the throttles to slow her way down. One of the fighters made a run at us but his high speed caused him to misjudge his trajectory and he slipped into the water, exploding in a ball of flame. The other two apparently got the message 'cause they took off for home.

"One night over New Ireland, flak hit our port engine and we had to feather it. We were heading home on the starboard engine when, just after daybreak, a Jap fighter jumped us. He flew around the Cat as if he was measuring us for the kill. But he stayed just out of range of our guns, flew parallel with us and let down his flaps and wheels to slow himself down to our speed. Finally, he looked over and grinned, waved and flew off. We figured he had used all his ammunition and wasn't crazy about joining his ancestors by crashing his plane into us. If he did all those things just to scare us, he more than succeeded.

"One evening we took off for parts north, running into rain squalls just as it was getting dark. About the same time, I picked up a radar blip on the 40 – mile range. The pilot said we had nothing in that area and to home in on it. The closer we got, the more I realized it was a big ship. About 10 miles out, the pilot readied our bombs for quick release, lowered our altitude and slowed the speed. We came up on the stern of the ship and dropped the bombs on both sides simultaneously. There was a terrific explosion, tossing us higher in the air but the pilot fought it off and got control again. We had just hit and sunk a large ammunition ship and were quite lucky the explosions didn't get us too.

"The Australian Air Force was in our area, some of their crews flying the amphibian PBY-5As. They swore by the planes. Those Aussie pilots flew the PBYs into Jap-held positions, bombing and strafing as if the Cats were fighter planes. Seeing them fly, we often wondered how the wings stayed on the planes.

"There were many mornings on off-duty days we waited for our planes to come in from all-night patrol. Some came in with only one engine turning, made good landings and made it to their buoy; others flew close by the ship to show bullet holes in the hull of their aircraft, knowing that when the plane hit the water it would sink. But the Tangier, the big tender, swung out its crane from the fantail and waited for the Cat to make a stall landing nearby. Then, as the PBY crew scrambled out of the plane and onto the wing, the pilot would taxi the Cat under the crane where it would be picked up with water pouring out of the hull like emptying a sieve.

"From Morotai we moved to Port Moresby where we faced the same set-up: Living in tents, lining up for chow — many times a meal of mutton stew served from a 50-gallon barrel — a real choice standard of living. There was a Red Cross building at Moresby with writing tables and hanging canvas bags with lemonade and ice and Red Cross women to serve the military personnel. One afternoon, a couple of us decided we would visit the center, arriving in our skivvy shirts, cut-off trousers and boondocker shoes. At the door, we were told we had to be in uniform to come in! Some of us hadn't seen a complete uniform since December 7th.

"The time came for rotation back to Perth and from there many of us were offered a 30-day leave in the states, or return for flight school, or other home duty. At this point, some of my buddies couldn't understand my thinking when I expressed a desire not to return to the states. But I was afraid that after a short leave I would be returned to a combat area and not back with a PBY squadron. I had faith in the PBY; it was slow and cumbersome but dependable.

"The idea of leaving my friends was troubling, but leaving the Catalina was like turning my back on a faithful guardian who had taken me though the thick and bad and brought me back safely. So, as VP11 was at Perth and readying for deployment back up around New Guinea, I asked for and received a transfer."

The Tender — Mother Ship To The PBY

Throughout the world of seaplane patrol squadrons, the seaplane tender mothered the aircraft with diligence and dedication and, more often than not, without a hint of protection from the enemy war vessels or attack aircraft.

In the South Pacific, their job was to steam alone into forward areas, locating usable landing waters for the big boats. As was the case with most

USS Pine Island, AV12. One of many aircraft Tenders which serviced PBY Catalinas in all oceans and seas of World War II activity. (courtesy Ray Wagner, San Diego Aerospace Museum.)

of the South Pacific islands, dependable charting of reefs, harbors and beaching areas was simply non-existent. To further handicap the tender captains, many of the island inhabitants had been cruelly abused by Japanese raiding parties and were anti-social to all comers.

But officers and crewmen of these tenders, some of the early ones converted destroyers or minesweepers, were proud of their responsibilities and they faced the inconveniences with a can-do attitude. Enemy aircraft attacks were beaten back time and time again, most often with a minimum of damage to the tender or its flock of PBYs. On occasion, green or trigger-happy fighter pilots of our own Army and Navy, thinking they had caught an unprotected enemy vessel at anchor, attacked the tenders, sometimes inflicting death and damage. Such cases of mistaken identity were few but they happened.

Ureparapara And The Island's USO

Ercell Hart adds a tale about a romantic South Pacific island and a unique USO group.

"PBY crews in the Pacific got acquainted — more or less — with some exotic place names; many of Polynesian, Melanesian or Micronesian origin. Funafuti, Kwajalein, Ontong Java, Truk, Kolombangara and Gizo, to name a few.

"European explorers, coming into the Pacific thousands of years after the original settlement of its far-flung skein of islands, struggled to put into writing the names given them by the native occupants. Many places were given names on maps and in journals by latter-day finders which were phonetic renditions of what they thought their native informants were saying. But the names were phonetic in Spanish, Dutch, English, or whatever the nationality of the map maker or journalist. Some places bear several names, often an unhappy record of a ship that wrecked there or of events that happened ashore. Discoverers gave their names or the names of other people to islands, harbors, passages and topographic features.

"Immediately north of the New Hebrides lies a group of islands called the Banks Group, named for Sir Joseph Banks, man of science, companion of the great Captain Cook and President of the Royal Society of England.

"In the northwest corner of this group, like a tipped-up horseshoe, lies one of those islands with a multiple name. Ureparapara, or Bligh, is the unsubmerged portion of a volcanic crater 12 miles in circumference. Its eastern rim blown away, the remainder encircles a fine harbor two miles long with a clear opening to the sea northeastward.

"It was here that Captain Bligh and his 18 loyal men of the Bounty made landfall some 12 days and 1000 miles after leaving Tonga in their 23–foot open launch. The mutineers had set them adrift some 3600 miles from the nearest European settlement, Timor in the Dutch East Indies.

"Bligh and his men didn't set foot on Ureparapara, however, as the appearance of fierce-looking natives made it imprudent. They continued westward, successfully reaching Timor after a 41 day gale-driven passage.

"Having seen the odd crescent-shaped little crumb of land from the air with its inviting harbor, and being stirred by the musical native name and significant English name, I had hoped to find some reason to inspect it more closely. Finally, one day, into ComAirSoPac's operations center came a request from the Anglican mission that a way be found to deliver a piece of mail to the head man of the Ureparapara village.

PBY patrols at that time were not passing near the Banks Group, so an air drop was not considered. Admiral Aubrey Fitch was not about to risk the staff PBY-5A getting into and out of what looked like a mouse trap of a harbor that had a 2000–foot escarpment at one end and a narrow mouth at the other. The seaplane tender, Curtiss, however, had an SOC single-engine float plane available for utility work and one off-duty assistant operations watch officer with the 'mission' already planned—me!

"A few hours later, with a borrowed seaplane, a borrowed but willing ACI officer, Lieutenant (jg) Cal Chipchase, and a couple of gas mask bags of cigarettes and other small gifts, we circled the bay, overflew the neat-as-a-pin village and landed in the calm and unruffled harbor. We taxied along the sandy shore to see what kind of reception seemed likely. A few people stood stoically in the shade of the trees fringing the sand and one very black man, dressed in a wrap-around skirt and shading hat, stood alone mid-shore, watching us but making no sign.

"I cut the engine and coasted up onto the beach. Lieutenant Chipchase and I hopped down to meet the one-man welcoming party. After a little struggle with what I thought was passable beche de mer pidgin, we produced the item of mail and were thanked in quite good English and invited to come into the village.

When I asked if we should tug the plane up higher on the beach or keep her afloat, he explained it was slack tide and we could leave her safely there. We got out two lines to tether one float and wingtip. It was then that the Ureparapara USO made its appearance.

"At a wave of the old man's hand, a chorus line of nubile, dusky maidens and frolicsome boys charged down the beach, tailed onto the painter and wing line and with lots of chatter and merriment followed our signals to secure the plane from going adrift. Surely, no beaching crew I'd ever seen matched this one in smiles, curves and willing vigor. Uniform of boys and girls alike was a kilt, an arm band or two and nothing else but a smile.

"The old man detailed a group to stay on the beach and tend the lines and the rest of us swept into the shady village with lots of chattering and giggling. Chipchase said later, . . . 'and lots of jiggling!'

"Our first stop was to inspect the stick-and-sand sketch that one of the small boys had made of our plane. It was unbelievably accurate. We inferred from what the headman said that it would have been kept as a report if called for later — friend or enemy.

"Chipchase's comment was, 'For a crew I'd like the USO girls, but this little guy could be my intelligence officer anytime.'

"After a visit to the small thatched church of the village (where the headman carefully tucked his snuffed-out cigarette into a crevice of the thatch before entering), and after bestowing our small store of gifts and receiving mementoes in return, we recovered our well-tended SOC, cranked up and pushed off the beach.

"As we taxied away, our bevy of USO volunteer beach crew members waved farewell. It might be pardonable poetic license to say we flew off into the sunset, but aerodynamic necessity and seamanship, combined with a near calm, dictated another course.

"The not-so-powerfully endowed SOC needed a long run and much persuasion to get unstuck from the calm surface, so we criss-crossed the bay at taxi speed to stir up a chop, aimed for the harbor entrance — the only low spot — and firewalled the throttle. I think she may have been reluctant to leave Ureparapara behind. But we made it, somehow, up, up and away, with a final salute to the dusky USO and to Captain Bligh's near miss of a century and a half before."

The Blonde Of Vanikoro

Ercell Hart continues with a story of a beautiful blonde on the island of Vanikoro.

"There she stood, gloriously nude, blonde and fair, hands raised at her side, looking down at us with a faintly bemused smile. I'll never forget that meeting with the Blonde of Vanikoro. Latitude 11 40' S., Longitude 111 54' E.

"Vanikoro, the southernmost of the Santa Cruz Group of islands, lies some 240 miles north of Segond Channel, Espiritu Santo Island, where PBYs of ComAirSoPac were based for operations supporting the Solomons campaign. It was proposed that a seaplane tender set up an advance base in the anchorage at Vanikoro. She would supply aviation fuel to top off the planes there, thus extending their possible search range northward toward the Carolines, Gilbert and Marshall Islands. Crews could be berthed and fed aboard so that a fresh crew could take over the patrol.

"LTCDR Paul D. Stroop, commanding the new small seaplane tender, Chincoteague who, after the war, became Commander Aircraft Pacific, was assigned the advance base operation and proceeded to Vanikoro.

"It was on the southwestern side of this island that the ships, Boussole and L'Astrolabe, commanded by the great French navigator, La Perouse, were wrecked in 1788. Survivors established themselves ashore while constructing a small escape vessel, then sailed away and were never heard of again. Now, in 1942, Australian interests had set up timbering operations to harvest Kauri pine trees. As the war moved into the northern ranges of the Pacific, and as manpower needs at home developed, their lumbering had come to a standstill.

"Part of the timber camp establishment was a clubhouse-recreation center for the Australian workers — now almost all departed — and it was here that I came upon the beautiful Blonde of Vanikoro.

"I had been assigned to ferry a J2F, a Grumman single-engine utility seaplane, from Espiritu Santo to Henderson Field on Guadalcanal. The J2F didn't have the range to make it all the way without refueling, so I flew up to Vanikoro, planning to refuel from the tender, then press on to Henderson.

"While aboard the tender and enjoying a fine meal with the PBY layover crews, Commander Stroop came in the wardroom with the word that a Japanese force was reportedly heading toward us. Not wanting to risk his ship being caught in an anchorage, he planned to put us all ashore, steam out to sea and return to pick us up when practical. The PBYs out on patrol could return to Santo, if necessary, and my J2F, not yet refueled, was towed into a wooded creek mouth where it was out of sight under the trees.

"A party of a dozen or more PBY crewmembers and myself were quickly beached, along with some hastily assembled rations, to make do until the tender's hoped-for return. As we prowled around our tropical refuge, my mind reflected on some of the things I had learned about the island before leaving Espiritu Santo.

"I had been impressed by some of the names on the chart: Deceitful Reef, Treacherous Reef, and La Perouse's two ships forever memorialized by the questionable honor of appearing in print as Boussole Reef and Astrolabe Point. The Pacific Islands Pilot had rather dolorously reported under climate: . . . 'damp, hot and unhealthy, even to natives, who are covered with ulcers and are often sick; therefore, it is deadly to Americans.'

"Meeting the lumber company's manager in his cheerful cottage surrounded by flowers dissipated any apprehensions about unfriendly ulcerous natives. As we made supper from our rations, supplemented with English tea from the manager's kettle, he told us of their hidden and provisioned company motorboat by which they would escape if the time came to evade the Japs.

"We had early supper while it was still daylight, for there would be no lights after sunset. 'Sorry,' the manager said, 'I haven't bunks for you, but you can all put up at the clubhouse if you don't mind sleeping on the floor.'

"So at least we felt welcome, if not optimistic about our forced stay ashore. In no way were we prepared for the company we would find waiting for us at the clubhouse.

"The clubhouse was a little green-painted frame building with steps leading up to a porch and a sagging front door. The last slanting rays of the setting sun shafted through the door with us as we swung it open and entered. There before us, glowing in the warm yellow light, stood the Blonde of Vanikoro, innocently unclad, wide eyes smiling slightly, though sympathetic to our gaping surprise.

"Surprise gave way slowly to wonder and admiration of the artistry and perceptive good taste that had inspired some Aussie to enshrine the beautiful life-size photograph of this gloriously endowed Venus in such a remote and humble temple.

"And so we shared a near-sleepless night with the Blonde of Vanikoro and a buzzing swarm of millions of vampire mosquitoes."

R. L. Summers: "His Parachute As A Souvenir"

R.L. Summers ended his stateside duty in the fall of 1942, piloting a PBY from San Diego to Pearl Harbor. His squadron was heading out to the islands in four-plane groups and Summers found himself thankful for the long-range capabilities of the Catalina on the flight over.

"On the way over, I went back to the bunk to get some rest. In an hour or so, I came back up to take over, asking as I did, where the other planes were. The second pilot pointed to a light and said he was following it. I couldn't see aircraft lights but I did see a planet. He had been following a planet for an hour or more and the other planes were nowhere in sight.

"We checked the navigation, corrected our heading and got there. But it took us 23 hours to make the crossing and we arrived with about one-half hour of gasoline in the tanks.

"Flying patrol out of Espiritu Santo, we frequently ran into our Japanese counterparts. We encountered one of their four-engine patrol seaplanes one time and they, being faster, promptly overtook us. We knew they had 20mm cannons but our 50–caliber machine guns had greater range, so we exchanged fire for about five minutes. When they tried to close, I put the Cat into a steep turn and kept going in circles, keeping out of range of their 20mms. We scored several hits with our 50s and each time the Jap veered off but came right back. They finally left and, unhit, we continued on patrol.

"Six of our planes were ordered out to night-bomb Nauru Island in the Gilberts. We were supposed to meet the Army's night bombers who were to attack first, then the Cats were to bomb and drop incendiary packets. Well, we arrived at about 5000 feet but no Army bombers had been there; they never found the island.

"Anti-aircraft guns began firing at us, so we decided to glide-bomb the place. I still have a mental picture of the incendiary bullets floating up at us. We hit the concentrated area with bombs and incendiaries and took off, flying at a few hundred feet above the sea. One of our planes was hit but got back all right. We were awarded Air Medals for the raid.

"My crew and I were sent on one mission to supply a coastwatcher on Vella Lavella Island. We took off in the early morning, flew very low — well out to sea — and came in low off our drop area, landing in an inlet where we were met by the coastwatcher. After unloading our supplies, we picked up four passengers to take back with us.

"Since the Japanese had an airfield on New Georgia Island, between us and home, we didn't know what to expect. But the Air Force sent a fighter escort with us for the return trip. After takeoff, we skirted Rendova Island and were just past it when one of the fighters developed engine trouble and had to ditch.

"We couldn't leave him so we landed at sea, taxied to where he was, and threw him a line. We had a dickens of a time pulling him in because he wanted to bring his parachute as a souvenir. I could have crowned the jerk. Here we were, very close to the Japanese air base and, by this time, the air cover fighters were getting low on gas and had left us out there on the water alone. When we finally got off, we stayed about 50 feet above the water all the way back to Guadalcanal."

13

Guadalcanal

In early July of 1942 the Allied Command received word from reconnaissance aircraft and Solomon Island coastwatchers that the Japanese were building an air strip on the northcentral coast of Guadalcanal. The news forced the Allies into immediate action to counter the enemy move. Allied plans had already formed to begin an offensive toward the Philippines and Japan but Guadalcanal had not been figured as an important stepping-stone along the way. A Japanese air strip on the 'Canal left little doubt that the enemy intended to use it as an offensive and defensive air terminal in the conquest of New Guinea and, eventually, Australia.

Thus, on August 7th, eight months after Pearl Harbor, the First Marine Division, covered by air and naval surface vessels, landed on Guadalcanal and Tulagi to begin the first American land offensive of the Pacific war. On August 8th, the Marines captured the unfinished air strip on Guadalcanal, renaming it Henderson Field. On the same day, they took partial control of Tulagi and two other islands of the Solomon group.

During the following six months, the Allies would wrest complete control of Guadalcanal, the Southern Solomons and most of New Guinea from the tenacious Japanese. But the price paid in men and naval vessels subdued the victors, convincing one and all that the enemy was cunning, courageous and far from defeated.

A preview of what lay ahead came early, just two days after the Marine landings, when naval vessels of the Emperor's Fleet out-maneu-

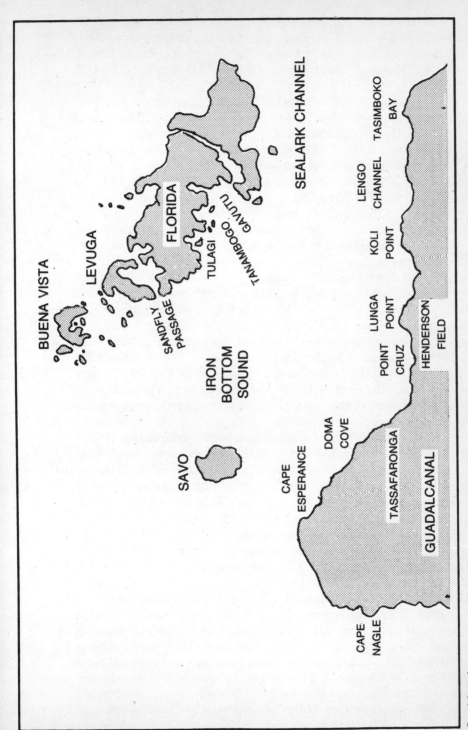

Guadalcanal.

vered and out-fought a near-equal Allied task force off Savo Island. When the adversaries backed off from each other, four Allied heavy cruisers had been sunk and another heavy cruiser and two destroyers were badly damaged. One Japanese heavy cruiser was sunk the following day, by a U.S. submarine.

There were other major naval battles during the conquest of Guadalcanal; in August, the Battle of Eastern Solomons; in October, the battles of Cape Esperance and of Santa Cruz Island. In each of these, American naval forces lost more fighting ships than did the Japanese. The U.S. carrier Wasp was sunk September 15th while covering reinforcements to Guadalcanal and the carrier Hornet was sunk by enemy planes October 27, as a result of the Battle of Santa Cruz.

Meanwhile, the enemy was losing naval vessels in greater number of a class they could ill-afford. Troop transports and freighters, with few exceptions, were turned back or sunk in battle after battle, as the Japanese failed to reinforce their beleagured ground forces on Guadalcanal.

In addition, a skimpy band of raggedy Marine and Navy pilots pieced together a few handfuls of American fighter aircraft and literally wrestled command of the air over Henderson Field, if not from the better part of Guadalcanal.

While this was happening, the pilots and crewmen of a growing force of PBY Catalina patrol bombers were contributing their all. During the early weeks of the Guadalcanal campaign, the only days off for PBY personnel were those forced by aircraft maintenance, or as a result of extra crews rotating with assigned crews. Otherwise, every crew flew every day and the flights were long and tedious.

To report that each flight resulted in an enemy task force sighting, or an encounter with a Japanese fighter or bomber, or a dramatic rescue at sea, simply would not be true. Hardly! The eyes of the pilots and blister-watch crewmen rarely cleared from the strain of searching endless miles of ocean; the surface of which was only occasionally broken by an island. When they were needed, however, the men of the Catalina squadrons were there to spot the enemy submarine stalking Allied convoys, to locate and report Japanese fleet movements and to pick up survivors from the many encounters in the area. Then their discomfort and inconvenience was forgotten.

Major General R. S. Geiger, USMC, had the dubious honor of leading the Marine fighters and bombers calling themselves the Cactus Air Force during the desperate and costly days of October, 1942. The Japanese were throwing every ship and aircraft they could muster into the recapture of Guadalcanal. They pulverized Henderson Field with sustained and accurate battleship bombardment, destroying almost half of the Marine fighters, blowing up stores and forcing the field's defenders into days and nights without rest or sleep. More damaging was the loss of most of their aviation gasoline, without which the entire island lay at the mercy of enemy air and sea attacks.

To make matters worse, word came from coastwatchers and PBY search planes that the Japanese were moving thousands of troops aboard six transports from Shortland Island. Their direction was Guadalcanal and they were obviously determined to recapture the precarious corner held by the U.S. Marines and Army forces. Eight Japanese destroyers escorted this troop movement. Further, as if to eliminate any chance of failure, Admiral Mikawa brought up the rear with his Eighth Fleet, including the cruisers Kinugasa and Chokai.

As the enemy sea forces approached, contingency plans were made in which each officer, pilot and ground crewman surviving the expected air and sea attacks would find his way into the American lines; there he would serve until returned to air service.

In the early stages of that battle for Henderson Field, facts pointed toward the probable implementation of those plans, as the Cactus Air Force's F4F fighters and SBD dive bombers were no match for the firepower of the attackers. But the ground crews kept patching planes and search groups miraculously located more and more barrels of precious gasoline stashed away by earlier field defenders against the bombings and naval attacks.

PBY Mission: Torpedo The Transports

Major Jack Cram, USMC, was General Geiger's junior aide and flew the General's private PBY — always. Never did the General fly without Major Cram at the yoke and rarely was there a pilot occupying the co-pilot's seat, except General Geiger. But the size of the PBY, and it subject to the constant bombardment of the General's area, prompted Geiger to order Major Cram to limit his activities to transporting supplies and personnel.

On the afternoon of the 14th of October, Major Cram landed his PBY between the bomb craters on Henderson Field with a torpedo attached under each wing, having picked them up at Noumea, New Caledonia for Torpedo Squadron Eight. But the TBF squadron had been bombed and shot out of service before the Major's arrival at the field and there seemed no apparent use for the torpedoes. However, the Major came up with a hair-raising idea that contributed to the defense of the United States' position on Guadalcanal and caused the General to write out a citation leading to the award of the Navy Cross to this brave man.

Jack Cram is currently in business in the San Francisco bay area of California, having long since retired from the Marine Corps but his dedication to the Corps and to his country carried him to the rank of General.

"I dodged shrapnel and bombs, most of the time from a foxhole, all night of the 14th of October. Our Operations Officer, Joe Renner, spent much of the time with me and painted a picture so critical of our chances that nothing short of a miracle could save us. But I was getting the hint of an idea and, as soon as there was a let-up in the bombardment, I approached General Geiger's aide, Toby Munn, with a request to let me rig a manual release for the two torpedoes still on my PBY and attack the Jap troop transports. As crazy as the plan was, Colonel Munn agreed there was little else left for any of us and immediately took me to the General. He gave his blessing and ordered us to find as much protection as we could from the remaining flyable aircraft.

"Jap troop transports were already landing reinforcements at Tassafaronga and they were all but unopposed. Only an occasional F4F or P-39 broke through the fierce anti-aircraft screen put up by the Jap destroyers. But the unbelievable ground crews began performing one small miracle after another as they, somehow, pieced together over a half-dozen bedraggled F4Fs and P-39s to give me fighter coverage for my run; about a dozen SBD dive bombers staged a simultaneous attack.

"By 1000 hours we were ready. I had just received a crash course in the art of aircraft torpedo bombing—from a PBY—with a makeshift manual release for the torpedoes, speed recommendations and proper drop altitude.

"My entire crew climbed aboard the Cat with me and we took off, heading out toward Savo Island where I took her up to about 6000 feet before pushing over into a long dive. I lined up between two of the transports and was concentrating so much on what I was supposed to do next that I forgot about my airspeed. When the plane began to shake, and the wings looked as if they were on a sea gull in flight, I chanced a look at the airspeed indicator. I thought, at that moment, I was dead for sure. The plane was ripping through the air at 240 knots—at least 60 knots beyond safe air speed for a PBY.

"Even though I eased up, we were still going so fast we passed over the destroyer screen before they saw us, and suddenly, there were my targets. I released one torpedo, waited a couple of seconds, then pulled the release on the other and started to get the hell out of there. I pulled the Cat up into a left turn and headed for Henderson Field. Back behind, one of our torpedoes scored a direct hit on a transport while the other one missed.

"But our troubles were just beginning. All at once there were Zeros all around us and we were taking a terrific pounding with some distance to go to the field. Duke Davis and his F4F fighter cover were doing everything they could to get the Japs off our tail and barely succeeded. One persistant Zero kept closing on us as we passed over Henderson but he was blasted out of the sky by a crippled Grumman, flown by Roger Haberman of Fighting 121. He was trying to negotiate a landing and already had his wheels down when he spotted our predicament. He poured on the gas and got the Jap, just before he got us. It turned out to be his first-ever kill.

"The PBY was the most versatile aircraft ever created. From air-sea-rescue, observation of the enemy, endurance, bombing and attack, the airplane was an all around workhorse. In the early stages of defending our positions on Guadalcanal, General Geiger used the PBY as a freighter. We flew supplies in — everything from toilet paper to torpedoes — and we flew out with severely wounded personnel. Later, we brought in VIPs and replacement personnel and flew out with fragments of squadron personnel who were being relieved.

"The great thing about the PBY was that it would take off with anything we could get into it, or on it. The day we came in with the torpedoes that we eventually fired at the Jap transports, we also had food, ammunition and replacement personnel. Everything was packed in and we took off: a long run, yes, but the Cat took off. Slow! Take off at 80 knots, cruise at 85 knots and land at 80 knots but always dependable.

"On one occasion, a flight leader named John L. Smith and his remaining pilots came aboard at Henderson Field to fly out in search of replacement aircraft. Just south of the field, one of my crew called out, 'Bandit at three o'clock!' Immediately, our guns were manned by my crew but before the bandit could be definitely identified, John L. Smith's pilots had taken over all the machine guns, having pushed my crewmen — none of whom knew the first thing about air-to-air combat — out of the way. I was impressed by their move; everything was so spontaneous. Even though they were on their way out, they were still in the fight.

General Geiger's Orders: Pick Up Joe Foss

"Another example of the PBY's flexibility came one afternoon when General Geiger, General Woods and, I believe, Colonel Parmalee, were sitting in General Geiger's tent and a call came in saying that Joe Foss, one of the top Ace Marine pilots of the 'Canal campaign, had been shot down but swam ashore to a small island where a coastwatcher had found him.

"This happened after the torpedo attack and the General had just accepted the return of his PBY, having been without it for two weeks while it was being patched up.

"The General discussed the situation with the others and finally said, 'Joe Foss has done so much, there is no choice.' He turned to me and said, 'Jack, get your crew together, get the details on where he is and go get him.'

"We did. We had no field to land on so we landed just off shore, in a bay, after circling and spotting Joe with the coastwatcher on the beach. We taxied in, put the wheels down and came up on the beach. There was Joe in a skroll skirt and white duck-pants, which the coastwatcher had given him. He had slipped out of his uniform to swim ashore.

"Joe jumped into the blister compartment, ran up to the front of the PBY and into the cockpit seat saying, 'Boy, am I glad to see you! Let's get the hell out of here!'

"And we did. Only the PBY could have made that rescue: no field, just water and a beach on an island.

"General Geiger was a man who wanted to be where the action was, regardless of the risk. He was briefing General Mulcahay, who was to relieve General Woods at Guadalcanal, when a message came in saying the Navy was going to shell Munda. General Geiger looked at the situation map and the location and said, 'You know? That ought to be a great show.'

"The more they talked, the more enthused they became. Finally, Geiger said, 'Let's go up and watch it!' All agreed. He turned to me and said, 'Jack, get the PBY ready and have operations get an altitude at which we can fly without being shelled. Tell the Navy that we will fly at that altitude and will be there during the shelling.' The altitude arranged was 8000 feet, which would give an excellent view of the entire operation.

"The shelling was planned for eight o'clock and everything went off on schedule: takeoff, flight to Munda, 8000 feet altitude and the shelling started on time, a real sight to behold. Then, apparently one of the ships hadn't gotten the word as anti-aircraft fire started bursting right near us; it got closer and more dense. Suddenly, the game was over and I had to make a move — fast!

"I kicked the PBY over into a spiral from 8000 feet to 500 feet; luckily, the shells were all behind us. As we went down I thought, 'What a Jap coup this will be if they shoot us down or cripple us on the water — capturing the three main Generals running the Guadalcanal campaign.

"We escaped. But then we were faced with another problem. Both fields at Guadalcanal had been bombed out of commission that day and an open – sea landing at night was much too risky with the value of our cargo. We had enough fuel, however, to fly until morning, and if the fields were still out, we could land offshore. Our plan worked, as the strip was back in operation the next morning and we landed without incident.'

Jack Coley: First U.S. Aircraft Into Tulagi

Jack Coley, a frequent contributor to our story, offers a brief anecdote about the Marine landings at Tulagi and Guadalcanal.

"I took the first airplane into Tulagi following the Marine landing on August 7, 1942. After being briefed that Tulagi was all secure, and that the Marines had the Japs on the run on Florida Island, I had gone up the 'Solomon Slot' as far as I could and still make it back to Tulagi before darkness. I was eager and since the enemy cruisers didn't come down the Slot that night, I pushed a little farther. Finding nothing to fight, I turned around and got back to Tulagi after dark. There were fires on the beaches and enough moonlight that I could make out the shore line.

186

"In the briefing I had been told about the Jap seaplane base on Tulagi, so now I knew where I could land. I could see well enough and turned on all my lights, figuring on landing among friends. I set up the blind landing procedure: set the PBY at 60 knots, 200–feet–per–minute drop and just held it till we touched down. It was a smooth landing.

"But as I turned around to taxi toward the seadrome, we were suddenly bathed in lights from all sides. Our ships were making sure of who we were. It turned out that the Marines had taken only half of Tulagi, none of Florida Island, and the seadrome was still in Jap hands. For some reason, they didn't want us to tie up there."

Allan Rothenberg: The "Experienced" Volunteer

Allan Rothenberg's account of the four-PBY torpedo attack on the Japanese invasion force at Midway described the before and after of the incident, leaving the attack itself for others to tell. What is only mentioned in his story is the fact that standard submarine type torpedoes used in the attack had never been dropped from an aircraft before. Since Ensign Rothenberg was "experienced" in this type of torpedo attack, he became the logical volunteer for another such effort in October of 1942, during the extended battle of Guadalcanal.

"A PBY had spotted four enemy cruisers headed for Guadalcanal and was shadowing them, waiting for Allied ships or aircraft to attack. But our forces were spread so thin, there was only a slim chance that elements of our fleet could reach the area in time to intercept. Admiral McCain, Commander of Air South Pacific, called me into an interrogation session and asked if I thought it possible to torpedo the Japanese cruisers at night with submarine torpedoes fired from PBYs. I told him that submarine torpedoes needed a long run for arming but that we had tried pre-arming them by manually rotating the propeller for 500 yards arming. Needless to say, I got the job!

"Two PBYs were scheduled to make the run but the other plane developed engine trouble and had to abort, leaving just 'that little Ensign in the back of the room' and his crew.

"The first PBY shadowing the cruisers was relieved by a second and we were given only sketchy bearings on a spot some 400 to 500 miles north — no navigational aids. When we were about 30 miles away, we requested MO's — radio signals sent slowly and repeated over and over — from the PBY on station. Picking up their signal on the direction finder, we flew in on a strong bearing.

"Drawing close, we dropped down to 50 feet off the water to make a controlled drop. Any higher altitude would have limited our accuracy; at least we surmised as much, since this was only the second attempt ever. At 15 miles, the radar showed what we thought were ships. But with the primitive models we had at that time, distances and shapes were hardly dependable; distance within two miles could not be calculated consistently.

"We strained our eyes in the darkness to make out a ship or ships ahead. Suddenly, there it was! Right in our faces! I yanked the Cat up over the ship and realized we had barely missed the first of four enemy cruisers. We flew for one minute — about two miles — then turned to make a torpedo run. There had been no firing by the Japanese, apparently no recognition. Then, about one quarter of the way into my turn, at about 500 feet ahead, were four more enemy cruisers heading in the same direction as the first group.

"I dropped the Catalina down to about 200 feet; still no fire from the enemy. This time I picked up the original four cruisers from about a mile out, steaming at about 100 yards distance from each other. I chose the second one — lined up — and made my drop somewhere around 500 yards off the bow of the cruiser; the torpedo travelled at about 30 miles an hour.

"Once more I lifted the plane over one of the cruisers, dropping immediately back to the water as soon as we were clear. This time the Japanese began firing. As we high-tailed it out of there, both blister watches reported a tremendous explosion on the second cruiser. Japanese records later confirmed major damage to the cruiser.

"Four nights later, patrolling alone with four 500-pound bombs under the wing, we came upon a cruiser escort guarding the unloading of a Japanese freighter at Kolubangara, Guadalcanal. With a good depth of broken clouds, I was able to climb to 5000 feet without the enemy detecting us and kicked the Cat over into a slow glide.

"With my bow gunner, Metalsmith Warren Tottem, visually lining us up, we attacked astern to bow, releasing one — two — three — four — in timed sequence. We scored at least one direct hit on the cruiser which had been moving before our attack; it now lay dead in the water.

"I was so intent on the attack and bomb release, I didn't realize that every enemy ship at the landing was firing at us by the time we dropped to 1500 feet. But I wasn't long in getting the word, as we were heavily buffeted by shells bursting all too nearby. To make matters worse, one of the crew reported a 'Washing Machine Charlie' on our tail.

"At this time, I issued a command to my radioman to send a message to base that would come back to haunt me over and over during the remainder of my tour. I said, 'Send a message that we have attacked and hit a cruiser and that the entire Jap Navy is firing at us, plus a biplane is on our tail and we're getting the hell out of here.'

"I didn't expect him to send it almost verbatim. Later, in the communication room of the tender, Tangier, I saw a copy of the actual report: 'Attacked enemy cruiser — hit scored — ship dead in water — entire Jap Navy firing at us — enemy biplane on our tail — we are returning to base, scared stiff.'

"Incidentally, dive bombers from Henderson Field went over the next day and finished off the cruiser.

"In early December, we were searching for survivors of a destroyer which had been sunk when my plane captain, C.G. Lawler, spotted debris in the water. We found several life rafts and counted over 70 men who had been hanging on for over 18 hours. Immediately, we took off for a destroyer some 30 miles away and, on the way, spotted four more men in life jackets. At the destroyer, we signaled with an Aldis lamp, 'Follow me, men in water.'

"An hour later, all of the survivors were being picked up."

For his courage and fortitude in the torpedo attack at the Battle of Midway, Allan Rothenberg was awarded the Silver Star. For his courage and leadership on those two days in October, 1942, he was awarded the Navy Cross. Following is the text of the Navy Cross citation:

"For extraordinary heroism as Commander of a Patrol Plane during action against the enemy Japanese forces in the Solomon Islands Area on October 16 and 20, 1942.

"Skillfully locating a hostile cruiser off Santa Cruz Islands in the misty darkness of early morning, Lieutenant (junior grade) Rothenberg, on his first attack, swept too close to the vessel for a release which would arm his torpedo. Coming back in a determined second run, he defied a tremendous hail of anti-aircraft fire to score a direct hit on the enemy ship. Later, off Guadalcanal, he located and attacked two other Japanese cruisers through a deadly screen of bursting shell, leaving one badly damaged and lying dead in the water. His superb airmanship and courageous initiative, maintained with utter disregard of personal safety, were in keeping with the highest traditions of the United States Naval Service." The above was signed, "For the President, Frank Knox, Secretary of the Navy."

14

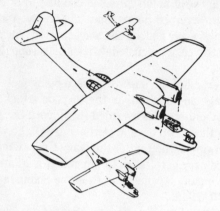

Patrol Squadron VP23

Patrol Squadron 23 was one of six PBY squadrons virtually wiped out by the Japanese bombing of Hawaii on December 7, 1941. It was one of three squadrons based at Ford Island and merged together with the other five to share the few flyable Catalinas left on the two naval bases after the raid.

With but a handful of Catalinas, the men of VP23 and their sister squadrons patrolled the skies for hundreds of miles around the Hawaiian Islands until assistance in the form of squadrons VP51, 71 and 72 arrived in Hawaii between mid and late December. But it was March of 1942 before replacement aircraft were delivered in sufficient quantities to rebuild VP23 and the Catalinas on the island.

By early January, 1942, another of the Ford Island squadrons, VP22, pieced together 12 PBYs and journeyed to the Dutch East Indies to reinforce beleagured VP101 and 102, who were retreating from the Philippines. Meanwhile, VP21 was scheduled for transfer to Perth, Australia in April, 1942.

Shortly after arrival in Perth, VP21 was decommissioned, joining the remnants of VP22 and VP102 to form a new VP101. And, aside from short detachments from VP14 and VP23, operating from Noumea, New Caledonia and Suva, Fiji, the bulk of PBY activities came out of VP101 and the Catalinas covering Hawaii, Johnston Island and Midway until preparations for the Guadalcanal campaign got underway.

Consolidated PBY-5. First model of PBY-5 seaplane, September, 1940. (courtesy General Dynamics.)

Tom Benton: Mutual Pilot-Crew Respect

Tom Benton, Santa Ana, California, earned his Navy Wings in Corpus Christi, Texas, and departed the United States from San Francisco in April, 1942, aboard the ex-Vichy French ship, the USS Wisconsin. He arrived in Pago Pago, Samoa, on Mother's Day, June 25th. Tom got his first taste of apprehension when the ship's captain plowed right through a mine field without waiting for a pilot boat.

Put ashore at Pago Pago, Tom's orders read: "To VP22 for flight duty." But he was soon to learn that VP22 had been wiped out in the East Indies. Tom and a couple of his buddies were enterprising young ensigns, however, and promptly wrote their own orders, had a Marine sergeant put a seal on them and they boarded the first ship to Pearl Harbor, the USS Indianapolis. At Ford Island, Tom was assigned to VP23, with which he remained until January of 1944.

Tom was best defined by his flying buddies as a man with super powers of concentration. A fellow pilot, Milton Cheverton, said that Tom could sit and read a book without so much as moving his head; he would lock himself into one position and read by the hour. He flew long night forays, seemingly with no regard for weather fronts. His favorite reaction to bad weather was to drop to about 100 feet altitude and go on instruments. Even in a PBY, it took ice in the veins to tempt fate in that manner.

Tom's loyalty to his crew, and the respect he won from them, though not unique in PBY squadrons, kept him flying with the same crew through two tours of duty in the South Pacific. But his crew first felt his wrath shortly after assignment when he discovered the aircraft was poorly maintained. After he had admonished them a couple of times, stressing the life-death nature of proper operating equipment, they became a tight team, completely at ease with each other under all conditions.

July, August and September of 1942 were busy months in the Solomons and Tom flew some form of flight every day of that period. On August 10th, his patrol assignment called for rescue of survivors after the catastrophic battle of Savo Island—the sea battle in which the Japanese "Crossed the T" and sank three American and one Australian heavy cruisers. But Tom found only the burning transport, George Elliott, and was waved off by supporting destroyers. All that was left of the Allied warships was a heavy coating of oil on the sea from Guadalcanal to Tulagi.

Once, when amoebic dysentary swept through the squadron, Tom and his crew were among a small group who missed it. Since the patrols had to go on, that group kept flying almost without let–up. Finally, Tom gave his men a day off only to have the order belayed by the executive officer of the squadron who set the crew to digging latrine holes. Tom, tired and frustrated, became so furious he had his exec' fearing for his life.

So many of the squadron became seriously ill from the dysentary it became necessary to evacuate them to Pearl Harbor for treatment. A Commander Ford, flight surgeon from Kaneohe, brought a Consolidated Coronodo to transport them back. But after the plane was loaded with stretchers of the ill, the pilot wandered out of the taxi lane and nipped a coral head, ripping a hole in the hull of the aircraft.

Chuck "Jerky" Rich, a close friend of Tom's was on the bottom bunk, nearest the hole and closest to the life preservers. He was also the sickest man aboard. Commander Ford ordered Rich to hand up the life jackets. Rich began handing them up but the water was rising around him rapidly, so he started to climb out of the compartment to the one above. Ford was positioned at that spot, and when Rich asked to join him, the Commander said, 'You have a life preserver on and I don't have, stay down there."

Roger Tittle, another of Tom's friends, was up on the next deck where he could look out and see a crash boat coming. He noted that the plane was no longer sinking and was resting on the bottom of the bay.

Rich said, "I still want to get out of here" and the Commander said, "Didn't you hear, we are not sinking anymore? Stay down there!"

But the water was still rising and when it reached Rich's chest, he started climbing out, only to have the Commander put his foot on the

Ensign's shoulder and shove him back down. As this was happening, Tittle sat at his perch giving a step-by-step account of Rich's efforts to climb out and the Commander's determination to keep him down below.

Finally, the water equalized just as it reached Rich's chin; only then did the Commander let him come up.

No replacement aircraft was forthcoming from Kaneohe, so Tom and a group of half-sick pilots fired up their PBYs and flew the seriously ill personnel back to Kaneohe. He stated that the Japanese could easily have followed the flight course of the Catalinas by the brown bags thrown out of the aircraft after-hatch.

Tom Benton continues his story with an example of the Catalina's ability to maintain an extended flight mode on just one engine.

"Flying co-chair to Hal Lough on patrols north of Espiritu Santo, we were introduced to further proof of the PBY's ability to stay in the air, even on one engine. "We had flown past Rennell Island, riding a strong tail wind all day and had started back a little early because of excessive use of fuel. No sooner had we turned back, and Hal had gone aft to sleep awhile, than there was a bang sound right at my left ear. I looked at the port engine and the number 13 piston was beating hell out of all the other pistons. I reached up and feathered the engine just as Hal came forward, asking what had happened. I pointed to the port engine and he went pale.

"Obviously, the engine had swallowed a valve and blew the whole head right off the crankcase, dumping it into the ocean. Pieces of the engine had gone through the port blister but had not injured anyone. We soon found that the poor old starboard engine wasn't keeping us airborne, even though I had the nose as high as I could with full power on.

"Hampy, my plane captain, was up in the tower reporting, 'Cylinder head temp' getting close to the red line'; then a little later, 'Cylinder head temp' is at the red line!'

"Finally, I said, 'Tell me when it gets 40 degrees over the red line'. He didn't call back.

"Meanwhile, Hal was in the after-station, throwing all the ammunition boxes out and all other heavy objects he could remove; but we were still losing altitude. We jettisoned all the gasoline in the left tank and that helped for a while.

"We had a new Ensign aboard, making his third flight and he was just about having a nervous breakdown — running around wringing his hands. He even took all the mattresses off the bunks and threw them out; they weighed about two pounds each. He threw out all of our cooking utensils, even a pair of the Mech's boots.

"About that time we looked at our charts. With the head wind, we knew we couldn't make it back to Espiritu, so we spotted Rennell Island. We weren't about to land at sea with water churning and high winds blowing. We eased around into a long, circular turn, away from the dead engine.

"About two hours later, Rennell came up. We looked at the chart and found there was only one harbor — one place to go in — with an approach from the southwest. The harbor was pretty big inside, the remains of an old breached volcano.

"I told Hal we would have to land down-wind because there was no way we could fly inside the harbor, turn around and come back into the wind for a landing with one engine. I kept trying to get him to take over, but he said, 'You're flying it, land it!'

"I took it into the harbor, and as soon as we got inside where the water was calm, I cut the throttle and eased the yoke back. We were going down-wind with a few rolling swells. When we saw one coming, we just eased the Cat down the back side of it and made a smooth landing.

"I taxied further into the harbor and could see nice coral sand beaches but there also were little hummocks all around the sand that looked like machine gun emplacements. I thought, 'Oh Boy,! We've landed on a Jap-held island.' Nobody said anything but all were thinking the same thing. We turned around again and kept the engine running. I had the sea-anchor out and ready, but was still holding. If something opened up, we could make a run for the mouth of the harbor.

"But nothing happened and pretty soon a little outrigger canoe came out with an old lady and a young couple aboard. When they reached the plane, the old lady held out her hand is if wanting something. One of the crewmen handed her a pack of cigarettes and a box of matches. She broke open the pack, stuck a cigarette in her mouth and lit up, puffing away like a chain smoker. All she wore was a "G" string and she had flabby, sneaker soles for breasts. She was 80, if a day.

"The young fellow with her was strong looking, named David, and could speak some English. We asked him if there were any Japs around. 'Jap — big thing, much grub — no Jap!' He said he would lead us to a safe anchorage, so we followed with the sea-anchor dragging to keep from running him down.

"He took us to a nice little bay with overhead palms and told us to drop anchor at one particular spot. The next morning, the tide was out and we found he had conveniently moored us with coral heads all around but none touching the aircraft. Now we could see that what we thought were machine gun emplacements were the tops of native huts.

"Before that, we had hardly anchored when about 20 canoes, loaded with what was probably the entire village, came alongside and villagers began climbing on the aircraft, wanting to see inside. But Hal got angry with them, so I told David to bring them all back in the morning and that no one could come inside that night. I told them to wait until the sun came up before coming back.

"Well, at the crack of dawn, here they all came. But, this time, they brought us fish and papaya. We told them they could come in the bow of the aircraft, walk by the navigator's table, then go out the after-hatch. We had

194

about 150 go through in an hour and a half. One of the few things our frightened young Ensign hadn't disposed of was the pencil supply, we had plenty. Each native was allowed to sharpen a pencil and take it with him as he passed the radio compartment.

"By 1030 they had all gone ashore, except for a couple of kids wandering around in an outrigger, when a sound came floating across the water from the direction of the village: 'Taboo! Taboo!' The word seemed to echo throughout the harbor. Looking toward a slight opening in the palms at the harbor entrance, we caught sight of a one-stack destroyer; for a moment we thought it to be Japanese. But we got ready with our blinker light, just in case, and the next ship slipping by the opening definitely was American.

"Before landing we had radioed our position and the Navy had dispatched a destroyer and a transport to search for us. They steamed right into the harbor and tried to tow us out. But we were fish-tailing around so much, I said, 'Cast off and I'll taxi the plane out of the harbor.'

"In a matter of minutes, we were attaching our big sling to the Catalina; the transport swung out a boom, picked us up, cranked up and we were under way for Espiritu Santo.

"After dinner that night, everybody was going below where they were showing a movie under black-out conditions. It was so hot and stuffy I couldn't stand it, so I was headed for the deck when General Quarters sounded. A submarine had been spotted and the destroyer escort was blasting away with depth charges before our ship had reached GQ. Seeing my chance, I went down to the officer's quarters, took a nice shower, found a clean bunk, and had the best sleep I had had in a couple of weeks. All this while the ship was still at General Quarters.

"When we got back to Espiritu, they took our plane to the beach for overhaul. The young Ensign? He turned in his flight orders and returned to the states."

Chuck "Jerky" Rich: Touch The Palms As Point Of Reference

Not all PBY pilots grew up in the coastal states. In fact, many of the best came from sparsely populated states such as Montana; and from Montana hailed Chuck "Jerky" Rich.

Graduating from Montana State College, Chuck found himself piloting a PBY for VP23 a short time before the Battle of Midway. As were so many others, in so many history-making battles, Chuck was one of the "also served" at Midway. He searched and searched for the Japanese fleet, patrolled for countless hours after the battle and never saw an enemy ship or submarine.

After the war, he settled in Mt. Holly, New Jersey. Chuck's story:

"In July, 1942, we moved to New Caledonia and started our move against the Japs. We patrolled toward Australia, losing a couple of PBYs to the enemy, then began operating from Efate before settling down in Espiritu Santo, New Hebrides.

"The night before our invasion of Guadalcanal, the squadron, with our tender, took up station in a little harbor at Malaita, across the slot from the 'Canal. We patrolled out of there the next morning. Either from the surprise of our attack, or a decision by the Japs to wait for the big guns of their fleet to mount a counter punch, the first couple of days were rather quiet, at least for the Cat people. But their fleet didn't take long in responding and they put up one hell of a fight.

"On August 24, the Jap fleet mounted the Eastern Solomons Battle in an attempt to retake Guadalcanal. We knew what they were up to but didn't know from where they would attack. It was the PBY squadron's task to locate and report the main body of the enemy fleet.

"I was flying co-pilot to Joe Kellum at the time and our plane found the Japs as we were returning from patrol. We came upon them so fast we were right in the middle of what appeared to be the whole Jap Navy before we realized who they were. They were spread out from one horizon to the other and we simply couldn't go around. The weather was clear and the seas fairly smooth, so we got through by getting down just off the water and jigging around quite a bit. Then we radioed all the data as to ship count estimates, types and course, to Espiritu as we headed back.

"On the way we ran across the American fleet which, at the time, was one carrier, the Enterprise, and a few basic ships. We circled them for a while, blinking out our information as to the enemy location, and they steamed off to intercept and turn back the Japs. Joe got the Silver Star for that episode.

"One time there was a Japanese submarine south of the 'Canal and we were furnishing Catalina patrols on 24–hour surveillance. I went out one night to relieve and take over the search. Suddenly one engine started pouring oil, causing us to abort the mission and return to Tulagi. At this time there were no night landing facilities and it was black. But the engine was freezing up and I had to land.

"I buzzed the tents where our squadron was staying and the boys got the idea, turning on the lights so I, at least, had some reference. But the camp was on the side of a hill. I started an approach and felt the palm trees scraping the bottom of the hull. I went around again and thought, 'Well, maybe that will be a good idea. I'll use the palm trees as a point of reference.'

"Lining up as best I could with absolutely no light, I let down until I felt the palm trees again, then held it until there was a break from them of a second or two. Immediately, I let down the aircraft and we landed all right."

"While the Battle of Eastern Solomons was developing into a U.S. Naval victory, of sorts, around Guadalcanal the Japanese were occupying

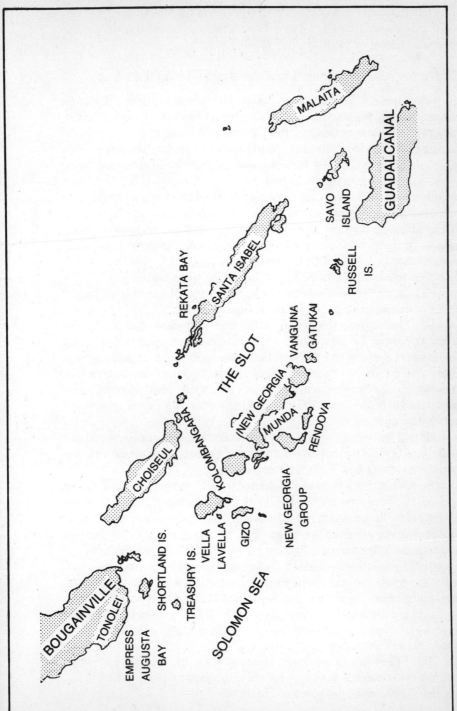

Solomon Islands.

the Gilbert Islands, Good enough Island, Ocean Island and Nauru. They were also landing forces at Milne Bay, New Guinea, all this during the three-day period of 24, 25 and 26 of August."

Cheverton And Blackman: Light the Night As Bright As Day

After the Battle of Midway, Milton Cheverton and Jeff, "Blackie," Blackman found their squadron, VP23, moving toward the South Pacific, though they knew nothing of the Guadalcanal plans until late July. In August their squadron was assigned to two small seaplane tenders operating out of Efate in the New Hebrides and the war closed in around them.

On August 4th, they watched the U.S. destroyer, Thatcher, hit a mine and blow up. Later, they were nearby when two American SBD dive Bombers mistook a small aircraft tender based at Santa Cruz Island for an enemy ship and bombed it, missing the ship, but killing about a dozen natives who had been playing in the area. About the same time, their squadron had the task of high-level night bombing the island of Nauru; each time they found the Japanese ready and willing to do battle.

Picking up the interview with Cheverton and Blackman, Jeff begins with events just prior to the Battle of Guadalcanal.

Jeff: "Just before the 'Canal battle started, flying out of New Caledonia, we took off for Efate, some 600 miles distant, stopped, refueled, had dinner on the lower end of New Hebrides, took off again and bombed Tulagi. We arrived over our target just as a formation of Australian PBYs arrived and together we gave the Japs hell for a while. Neither group knew until arrival over the target that the other was attacking Tulagi, let alone at exactly the same time."

Milt: "I was flying the night the Japs sank three of our cruisers and one Australian. Our patrol took us within sight of the battle but we didn't know until the next day how badly we had been beaten.

"Much fighting was done at night and wasn't limited to the islands. We made candle-flare runs for the PT-Boats with their match-box attacks on the Jap fleet. We carried flares with five-million candle power in canisters with parachutes attached, set to go off at 4000 feet altitude. We dumped them out one after another, lighting up the area almost like daylight."

"Jeff: "The islands around the Solomons hadn't been charted since the 1600s and sometimes the charts were just dotted lines without locations of bays, reefs, or anything. One such island was Stewart, just north of Santa Cruz. Flying over it became great sport for PBY crews; the native lovelies developed the habit of taking off their skirts and using them to wave at the passing American fly-boys.

Milt: "They were Polynesian. Most natives in the area were Melanesian, but these were Polynesian and quite handsome."

Jeff: "Rennell Island was also Polynesian."

Milt: "Yea! We had two Marine coastwatchers there. Seems the native chief picked two of his most luscious young ladies and turned them over to our boys. When we landed to pick them up, here were two short-haired native girls among all the long-haired beauties. The Marines had cut their hair."

Jeff: "There was a bay on Ambrym Island in the New Hebrides with the shape of a cul-de-sac, very narrow entrance, and a big bay inside. We had a rubber floating-dome in there as a standby reserve supply for gasoline.

"Also on the island was a French Catholic church with two nuns and maybe a priest, though I never saw him. A story came out about Roosevelt's Raiders, or someone, stealing all the sacrificial wine from the church and having a big party. The Bishop down in New Caledonia raised hell with the United States government, so it was our job to go in and appease the nuns.

"I flew an American intelligence officer and two U.S. Army priests through palm trees that were quite close together, doing a real job of scaring the puddin' out of them before I finally spotted the bay inside. Once on the water, we anchored the PBY and walked about two miles to the church compound where our guys made peace with the nuns."

"Jeff: "We were in the Battle of Santa Cruz and saw the carrier Hornet burning. After the battle, we picked up Commander Gus Wildhelm, an air group commander on the Hornet who had been shot down. He was belligerent and badly sunburned after two days in a raft; kept asking about his ship. We were a little apprehensive about telling him, and held off for a while, feeding him a few drops of booze and some food before finally breaking the news. At that, he let out a wild sob, spewing language worse than a sailor.

"I remember my good friend here going ashore and bumming wine off the French planters."

"Milt: "Got sick on it, too! It was my 24th birthday and I wanted to celebrate.

"On our second tour, I brought along case of Ancient Age. I knew that when you go aboard ship with booze, the Doc said, 'Thank you very much, Sir!,' then took it away. Well, I left my liquor aboard the plane, going back after it with my green pack-bag. All went well until about halfway up the gangway when the guys with me started horsing around and wanting to hand the booze up the ramp.

"It fell, of course, and I heard the bottles breaking. In desperation, I grabbed the bag and went tearing up, said, 'Permission to come aboard, Sir,' and ran up two flights up to my quarters, with this liquid dripping every step of the way. In my room, I hurriedly stuck the unbroken bottles into my safe and destroyed the broken ones; then it was off to the shower to destroy the aroma of the evidence."

Jeff: "The odor permeated the whole ship. It must have gotten up to the flag deck but they never said a thing to us."

Jeff had this to say in praise of the Catalina:

"The PBY seemed to know how long a crew needed to stay airborne and rationed its gasoline to compensate for it. As an example: I was flying a PBY from San Diego to Honolulu in heavy weather with a crew I didn't know and a co-pilot who had been a yoyo champion in high school; he couldn't even navigate. I had to fly the ship, navigate and everything else; and this was my first flight as a Patrol Plane Commander.

"Because of the uncertainty of headwinds and weather, the squadron had installed 400 – gallon auxiliary tanks in the hull. An electric pump was supposed to pump gasoline from the auxiliary tank to the wing tanks. My instructions were that those tanks had to be emptied first.

"But the crew didn't start the pump until we were almost at the point of no return, and when they did, the electric pump wouldn't work. Here we were: 400 gallons of gas, an extra 2400 pounds of weight, and shortly after turning around to head back, we flew into a hell of a storm. It was so bad, I had to put my hands through the yoke to hold on to it. When we landed in San Diego, we had about 50 gallons of usable gas in the tanks. The Cat was simply unbelievable for sustained flight."

Milt: "I was so proud of my plane, I named it 'Pugnacious Polly;' later I married the girl I named it after. My crew didn't like the name, thinking it was sissified and painted it out as soon as I left the squadron. On their next flight, they were going out for a patrol hop, hit a submerged log, and sank the plane in the bay."

Robert Elberg: The Cat Formed-Up with Enemy Bombers

Robert Elberg, Carmichael, California, graduated from flight school at Corpus Christi, Texas. He earned his wings and Ensign commission in August of 1942. His travel orders read: "San Diego, California, for transitional training." His story begins with assignment to VP23 in September of 1942.

"My transitional training lasted approximately one-half day before orders came down to be in San Francisco in 24 hours, ready to catch a ship to the islands. I joined VP23 in September of 1942, just as the squadron arrived back at Kaneohe after taking quite a pounding in the South Pacific. They had experienced the complete spectrum: search patrol, open – sea rescue, convoy, air-to-air combat, bombing and even torpedo bombing. Comparatively, the first four months I served with the squadron were quite boring; we flew 11 – to 13-hour patrols in sectors to the north, west and south.

"There followed detachments to Midway and more patrols. Then, in February, some of the Patrol Plane Commanders returned to the states for retraining in Liberators for duty in England. At about that time, Roger

Tittle and I were promoted to plane commanders and were reassigned to Canton Island.

"The Japanese used Canton for frequent high-altitude night bombing practice and were pretty accurate with their aim. When we got an alert, after the first half-dozen raids, we flew the PBYs off to a little island south of Canton and waited out the attacks. It was on such a deployment that Chuck Rich had an experience that had a chilling effect on all of us.

"On this particular night, Chuck, Tom Benton and I circled three PBYs around that little spot of ground in the ocean until we received the all clear and started forming up for our return to Canton. We were hardly under way when Chuck came on the voice radio asking that we slow up a bit, so that he could catch up. He said he was flying on our port wing, but when we looked around, no PBY, no anything! I called back to say we couldn't see him and it was then he discovered that the Japanese had chosen that same island to reform for return to their base; Chuck had tried to form up with the enemy, thinking it was us. But no shots were fired and Jap Bettys and American PBYs returned to their respective bases.

"Just before our squadron was transferred to Espiritu Santo in the New Hebrides in May of 1943, we were taking orientation training flights in PBY-5 seaplanes. Most of our flight hours had been in PBY-5As, the amphibious version of the Catalina. On the final day of practice, Roger Tittle, a Chief Aviation Pilot named Woodsack, and I went out on torpedo practice runs. The torpedoes had practice war heads painted a bright red to make recovery easier. At our briefing, the main stress was on 'not losing the torpedoes.'

"After we got rid of the fish, Roger and I decided to pull a little 'loop-de-do' and make a run on Waikiki Beach. Chief Woodsack declined to go along, so Rog' and I headed for the beach. About then, Rog discovered he still had one of his torpedoes; it obviously hadn't released.

"We flew so low that people in several outriggers jumped into the water just ahead of us, while others weren't running on the beach, they were crawling. Out of the corner of my eye, I could see Rog and he was even lower than I. His wing, the one with the fish dangling from it, was practically in the dining rooms of the hotels.

"After our fun, we made a couple of runs on ships in the harbor, then landed at Kaneohe.

"As we came up on the beach, two jeeps were waiting — one for Rog and one for me — to take us directly to the commanding officer of the base. He was a little upset, to say the least, but asked when we were shipping south. We said 'Tomorrow.'

"He said, 'You're excused. Good luck!'"

VP23, active through most of the Pacific action, found the summer and fall of 1943 to be a very busy time.

After the beach-buzzing incident at Waikiki, Robert Elberg and his buddies, having recovered from their bout with amoebic dysentary, found themselves once more flying PBYs for VP23 in the Solomon Island zone. Working their way from seaplane tender to tender, they performed the multiple duties of a PBY squadron now turned Black Cats.

Bob Elberg picks up his story on a day in September, 1943.

"Operating from a seaplane base at Tulagi, my crew was activated from stand-by duty and told to pick up a group of Marines — a Lieutenant, a Sergeant and four Raiders — and take them to Rekata Bay on the island of Choiseul. Australian coastwatchers had reported that the enemy seaplane base at Rekata had quieted down and that it appeared the enemy was beginning to evacuate. This Marine bunch was to go in and finish off what was left.

"We loaded everybody into the plane with all the Marine's attack gear, including rubber boats, and took off. We had air protection from six F4F fighters, which we appreciated for their close-in coverage, as opposed to P-38s. We called the P-38s 'High altitude fox holes;' when they gave you coverage, you never saw them.

"We got in pretty close to the beach — close enough to see the Japanese seaplanes lined up on their ramps — and unloaded our boys with all their gear into the rubber boats. They had so much gear, they couldn't make way against the tide. So to help them along, we cranked up our engines and got in behind them, literally blowing them ashore.

"Although we didn't pick them up, we followed reports of their mission and they really did a job: cleaned up what was left.

"We were trying to secure Rendova Island about this time and had established a PT-boat base there. It was a necessary maneuver for position on the way to the capture of Munda and its strategic air strip. We would land out in the lagoon, set up temporary residence with the PT boat sailors, then join them in a lot of their hunter-killer and rescue activities. And when New Georgia was secured, we moved to a base called Ondonga where we shared quarters with the fighter boys. Fighting 17, a skull-and-crossbones squadron, did a terrific job around Bougainville.

"Those were exciting missions. Each time we flew into Rendova, the PT boats were lined up in a row. We buzzed the line to alert them to send a boat to where we buoyed. As the practice became routine, the Cat pilots buzzed the PT line lower and lower. Finally, a PBY took off a couple of antennas and that was the end of the buzzing.

"By November, the Northern Solomons were the subject of one big battle after another. On the first of November, our troops landed at Cape Torokina, Bougainville, and the next day the battle of Empress Augusta Bay cost us one destroyer sunk and two light cruisers and two destroyers damaged. There was also a collision involving our destroyer, Thatcher. The Japanese lost a light cruiser and a destroyer.

"On November 11, my crew and I were on stand-by duty on the base at Rendova Island. We were sharing flight duty with another PBY squadron at the time and were just starting the day at a leisurely pace when the word came down for us to get our tails out to the plane for immediate takeoff. The other squadron's plane had hit a reef and was out of commission; so we had to take its flight.

"In the briefest of briefings, we were told to land at Treasury Island where we would receive instructions. As far as we knew, Treasury was still in Jap hands, but we got airborne and knew right away that something big was coming up. Suddenly, we had around 18 Navy Corsairs, 10 F4Fs, and a like number of P-38s escorting our lonely little PBY.

"When we landed at Treasury, this big tank-lighter came up alongside and, after some jockeying around, we got into position to receive passengers. The first man to come aboard was Admiral Bill Halsey, the Commander of South Pacific Forces, then General Geiger, his Marine counterpart and, by now, I didn't care who else. There was the usual supporting brass for high-ranking military, plus a host of *Life* photographers and reporters. As I said, I didn't much care as the worst had already happened when Admiral Halsey came aboard. I sat at the controls, with nothing more than a pair of shorts, a shirt — no insignia — and a ball cap, between the military leaders of the entire zone and my birthday suit.

"The plan was to fly these famous leaders into Empress Augusta Bay on Bougainville. There was little question that danger surrounded this move, as we had hardly secured our early positions on Bougainville, now these guys wanted to take a look-see. But General Geiger was thinking ahead when he ordered me, emphatically, to be back the next day to pick them up. Well now, that was before we landed.

"Everyone knows an open-sea landing in a PBY was no simple thing, especially in rough water. The sea was fairly calm that day, which wasn't the best of conditions because a calm sea means huge swells. But I spotted the pick-up boat and thought, 'We'll make a terrific splash right alongside that baby and show these boys that we can really fly the old birds.'

"I made a pass to check the size of the swells; they didn't look too bad but there were a few big old ground-swells. The next time we came around, I told my co-pilot, Jonesy, 'I'm going to bring this Cat in with a full, power-stall, landing and we'll just plunk it right down alongside that boat.'

"Everything was going fine and I said, 'When I give you the word just cut the throttles and she will suck right in.' The way we had done it a number of times before, we would hear the tail kind of click about three times in the water. If it was slow enough and the nose was high enough, the plane would kind of mush right in and stick, no jerking or bouncing. We were in a good attitude, and our pick-up boat was right along side of us, so I gave Jonesy the signal to chop the throttles. When this happened, there was a great silence for several seconds.

"Somehow, someway, we hit one of the swells a little wrong, and the next thing I knew, we were 50 to 100 feet in the air, with the nose sticking straight up and no power. I reached over and gave her full power, but all we got was a big cough just before the plane came down on its hull. We hit so hard, all the radio gear was jarred off of the bulkhead. But that's nothing to how it jarred the passengers.

"Nobody was hurt. The plane leaked like a sieve but we discharged our passengers and took off. We didn't have to go back for them; I guess they asked for a different pilot.

"A lot of fun things happened and many times we were scared half to death. For example: One night I was plane commander of a Black Cat snooping mission around the Truk Island group. On the way back, we were picked up by two Japanese Betty night bombers. It was one real experience bringing that old bird home with those guys right on our tail all the way.

"We sort of overdid it as far as engine ratings go; we were wide open all the way home, most of the time in dives and climbs or tight turns. When we finally shook them, got the plane back on the beach and tried to crank the engines, there was a strange rattling sound. This had been a four – to five-hour ordeal and those engines held together long enough to get us home.

"Tom Benton and I went back to Espiritu Santo shortly after the Bougainville activity died down. We spent a while flying general purpose patrols before the order came down to ferry our PBYs back to Hawaii and, hopefully, home. It was at this time we learned how almost indestructible the PBY Catalina really was.

"We ran into a hurricane at Suva, Fiji, and were instructed to turn back to 'Santo to avoid the storm. We didn't want to go back for fear of an order change that would abort our ferry-hop to Hawaii. So we landed at Suva and decided to weather the hurricane there in the harbor. We tied the Catalinas to buoys, started the engines, turned the planes into the wind, and kept them just about even by increasing and decreasing the throttles according to the wind. There were times at the height of the storm, with the winds topping 100 knots, when we were almost flying in a tied-down position. And this went on for a couple of days before the storm passed, with no major damage to either aircraft. With the storm behind us, we flew on to Hawaii.

"The PBY was some kind of aircraft, especially for the men who flew them. You got to the point, somewhere along the way, where you felt it could do anything you asked of it.

"When I first arrived overseas, I flew with an Aviation Pilot whose name was Pierre La Ponte. He had been in the Navy for a long time and was a long drink of water — better than six feet tall. He logged many hours in Catalinas. One of his claims was that he could make a 180 – degree turn in the length of a PBY. He would put the Cat in a little dive, jam the rudder, wrap the plane up and almost roll it on its back.

"Flying with fellows like him, and others I met along the way, helped me to gain the confidence to trust the PBY. So when I trusted it and asked the impossible of it; the old Pratt-Whitney engines just kept right on singing away. And the Catalina always brought us home."

15

Patrol Squadron VP11:
Part One

John Byrd, Elizabeth City, North Carolina, retired from the Navy after the war as a chief Aviation Machinist, having begun his military career before the war in the U.S. Marines. He joined VP11 in November of 1941 and was with the squadron until February of 1943.

"I spent the first four years of my military career in the Marines because of a mistake. Being a boy off the farm in Mississippi, I got into the recruiting office in New Orleans and was listening to the recruiter painting the exciting life of a Marine. When I asked how much I would make per month, he said, 'Semper Fideles' and I thought he said $75.00. So I signed up. For that mistake, I spent four years in the Marines and earned $21.00 per month and a horse blanket.

"I was in VP11 at Kaneohe on December 7, 1941 and I remember asking someone to give me something to shoot with, or a pair of track shoes. After the attack the work really began, so I wrangled crew assignments and flew patrols as often as possible. One of the few PBYs flyable after the attack still had camouflaging on it and the Army shot at us every time we returned from patrol.

"During the Midway battle, I flew eight days straight. I found that if the Cat could fly in, it could fly out.

"When the squadron went south in July of 1942, 11P7 did all right, even if we didn't get any medals. We rescued 23 survivors: one PBY crew from VP14, which had been shot down by Zeros, one crew from a B-17 and two airmen off New Georgia. We had our thrills, too. Once, after we had dodged Jap patrol craft to drop off two coastwatchers on Ontong Java, we were attacked by a trigger-happy gunner on an Army B-17. At the same time we were reporting their attack on us, they were reporting to the same base that they were attacking a Jap patrol plane.

"Their gunner was pretty good. He scored three hits on the starboard wing, one in the port engine propeller, one through the engine cowling and three through the hull. These hit a box of ammunition in the radio compartment, exploding it and injuring the radioman and a New Zealand Major who was just going along for the ride."

Leon Freeman: Friend or Enemy?
Answer—Red Flame And Black Smoke

"Leon Freeman began his naval career in November of 1935 and soon joined the old VP6 squadron, flying PBY-1s out of Ford Island, Honolulu, Hawaii. He was accepted for flight school at Pensacola, Florida, became an Enlisted Pilot upon graduation and was returned to duty with VP11, the PBY squadron which had evolved from his original VP6. Leon gives a few highlights of his South Pacific tours.

"We went south in July of '42—Kaneohe to Palmyra, to Canton Island and to Suva, where we lived in the town hall and bath house. That was most of us. Some had met New Zealand girls and lived with them. The officers lived in the Grand Pacific Hotel, having champagne cork fights and generally living the 'good life.' But that didn't last long as the squadron moved around the island to Lautoka where we flew northern patrols toward Ocean Island; the game playing was over.

"On the 27th of August, I was flying co-pilot to George Poulos. We sighted a task force but couldn't tell whether they were Japanese or Allied. We flew right down the side of the whole bunch of them—from bow to stern. I stood up in the bow, my gun station, with an Aldis lamp to give a recognition signal. But when I blinked at them, the whole line commenced firing. Red flame and black smoke belched out of every ship. Somehow, we knew they weren't ours.

"Poulos immediately started evasive action. I looked out under our port wing and saw a shell coming right at us; all I could think to do was wave it off. We were flying at about 50-foot altitude when the shell hit the water with a giant splash and the casing came tumbling up toward us. I swear, if I had had a boat hook, I could have reached out and caught it. The thing didn't miss our port propeller by more than five feet.

"In our haste to get out of there, we somehow lost that entire task force until after dark; we finally found them and reported their position.

"One morning out of Ndeni, we had taken off real early with the lizard-line—the line used to haul up the anchoring pendent—still outside the aircraft. It was my job to unshackle the pendent and stow it away. Now the lizard-line was beating against the hull. It was still dark and we had a full load of gas, so we didn't want to land.

"I had Leo Zok, our Chief Ordnanceman, hold me by the belt while I got up on the step going around the bow. I went back, opened the anchor locker and brought out the anchor pendent, this so I could get hold of the lizard line. All the while, my fanny was just inches from the propeller. It must have been quite a sight with me outside the pilot's window. But I got the lizard line, put it back in the box, tightened up the anchor pendent, closed the compartment and got back inside."

Bill Barker — The Apple Orchard At Sea

Sometime after he finished digging and filling in holes, as told earlier, Bill Barker, Marshall, Texas, became a crewman aboard a PBY, flying for VP11. Bill picks up his story in July of 1942 when he was flying with Lieutenant Flannery out of Suva, Fiji.

"We were making all-out searches for Eddie Rickenbacker after he went down at sea in an Army Air Force plane. On one of these searches, we lost an engine and flew into Tongatapu where we stayed four days, waiting for parts. While there, I got acquainted with a very good looking native girl whom I visited and swam with frequently. One day, while we were walking together on the beach, she reached over in the surf at the edge of the water and picked up a crab, broke off a leg, cracked it with her teeth and started eating the live meat. Instantly, I was no longer interested in the girls at Tongatapu.

"After abandoning our search for Rickenbacker, we flew back to Suva and soon moved on to Noumea, New Caledonia. At Noumea there was a very bad downdraft in the landing approach. It was unavoidable and quite an experience, especially to a new crewman. Gentle, compassionate souls that we were, we wouldn't warn a first-timer about the downdraft and just watched his reaction his first time through. One of our crews almost lost one of their new Aviation Pilots out of one of the blisters when they hit that thing. I understand he was thrown completely out but was able to hold on and climb back into the plane.

"Shortly before we began our assault on Guadalcanal, part of our squadron moved to Ndeni in the Santa Cruz Islands. My crew made the trip in the USS McFarland, which was an old four-stacker destroyer, converted to a seaplane tender. On the way, we went through a major storm and on one particular night the cook was making cherry pie for the entire crew. Well, the ship listed badly and one of the big pots of cherries tipped over in the galley, spilling cherries and cherry juice from one end of the room to the other. I'll never forget the sight of that big, burly cook and his mess-cook, sitting in the middle of all the mess, crying like little babies. Incidentally, we didn't have cherry pie on that trip.

"On August 6, the eve of the Marine's landing on Guadalcanal, with Lieutenant Flannery in command, we were returning from an all night patrol around Guadalcanal and ran out of gas. We sat down at sea with no damage but spent four days floating around the ocean in that PBY. We fed our old bacon to the sharks and spent most of our time pumping bilges and being sick. Finally, a destroyer, the USS Stack, picked us up. Their skipper said he had extended his search by 30 minutes beyond the limit he was allowed on a guess that he would find us. The question lingers: Was it a guess, and what would have happened had he not followed that 'guess'?

"Lieutenant Flannery took a position aboard the Curtiss and I flew with a couple of other pilots before joining the crew of Lieutenant Genta, a new Patrol Plane Commander, in early September. Long, routine patrols, boring to the point of frustration, marked the month of September and early October. But, about that time VP11 began an exciting new approach to fighting the war. Borrowing from the Japanese 'Washing Machine Charlie' tactics, we initiated nuisance raids to hit targets of opportunity — armed and ready to attack with bombs and torpedoes. We began painting the bottom of the wings and hull with a dull black paint.

"We made bombing raids over Japanese installations such as the airstrip they were building at Munda, on New Georgia Island. When we ran out of the many two- and five-pound personnel and fragmentation bombs we carried to toss out at intervals, we threw out Coke bottles; they made an eerie, whistling sound, much like bombs on the way down. We did anything that came to mind to harass the Japanese.

"On several occasions, we flew supplies in to the Australian and New Zealand coastwatchers stationed on the island of New Georgia. We thought then, and still do, that they had to be some caliber of men to stay up in those mountains, spying on the Japs, reporting ship movements and air activity headed toward Guadalcanal and the Southern Solomons, especially the activity through the 'Slot'.

"In November, I began flying with a Lieutenant Reese and his crew. One of our missions was to Rendova Island to pick up some survivors from a recent battle. On the way, we swung by Guadalcanal and picked up some Army P-38 fighters as escort — a first for most of us. We landed in a little lagoon where an SBD pilot off the Enterprise and a Guadalcanal Marine Sergeant, who had been shot down in a battle, were waiting for us. The natives had found and hidden them from the Japs until we could get there. They had also 'liberated' a Jap machine gun, with some ammunition, and were sending it back with us to be examined by Intelligence at the 'Canal.

"A Lieutenant from the Royal Australian Air Force was flying with us at the time as an interpreter and could speak the native language fluently. He was with us one time when we took some spotters and a radio crew up to Ontong Java, an island about 300 miles north of Guadalcanal.

"Landing late in the evening, we unloaded all of their gear, then spent the night in the native village, sleeping on mats stretched out on the sand, with a rock as a pillow. Next morning, we flew back to Tulagi. But having that Aussie Lieutenant with us really opened our eyes to the treatment the natives of that region had been receiving at the hands of the Japanese. Those people felt sincere respect for their Aussie protectors and the respect was mutual.

"During the period of late November and early December, we had a number of comical incidents aboard the tender. Several of the guys were acting crazy, pretending to catch flies and eating them; pretending they were painting everything they came across. They stole spoons from the galley and broomsticks and beat the spoon handles around the broomsticks, made golf balls out of electrician's tape, took plugs out of the tie-down holes on the fantail and played golf.

"One day we had a 'Man Overboard' alarm. Everyone ran to the fantail to see what was going on and, sure enough, there was a man swimming away from the ship. The Officer of the Deck called for a whale-boat and a rescue crew to go out and pick him up; by then he had swum quite a distance from the ship.

"They brought him back and when he came aboard the OD asked him why he jumped off the fantail. The young body said he went out to the apple orchard to get an apple. The OD hit the ceiling, raving and ranting. Then the kid reached in his pocket, pulled out an apple and showed it to him.

'See,' he said, 'I got one.' The strange thing about that episode was, at the time, there were no apples aboard the USS Curtiss."

Glenn Chase: Confirmation — Two Subs Sunk

Glenn Chase was an Aviation Chief Machinist Mate and Naval Aviation Pilot assigned to Patrol Squadron Eleven when the first shooting started at Kaneohe Bay, Oahu, Hawaii. During the two-plus hours of the attack, Glenn saw two of his buddies machine-gunned to death in the PBY hangar. He helped set up one of the many improvised machine gun nests intended to provide defense against an expected land invasion that never came. He was one of a number of VP11 crewmen who returned for the squadron's second tour of the Pacific campaign. Here are brief anecdotes of his two tours.

"From the 14th to the 28th of August, 1942, we were stationed at Suva, Fiji, then to Espiritu Santo in the New Hebrides. On September 7, we bombed a Japanese submarine and got confirmation that it sank. Two days later, flying out of Ndeni, we tore the hull out of our Cat on takeoff, finished our patrol, then lost the plane when we came in to land; it simply sank.

"On the 12th of September, a Jap submarine shelled our tender, the Mackinac, but backed off when we weighed anchor to pursue. On the same day, Lieutenant 'Dopey' Clark and crew were shot down and captured by the Japs.

"These were busy days for the PBY boys. There were but a few of us and we had thousands of miles of open sea and hundreds of islands to patrol.

Glenn Chase and crew, Patrol Squadron VP11. (courtesy Glenn Chase file.)

"Flying off the USS Curtiss, a classy aircraft tender, on the 29th of October, we sank another sub. On November 8, we rescued an Air Corps crew who had survived the crash of their plane and were stranded on a reef.

"We boarded the USS Grant on January 9, 1943 for a slow-boat ride back to the United States.

"After reforming in San Diego, getting new PBY-5s and extensive retraining, we found ourselves en route back to the South Pacific and a new home base at Perth, Australia.

"Though most of our flights were long and boring, some were hair-raising; like the time a flare exploded in the tail section and we barely made our open-sea landing before the plane literally exploded and burned. Island natives rescued us, sent word through the coastwatchers, and a torpedo boat crew picked us up.

"On the third of October we strafed a Jap seaplane, a destroyer and a cargo ship. On the fifth, we were attacked by Jap fighters but got down just off the water where they couldn't get to us.

"On December 15, flying out of Port Moresby, we took part in the rescue of over 2000 Aussie Commandos and all their equipment. No big thing! We just flew back and forth over the 15,000 foot Owen Stanley Mountains, time and time again, until all were safely removed. The last plane left with Jap foot – soldiers less than a couple of miles from camp.

"I think the old PBY Catalina was one of the greatest aircraft ever created, but then I'm prejudiced. It took me through some 2900 wartime flying hours."

George S. Clute: Cats Down At Sea
— Sharpened Pencils, Plugged Rivet Holes

George Clute retired from the U.S. Navy in 1968 with the rank of Commander. During 1942, flying PBY Catalinas for VP11 around the Solomon Islands, he was a Lieutenant (jg). George logs the following typical highlights of his crew's activities between August 5 and December 13, 1942.

"August 5, 1942: Several planes flew to Ndeni, Santa Cruz Islands, to operate off a small seaplane tender. My plane was among them. The next morning we patrolled as far north as possible to ensure that the Japanese fleet would not interfere with our landings at Guadalcanal. Upon return that night, a tropical front lay across Ndeni. Our radar and voice radio were out, and since we were the last to arrive back from patrol, we had to wait our turn to be vectored to the island via the lost-plane procedure. The tender had just started our vector pattern when we ran out of gas and had to land in 25 – 30 – foot swells.

"I was an extra pilot with Lieutenant (jg) Moss Flannery and his regular crew on this flight. Moss did a marvelous job of landing in a heavy sea; the plane suffering no more damage than some popped rivets and a drooping engine mount. Following standard procedure, we sharpened pencils and plugged rivet holes and, by bailing about 30 minutes of each hour, we stayed afloat until picked up.

"September 20: Sighted Jap Kawanishi flying boat. Chased it for six minutes — fired at us with tail cannon — out of range, too far from base to chase further.

"October 19: Night bombing raid on enemy ships off Guadalcanal. Dropped spare torpedo fuses to U.S. PT boats. Made skip-bombing run on Jap destroyer off Guadalcanal air strip. Bomb failed to skip but scared him off from shelling air strip. Looked for larger target but found none, so went after destroyer again since he was escaping to the north.

"A downdraft caught us just as we entered a squall, causing us to almost collide with the destroyer. We were below masthead height and so close we could see men on the bridge as we went by, even though it was near midnight and raining. Needless to say, I had nightmares about that one for awhile.

"October 25: Night torpedo attack on enemy cruiser 500 miles north of Espiritu Santo. To our pleasure, we penetrated the circular destroyer screen at masthead height and made our drop without being fired on until we were making our escape turn to stay down-moon of the cruiser. At that point, the cruiser fired one AA salvo which burst harmlessly off our port wingtip. We went back through the destroyer screen without another shot being fired. The only thing we could figure was that they didn't want to expose their position with gun flashes.

"We had reported their position before attacking and circled out of range afterward for a couple of hours, reporting their movements. A few days later, a Jap cruiser was reported limping north with a starboard list and trailing oil. We like to think it was the same one, though it was never confirmed.

"Anyway, the Navy gave me my first DFC for this and the Guadalcanal job of a few nights earlier.

"December 13: Flew anti-sub coverage for the battle damaged USS Minneapolis off San Cristobal in the Solomons. That was some night — a cruiser with no bow forward of the bridge and steaming under her own power."

Jack Coley: Nuisance Raids

Jack Coley, VP11, and his crew had the distinction of making the first of hundreds of night harassment raids on Japanese positions, beginning with the enemy troop camps on Guadalcanal.

"On the night of October 18, with Max Ricketts flying as my co-pilot, we spent two hours over the Jap positions west of Point Cruz. There was a big moon which was ideal for our purpose: harassing the Japs. The enemy, with their 'Washing Machine Charlies,' had strafed and bombed the Marines and generally made a nuisance of themselves almost every night. But nobody had heckled them.

"I asked the boss to let me try and he, reluctantly, okayed it. The Japs were so ill-prepared for a night sortie that we had a picnic strafing their watch fires. In direct contrast with our Marine positions, which were blacked out, the enemy had fires everywhere. We flew over at 2000 feet and the Japs were blazing away at us, then we dove down and strafed their fires, scattering the troops but never knowing what damage we did, if any.

"We took parachute flares, put them on maximum delay and dropped them from about 1500 feet. They lay on the ground, lighting up everything for hundreds of feet all around. In the middle of a large coconut grove, we spotted a stack of supplies which we promptly attacked and set ablaze. This was especially gratifying to the Marines as most of the pounding had been coming the other way.

"We were carrying two 500–pound bombs, one under each wing, and a dozen 100–pounders stacked on a bunk. We had a pretty sturdy ordnanceman who could stand over the tunnel hatch with one of those babies cradled in his arms and when we yelled, 'Ready? Drop!, out it would go. So, that old PBY was just huffin' and puffin' and zooming down toward them; the ordnanceman standing in the aft compartment with those 100 – pound bombs, letting go over their bivouac and supply area.

"We were flying out of Ndeni one day when I ran an overlapping patrol with a Jap Mavis. It looked like an old Skorsky four-engine, high-wing boat. They had about 15 – knots speed advantage on us and though I had everything bent forward on the firewall, he just stayed out in front of us. We tried lobbing some shots but to no avail.

"Cloudy Joe Riley, in VP12, shot down a Jap patrol plane. His crew spotted it on an overlap patrol before the Jap spotted them. The sky was about five-tenths cumulus base at 1800 feet with tops at 2500, so he went above them and continued on a converging course, making one pass, just like in aerial gunnery practice. He came down with the bow and port waist guns firing, then pulled over and the starboard waist and tunnel fired. The Jap spiralled into the water.

"Whisky Willis flew one of those overlapping patrols but wasn't so fortunate. They ended up side-by-side, shooting hell out of each other. Whisky's first Mech, Frankovich, was in the starboard position and took a freak shot that came between the armor shield around the gun, hitting him in the chest and mortally wounding him. They later named a destroyer after him.

"Whisky landed in the open sea and was picked up three or four days later. He said the Mavis was smoking severely when it broke away; he was convinced it never made it back to Truk."

Joe Hill: PBY Down At Sea — Crew Captured

Joe Hill, floral City, Florida, VP11, completed flight training at Pensacola, Florida, in July of 1940. His activities parallel those of most other pilots of VP11 during the rebuilding months following the Japanese attack on Hawaii. When the time came to move south, Joe's PBY developed engine trouble and required a change.

"Before deployment to advance bases, each pilot was alloted one gallon of spirits, in lieu of the one – quart – weekly ration. George Poulos and I duly received our allotment, told two girl friends about the engine, bought some groceries and made plans for a last farewell party.

"With a bag of groceries in one hand and a gallon of Ten High in the other, I opened the screen door to the ladies' house. Promptly, the gallon of Ten High slipped to the floor, making about a one-inch puddle of booze throughout most of the living room. I doubt if the Guiness people were keeping records then, but if this wasn't a record, it sure made a young Ensign cry. We couldn't get another ration, so George broke out his gallon and the party was on.

"On September 10, 1942, I ran a sector where four-engine Jap patrol planes had been spotted. My crew reported one at about 1000 feet when we had the sun at our backs, a good broken cloud cover, and we were flying at 3500 feet. I pressed the attack and we got in several good bursts from our 30 – caliber guns. I don't think we hurt them, and with their superior speed, they quickly outran us.

"The next day, Dopey Clark was on patrol, sighted a Jap cruiser and was shot down by Zeros. He radioed the tender, McFarland, that he was under attack by Zeros on floats and that was the last we heard from him. We learned after the war that he and his crew were taken prisoners and spent the rest of the war in various Jap prison camps. All but two of his men successfully withstood the rigors of exposure, hunger and daily beatings for three years, returning home after the war.

"On October 29, about 250 miles into our patrol, at about 0800, we were flying through broken clouds at about 1000 feet when we spotted a Japanese submarine on the surface. We flew into a light squall and when we came out he was no more than three miles away. I put the plane into a dive and made a depth charge run before he had completely submerged. Our run was good and the drop right on target. After reporting the attack, we circled the area for 15 minutes, leaving after a tremendous oil slick convinced us we had sunk an enemy submarine.

"Throughout the fall and into December, VP11 Catalina crews made night bombings and torpedo runs on Jap ships at anchor in various ports, lagoons and near enemy islands. These were all low – altitude attacks that achieved complete surprise and did considerable damage."

George Poulos: Out-Wile The Wily Enemy

George Poulos flew patrols and trained then trained some more, just as his buddies in VP11 and in their sister squadrons did, with little to create a diversion until the Battle of Midway. When VP11 was passed-over on a Midway assignment, most personnel of the squadron felt they were discriminated against. But they would soon learn that long-range planning not only included them, it required them.

Poulos picks up his story just after the Battle of Midway.

"The Japanese were in the process of building a landing strip on Guadalcanal Island, with obvious plans. In conjunction with the excellent harbor at Tulagi, some 20 miles across the channel, they would establish a major base from which to launch their attacks on New Guinea, Australia and New Zealand.

"Across the island from Suva was a natural harbor named Saweni Bay. It was near Lautoka, the second largest city in Fiji, in an area generally known as Nandi. The Seabees were assigned to build an operating base on Saweni Bay for the VP11 group. An advance contingent of officers, chiefs and enlisted men were sent to provide advice regarding our maintenance requirements, anchorage, ramps and boating facilities. The Seabees, by the way, were well-qualified for the assignment.

"In the meantime, the main section of the squadron patrolled from Suva. On August 2, 1942, the entire group moved to Saweni Bay and a daily three-plane patrol was set up. Sectors were chosen to guard for a possible 'end-around' sweep by the Japanese fleet, to cut off our fleet.

"It was during the Saweni Bay operation that once more we realized what a great machine the PBY-5 was. There were six airplanes and six crews and we were required to fly our three sectors every day for a duration of 12 to 15 hours. We could beach only one airplane at a time in our small facility. This meant that practically all maintenance had to be performed while the planes were floating at the buoys.

"On August 25, 1942, we learned that the Marines had entrenched themselves at Henderson Field on Guadalcanal and that they intended to stay. By the morning of August 26, all of our equipment had been packaged for shipment and the airplanes and crews were ready to go. Orders were to proceed to the island of Espiritu Santo to join the remainder of the squadron, which was based on the aircraft tender Curtiss.

On arrival, we found that although the Curtiss was considered home-base, the rest of the squadron was operating from smaller tenders 400 miles closer to Guadalcanal at Graciosa Bay, on the island of Ndeni, in the Santa Cruz Island chain. We immediately took off again for the new destination.

"On August 27, my crew and I had our first encounter with the Japanese since December 7, 1941. One of the early morning patrol PBYs had made contact with a Japanese battleship fleet, which was sailing without cover of aircraft carriers. Since it was at the extreme end of his 700-mile sector, he was not able to track them for longer than two hours. The importance of the course this fleet would take late in the afternoon, and during the night, was obviously very important to the Navy high command.

"I drew the assignment for the night tracking. Takeoff had to be timed just right to make contact before dark, or it would greatly reduce the possibility of making contact at all. I could not take off too early as I would run out of fuel before daybreak. There were no provisions for making a night landing at Graciosa Bay or at any other sheltered water.

"During August, at these southern latitudes, sunset occurs at six o'clock, local time, and it occurs fast, with almost no twilight time. Likewise, sunrise occurs at six o'clock in the morning with very little elapsed time between total darkness and full daylight.

"Based on my prior experience with a maximum-endurance flight on Christmas Day, 1941, and calculating the distance involved, I decided on a noon takeoff. I anticipated contact at darkness, tracking till midnight and a landing at Graciosa Bay just at daybreak.

"Plans went like clockwork. The sun had set when we first saw the line of battleships on the horizon, escorted by cruisers and destroyers on the periphery. Immediately I reduced altitude to water level, hoping that they had not yet detected us. My plan was to get within two miles, quickly increase altitude until we could see the entire fleet, take a ship-type and count, then retreat to send our messages.

"But we were not that lucky. At the time I considered we were two miles away, a destroyer appeared headed straight for us, firing his forward guns as rapidly as possible. We had been detected. Within seconds, geysers of water were spouting on all sides of the aircraft, the result of shells hitting the water and exploding. We were just high enough to skim over the waves and the water spouts towered considerably above us. In one instance, it was necessary to maneuver rapidly to avoid flying right into one that shot up directly in front of the airplane.

"The accuracy of the destroyer's fire caused me to reconsider getting an exact ship count. We sent an initial contact message. The exact battleship count had been established and we could approximate the peripheral ships.

"By the time we had safely retreated, gained altitude to let out the trailing wire antenna and sent a coded message, it was totally dark. I told the crew to have dinner. We would loiter for one hour then proceed to the point where the Japanese fleet would be if they did not alter course. Then, we would try to make contact again. This attempt failed. Obviously, the Japanese commander, knowing he had been detected and suspecting that it was our intent to track him, had changed course.

"To make a meaningful search, we had to consider what the objective of the Japanese fleet was. Were they retreating to refuel and reprovision after an encounter with our fleet units in the Solomons, or was this a new force heading into battle? Now the most important information for our fleet commanders was to determine if they were headed toward the Solomons. After two hours of searching, we still had not made contact.

"I considered the next possibility, that this fleet was waiting to rendezvous with provisioning ships and that the most likely course was on toward a major fleet base; that had to be the island of Truk, their largest base outside of Japan.

"This meant flying farther away from home base and aggravating our already tight fuel–management scheme but it had to be done. If we could make just one more contact, and find them retreating from the battle, they would not pose a threat for at least two more days. In about an hour and half we found them — headed for Truk.

"It is somewhat eerie to come upon a large enemy battle fleet in the middle of a large ocean in a very dark night with a solid overcast above you and not a star nor a flicker of light showing anywhere. At first we sighted the phosphorescence of a wake, then the full wake. Gradually, more wakes emerged on all sides and the dark silhouettes of the ships were discernible. Suddenly we were in the middle of a battle fleet which had enough fire power to destroy a city. I wondered why they hadn't put a searchlight on us and opened fire. Now, at about 30 degrees off the port bow, the big wake was visible — five battleships, still in a line. If they are going to be this docile, why not attack them? We had four 500 pound bombs under the wings. But we had a position and heading report to make and if we loitered to transmit the message to base, then attacked, our fuel reserve would be depleted. I chose to make the report.

"The night turned stormy and as we headed back to base, we could see neither sky nor water. Only dead-reckoning navigation was possible, and in our slow maximum-range flight regime, the high winds could drift us off course if they came from either side or could reduce our ground speed significantly. Either way, fuel management was our biggest concern. Again the engines performed magnificently with severe fuel thinning.

"About an hour before daylight, I smelled the navigational aid we were waiting for. Some 80 miles north of Graciosa Bay was an active volcano jutting out from the ocean to about 3000 feet. Fumes from the eruption contained a very severe hydrogen sulphide smell that permeated the air for several miles in all directions. Notwithstanding our inability for precise navigation, if we could smell the volcano, we were close enough to find our way to Graciosa Bay at daylight, providing we took every precaution not to fly into the volcano. Fortunately, our crude radar could detect an island within five miles.

"We landed just as the daylight patrol PBYs were taking off. The duration of the flight was 18.4 hours. Fuel remaining from a full load of 1430 gallons at takeoff was 30 gallons. Only a PBY could have fulfilled such an exacting mission. A great, great airplane. At the same time, only a great crew could plan and execute a precise mission like this. I was proud of each and every one of my crew members."

Vernon Koenig: Face-To-Face With Pygmy Cannibals

Vernon P. Koenig, now of Deakin, Canberra. Australia, began his Naval aviation career as an aviation radioman with Patrol Wing One. He was assigned to North Island Naval Air Station at San Diego. Later, on duty in PatWing One Communications at Kaneohe on December 7, 1941, he remembers it "as the longest day of my life." He felt extremely helpless until they handed out Springfield rifles with bandoleers of ammunition.

"In April of 1942, we began installing ASE Radar in the PBYs and I had a chance to enter an Aviation Radar School set up by the Wing. Six weeks later, I graduated and was immediately assigned to VP11.

"One day in September, we sighted an enemy seaplane tender and came under attack by two Japanese single-engine seaplanes. I was in the starboard blister and got a number of hits on one of them. He disappeared into the clouds and never came back. His tracers had gone above us, but the plane on our port side made several hits on our tail section. The following morning when they hoisted our Cat onboard the Curtiss for repairs, we found the lower bearing plate of the vertical stabilizer had only one bolt holding; still the plane had brought us back.

"There was always plenty of excitement, even in the safety of Espiritu Santo. A picket boat pulled up the gangway one day to drop off some visitors from another ship and as it pulled away, one of its depth charges fell into the water. The Officer-of-the-Deck announced over the public address system that a depth charge had fallen off the port gangway. Aircrew quarters were in that part of the ship and I have never seen a place evacuate in such a short time. The ship's diver retrieved the depth charge where it rested on the bottom, its safety pin still in place and quite harmless.

"Enemy submarine activity increased in the month of November. On the 5th, in a Catalina borrowed from VP23, we sighted an enemy submarine and bombed it with 'probable' results. On the 21st, 25th and 29th, we sighted more enemy submarines but, for some reason not explained by our high command, we didn't have torpedoes or bombs to drop. We had to be content to strafe with our machine guns when we were fortunate to get within range before they submerged.

"The greatest fright I experienced in the New Hebrides wasn't caused by the Japanese, it was coming face to face with a group of cannibal pygmies. We had a Catalina, with beaching gear attached, up on the beach for a major engine overhaul. The work had been completed and I was inside the hull carrying out a final check of the radio and radar equipment, when I heard a strange chattering outside the plane. Sticking my head out of the navigator's hatch, I came face-to-face with about 16 pygmies with long spears, bones through their noses and feathers in their hair. Now, it's one thing to be shot at by the enemy, but to face consumption by a band of cannibals is something else. It turned out that they were only curious and wanted a closer look at one of the large birds that had taken up residence on their island."

16

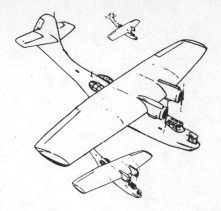

Patrol Squadron VP11: Part Two

After returning to the United States for new aircraft, and training on new equipment, Patrol Squadron 11 reformed on March 16, 1943. The squadron had served well during the Guadalcanal campaign and would soon return to the South Pacific to begin again its destruction of enemy shipping and shore installations. On their second tour, they would sink over 75,000 tons of Japanese shipping. This time, too, they would perform near miracles in rescue and evacuation.

From April until October, VP11 trained and moved on, trained and moved on, until they had moved from Hawaii and the Midway–Johnston Island group through Perth, Australia. During their stay at Perth, they patrolled the western and northern coasts of Australia.

In October they transferred to the USS Half Moon and USS San Pablo aircraft tenders anchored in Jenkins Bay, Samarai, New Guinea. Assigned to ComTask Group 73.1 and the Army Fifth Air Force, VP11 worked under ComAir Seventh Fleet, FAW17. The squadron moved frequently during the balance of 1943. Their patrols reached all active shipping zones of the Japanese fleet around New Guinea and the Bismarck Sea. Night after night VP11's Black Cats searched for enemy shipping, but as the year ended and a new one began, fewer and fewer targets could be found. Finally, after following the Allied advance back to the Philippines, and after compiling a service record second to none, Black Cat Squadron VP11 was relieved in December, 1944 by a squadron of PBM Mariners.

Papuan Peninsula, New Guinea.

Bill Barker: A Hair-Raising Short Flight

Bill Barker tells of a hair-raising short "flight" by a Catalina with two of its crewmen clinging to the outside of the aircraft.

"The story of 'Whisky' Willis taking off with part of his crew outside the plane has been told many times over the years. As with all stories, the facts have been changed by the age-old act of retelling in one's own words. I was there and here's how I saw it.

"Whisky was allowing a new pilot to make a pre-dawn takeoff out of the channel at Espiritu Santo. The Cat was heavily loaded with bombs and fuel for a long patrol. As the plane got close to lift off, it started to porpoise and just at lift off, one of the floats dug into the water and was ripped off the end of the wing. Whisky took over the controls and completed the lift off successfully. After observing the damage to the wing, Whisky flew out to sea to jettison his bombs, burn off some fuel, and wait for full daylight before attempting a landing.

"Whisky instructed his plane captain, Bill Sinclair, AMM2c, to get some men up on the good wing as soon as he landed so as to hold that wing float down and prevent the damaged wing from dragging in the water.

"As soon as it was light enough, Whisky made the landing and three men, Charley Knauff, AMM2c, Bill Sinclair and Denny Garchow, AMM3c, started out of the blisters and up on the wing. In the meantime, Jim Steadman, CAP, saw that the plane was taking on a lot of water through holes left by rivets popped out during the takeoff or landing. He reported this to Whisky, who immediately applied power and made another takeoff. By this time, Charley was midway up on the wing, between the engines. Bill Sinclair was just starting up on the trailing edge of the wing between the blisters and Denny Garchow was on the turtle-back between the blisters waiting to follow Bill up on the wing.

"When Whisky started the second takeoff, Charley dropped down and grabbed a hold on the hoisting eye protruding from the center of the wing between the engines. Bill was blown off the plane into the water and Denny grabbed the handles between the blisters. The takeoff was completed with both Charley and Denny hanging on for dear life.

"When Whisky realized he had two men riding on the outside of the Cat, he immediately circled the channel and started an approach to land. He made the landing successfully with both men still hanging on.

"While the plane was in the air after the second takeoff and before the landing, the radiomen, Walt Banisky and Joe Damato, plugged the rivet holes with sharpened pencils to keep the plane from taking on any more water.

"While Whisky was circling to make his second landing, the Officer-of-the-Day of our support tender, USS Curtiss, sent a rescue boat out. The boat crew found the float that had been ripped off, picked it up and returned it to the ship without ever seeing Bill thrashing about in the water. However, some Marines on the beach saw Bill waving his arms, took out a landing boat, and brought him back to the Curtiss. Bill was so mad; he was livid when he came up the gangway. He stopped and 'told-off' the young O.D. in no uncertain words, then went below to put on dry clothing. The O.D. had nothing to say.

"During the second landing, Charley and Denny continued on up the wing and successfully held the good float down in the water.

"The standby crew, waiting for all scheduled planes to take off before securing, saw the whole show from the decks of the Curtiss. On their way out to another PBY to take Whisky's patrol, they went by the beached plane. Charley Knauff was sitting on the end of the good wing smoking his perpetual cigar. He held the cigar up and yelled that it had not even gone out. Denny was 'chipping-his-teeth' about losing his wallet and a shoe. There were no injuries to any of the crew and only Bill and Denny were the least bit upset.

"This is probably the only case of men flying on the wing and turtle-back of a PBY, even for the few minutes they were in the air."

George Poulos And Jack Coley: Longest Torpedo Run In History

Of the many missions flown by PBY Catalinas during World War II, none topped in sheer audacity, contempt for the enemy and nerves of steel, the moonlit, early morning raid by three PBYs of VP11 on a major Japanese fleet formation which had rendezvoused at Tonolei Harbor, Bougainville.

For audacity, the three PBY crews flew 900 miles, heavily loaded with fuel, bombs and torpedoes; attacked their targets, then flew back to base. For contempt of their enemy, they took on a major portion of the Japanese fleet with the slowest, lightest armed bombers in the U.S. Navy. And for nerves of steel, they volunteered, pilots and crewmen, to fly for some eight hours with the almost certain knowledge they would be blown out of the sky.

Two of the three Patrol Plane Commanders offer their memories of that attack:

George Poulos, Fallbrook, California, picks up his story in the Solomons during September and October of 1942.

"When a night battle was anticipated in the 'Slot,' PBYs performed all-night patrols along the northeastern gaps between islands to detect or otherwise prevent Japanese submarines from making 'end around' sneak attacks on our ships. If nothing else, the presence of the PBY caused the Japanese subs to submerge and upset their time-table for meaningful attacks.

Witnessing a night fleet battle in the slot was an awesome experience. A typical event would be a calm, quiet night, then a searchlight would flash for a brief second and all hell would break loose. The intensity of the fire from both sides was unbelievable. Giant explosions could be seen aboard

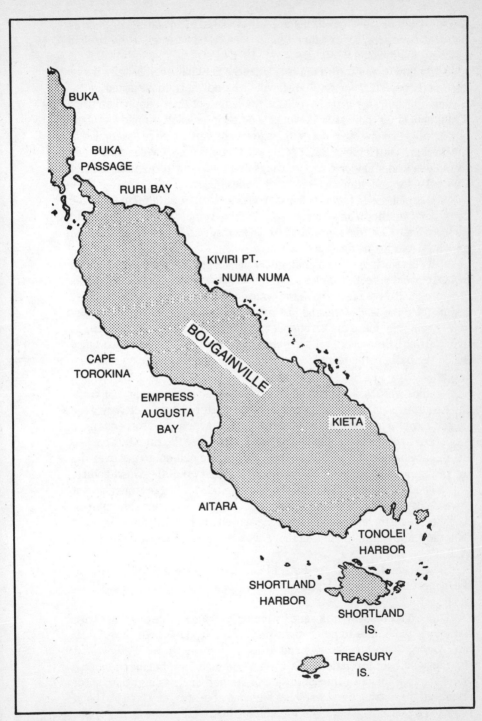

BUKA

BUKA
PASSAGE

RURI BAY

KIVIRI PT.
NUMA NUMA

BOUGAINVILLE

CAPE
TOROKINA

EMPRESS
AUGUSTA
BAY

KIETA

AITARA

TONOLEI
HARBOR

SHORTLAND
HARBOR

SHORTLAND
IS.

TREASURY
IS.

Bougainville.

the ships of both sides. In one instance, I witnessed a ship, later identified as one of our cruisers, suffer a direct magazine hit and blow up, with a fireball climbing to at least 10,000 feet.

"By now it was known that the Japanese fleet had established a major base at Tonolei Harbor on Bougainville, the northern-most island in the Solomon chain. This greatly reduced the length of their supply line from Truk, indicating their attacks would soon be intensified. In mid-October, our intelligence discovered a very large enemy carrier force assembled in the harbor. On October 22, 1942 Jack Coley, Whisky Willis and I had torpedoes loaded under our port wings and made our plans to fly almost 900 miles for a night attack on that Japanese fleet.

"Our plan called for takeoff just at dusk and attack at 0200 to 0300 the next morning; then a dawn landing at Tulagi to refuel for the flight back to Espiritu Santo. En route, a landfall would be made on Rennell Island and an unnamed reef for navigational purposes.

"It was a bright, moonlight night with exceptionally good visibility. In order to avoid detection under such conditions, we flew the last 150 miles at approximately 20 feet above the water in a tight formation. Jack Coley commanded the lead plane and his navigation was perfect. We found ourselves going right into the harbor inlet undetected until we had to pull up to avoid hitting a destroyer that was doing sentinel duty at the entrance. Once inside the harbor, the formation split up, with each of us seeking his own target.

"Ships were visible everywhere: mostly destroyers and harbor craft, then a larger ship, a heavy cruiser in an uncluttered area — a very good target. I swung to the right to allow enough room for a good torpedo run, a quick turn to the left with just enough time to stabilize the run, then I pulled the release handle at about 300 yards. During the pull-up, to get over the top of the cruiser, I pulled the handle to release two 500 – pound bombs.

"The PBY shuddered as the weapons exploded. The crew members at the waist hatches reported direct hits but could not determine the extent of damage. Nevertheless, we knew we had scored, that we had hurt them and that they now knew their sanctuary was not safe from the workhorse PBYs."

The second of the three Patrol Plane Commanders to participate in the longest torpedo run in history was a pilot who reported previously, Jack Coley:

"George Poulos, Whisky and I went up to Bougainville one night with torpedoes and bombs to pull a night raid on the Jap fleet at anchor. I flew lead, George was number two and Whisky, number three. We flew in a tight, blacked-out formation with a full moon night — a bomber's moon.

"We flew up along the south side of the harbor, passing a number of islands off the entrance and watching for a picket destroyer which had been reported by coastwatchers. We found it at the mouth of the channel. But our prime target was a carrier which had also been reported in the harbor that night.

"Either George or Whisky attacked the destroyer, sinking it right there, while I went charging on in, looking for the carrier. I must have flown around that harbor for five or 10 minutes searching for that flat-top, with searchlights lighting up the sky and the Japs starting to shoot. Finally, I lined up on a big battleship that we spotted and lobbed a torpedo into it, made a turn-off to the left and dropped two 500–pound bombs into, or alongside, a transport. Then I spent 15 minutes dodging searchlights. I turned that airplane everyway but inside-out. There must have been 60 to 80 ships, a major anchorage, and they were all firing at us. It looked like the Fourth of July, with us the center of attraction.

"We could see tracers coming up at us and we would say, 'Oh! That guy's got the right lead this time.' But they would curve around us. All the while, we were gradually working our way out, ducking down several times behind an island to get out of the searchlights, only to find another ship anchored there. Of course it began shooting at us and we were off and away again. At last, we got far enough out to where there were no more ships hiding behind the small islands. We timed the searchlights, slipping by them until we broke into the clear, open sea.

"There was a big hole in the starboard wing and a number of others throughout the airplane; some went through the tanks and I lost some fuel. But we landed safely at Tulagi and gassed up for the final hop to base."

George Poulos picks up his story following the torpedo attack.

"A massive Japanese carrier fleet took to sea from Tonolei sometime within the next two days. It was the job of the PBYs to find them and enable our carrier force to attack. This was the prelude to what became known as the Battle of Santa Cruz, where we lost our carrier, Hornet. Losses to the enemy were also severe and history records the battle as a toss up. But it blunted their sword, crippling their effort to retake Guadalcanal and Tulagi.

"In the early morning darkness of October 26, 1942, the PBY patrols were launched two hours ahead of schedule. We were aware that a major battle was brewing but our pre-flight briefing left the question of the location of the Japanese fleet unanswered.

"At dawn, my alert crew saw a submerging submarine's swirl about five miles ahead and a bi-wing seaplane taking off in a swirl. This was a feature the Japanese had that we lacked. They would make a wake to smooth out the water for the plane's takeoff, submerge while it patrolled a limited distance, then surface to let it land in the wake and retrieve it.

"We were too far away to make a meaningful attack on the submarine and, although the crew was disappointed that we did not chase and kill the biplane, the seriousness of a pending carrier battle without knowing the exact location of the enemy fleet dictated that we proceed with our primary mission. In retrospect, the fact that the submarine was in this sector on this day may have been a diversion; he had no other reason to be there.

"At about 0700 hours we found them, a large force, with four carriers and their escorts. It was apparent that the carriers had already launched their planes because the flight decks were clear. The only airplanes in sight were several Zeros flying overhead coverage. They apparently knew where our carriers were and we had to send their position to enable our carrier planes to attack them.

"I climbed a few hundred feet to see the entire fleet and ordered a quick count, then a retreat to extend the trailing wire antenna to send the position report. Because of harassment by ship fire, there was an honest difference in the ship count among the crew. All agreed concerning the number of carriers and that was most important.

"We were later to learn that our carriers, Hornet and Enterprise, had launched blind to clear their decks in anticipation of an attack and did not know the position of the enemy until they received our message. By then our carrier planes had burned some of their fuel and were not as effective as they might have been. But, if we had not found the Japanese fleet, the whole day would have been a complete disaster.

"Having sent our message, we returned for an exact ship count and had agreement before we left this time, but too late. Four Zeros left their umbrella cover and took after us. I did not anticipate this since I considered the Japanese umbrella cover planes only concerned themselves with attacking carrier planes. But, here we were.

"We had knowledge of nine previous PBY crews having made contact with Japanese carrier fleets and all had been shot down. Would we be the 10th? I was determined that we would not. There was very little wind at sea, with no discernible white caps. Instead, there were huge swells in the water that rose 15 to 20 feet and by the time the first Zero was making his firing run on us, I was at the bottom of a trough, looking up at water on both sides. One of the crew members remarked, 'Hey! We're making like a submarine!'

"As a swell terminated, I picked up either the port or starboard wing and slid into the next trough. As a Zero came in on a firing run, I turned quickly into his line of flight to shorten his run. He tightened his turn as much as he dared, flying ever so close to the water. The zero attack was totally ineffective. The closest they came was a splatter of bullets 20 to 30 yards behind us. Apparently sensing their ineffectiveness, and having no desire to be drawn miles away from their fleet, they broke off and left us. We had broken the string and were not the 10th victim."

Bill Barker: Champagne Ride In A Wheelbarrow

The long, boring patrols, some lasting 14 to 16 hours, coupled with relatively few sightings or action, had the effect of winding up the nerves of

PBY pilots and crewmen. The tension of remaining on the alert at all times demanded release. There was a definite need for rest and relaxation away from the endless sea, the jungle atolls and native islanders, regardless of their friendliness.

Well – trained squadron flight surgeons kept a wary eye on the crews and followed the mission reports of each debriefing. When the time was right, the crew was "excused" for a week or so and sent to Aukland, New Zealand, or Sidney, Australia.

Stories emanating from these R&Rs, as they were known, reflect the degree of release these men found, and are classic examples of the deep humor every present in the American youth of that war.

There is a story of a group of VP11 pilots spending an R&R in a downtown hotel in Aukland, New Zealand. After trying to consume all the alcohol in the city, they discovered that many of the young ladies entering and leaving the hotel were wearing girdles. Feigning utter dismay, they held a strategic briefing session and resolved that the girdles had to go. A short search produced a number of 50 – gallon barrels which our heroes placed at plotted locations near elevators and stairways of the hotel. Then, as the unsuspecting young ladies approached, the "inspectors" asked if they were wearing girdles. If the reply was "Yes!," they were advised, by decree, that they were out of uniform and asked to remove their girdles and place them in one of the barrels. As the story goes, most of the girls went along with the edict, much to the delight of the pilots.

Bill Barker adds an Aukland chapter to the story of R&Rs, this from the enlisted men's viewpoint.

"VP11 and our sister squadrons were catching hell in the fall of 1942 but it wasn't all fighting and killing and rescue. In November, we started sending crews down to Aukland, New Zealand, for five days of rest and relaxation. Several crews had gone down before my crew went and our buddies brought back the names and addresses of the best dates. Before I left, one of my buddies gave me the name of a girl. He said, 'She's all right! Pick her up.'

"On arrival in Aukland, some of us rented rooms in a boarding house. I called the girl and right away a big party was planned. Good whiskey was hard to come by in Aukland; their New Zealand brand tasted awful but you could get pretty good champagne. So I decided I was going to have champagne. I bought seven magnums of the stuff, stashing it away in the closet of my room. We bought beer and port wine and fish and chips, preparing for a grand party.

"We were dancing to the radio and playing around when, about 10 o'clock, my girl disappeared. I decided, 'Well, she got tired of the party and left,' and I didn't think much more about it. At the time, I had opened one bottle of champagne.

"Around midnight, we ran out of whiskey and beer, so I said, 'it's time to break out the champagne!' I went to the closet and opened the door.

There, passed out on the floor, with two empty bottles of champagne beside her, was my missing girl friend.

"It was pouring down rain outside, and at the moment she didn't look too uncomfortable, so we went on with the party. But about two o'clock in the morning the champagne was gone and I realized it was time to get that young lady home.

"I went outside and tried to get a taxi but they weren't running much at that hour and the phones were disconnected. However, I noticed a wheelbarrow parked alongside the building next door. Since the girl lived about five or six blocks down the hill, I decided to put her into the wheelbarrow and wheel her home.

"I 'borrowed' the wheelbarrow, carried the girl down, emptied the rainwater out, then put her inside as gently as I could. At that point, she was sleeping quite peacefully. The sidewalks were bumpy and rocky going down the hill. But, since there were no cars, I pushed her out into the street.

"We started to move and I felt the wheelbarrow moving faster and faster. The wheel was made of iron and had no rubber tire on it; somehow it slipped into the tram-track. Now it was impossible to keep up with. I was just hanging on.

"As we passed one corner, out came a Bobbie — running behind us and hollering, 'Hi there, Yank! Where ya' going? Whatcha' got in the wheelbarrow?'

"I couldn't stop and I couldn't talk. I was winded. Anyway, we got to the bottom of the hill, the tram turned, the wheelbarrow turned, the girl went one way and I went the other. I just kept on going around the corner.

"I never found out what happened to that girl. I sure didn't look her up again.

"Not enough can be said about the Royal New Zealand Air Force. They were an outstanding group of men. Anyone who flew those old planes had to have a lot of guts. And they had a sense of humor that wouldn't wait. We had a lot of fun with them, enjoyed operating alongside them.

"Australian and New Zealand men of 16 to 50 were spread from the islands of the South Pacific to North Africa and into Europe. These were countries totally involved in a World War. They committed their troops to the Allied needs, whether that need was at home or a continent away.

"At Perth, Australia, we met the home guard, a group of men 50 or over, called Diggers. These men were Australian soldiers but were restricted to guard duty at military establishments of the area.

"One night a drinking buddy of mine, who had met some of the Diggers, talked me into joining him at one of their bars. I had heard about their hob-nailed boots that could stomp you to death if you got into a fight with them. So I stayed clear of the activities, choosing to sit at the bar.

"After I had finished one glass of beer, my buddy said, 'Turn your glass upside-down on the bar.'

"I said, 'What for'?

'Well, that tells these guys you want to be friends.'

"I didn't give it any thought and turned my glass upside down. I didn't know what hit me. It seemed they all hit me at once. The tradition with the Diggers, I soon learned, was that if after you drank your beer you turned your glass upside down on the bar, you were challenging anybody in the bar to a fight.

"My buddy stood there laughing at the mess they were making of me. Finally, he told them what he had done and that I didn't know the meaning of my move. They picked me up off the floor, dusted me off and we got drunk together. Of course, I was pretty sore and miserable for the rest of the time I was in Geraldton."

Cash Barber: The Cat—A Mechanical Hero Of The War

Cash Barber, Olympia, Washington, began his PBY career with VP11 in December of 1941 as a seaman second class. He advanced through the ranks to become Aviation Machinist's Mate First Class by the time he left the squadron in December of 1944. But Barber wasn't finished with the Navy. He continued in various duties until retiring after 30 years of active duty as a Lieutenant Commander.

His lasting fondness for the PBY is reflected in the following entries.

"The 'Cat' was one of the greater mechanical heroes of the war. I can remember many 15–hour patrols, takeoff at sunset and return after sunrise, while operating from an aircraft tender parked in some small bay.

"We made radar contact one night about midnight. After closing in, we dropped a parachute flare and brightly illuminated a Jap light cruiser. But they lucked out and doused the flare. Lieutenant Williams, our plane commander, decided to climb up and make a dive–bombing run. We could see the cruiser's wake and made our run from the stern. The Japs were still lucky, as we dropped our bombs too short of the target and had to abort the attack.

"On another night flight, we stripped our PBY of guns, bombs and loose equipment to load 'Christmas Packages.' These were supplies to be dropped by parachute to some Aussie Commandos near Rabual. We spotted our drop area by small flares marking the perimeter. As we made our run to drop, we noticed a single–engine aircraft flying above us, taking in everything, but making no effort to attack. We learned later that the Commandos had considerable company from the Japs the next day.

"There was the time we landed at sea with 200 cases of beer loaded in every spot of the aircraft. A small, five-man crew had been chosen to fly to Manus Island to pick up a replacement PBY for one the squadron had lost.

"At this point in our tour of duty, liquid refreshments of any sort were hard to come by. But it should be pointed out to never underestimate the ingenuity of the Navy. We rounded up enough money to buy 200 cases of canned beer; its solid boxing made it easy to load the bilges from the nose to blisters.

"Takeoff was slow and laboring but we made it and seemed headed for a safe trip back to base. Then things began to fall apart. About two hours out of Manus, I noticed we had lost oil pressure in the starboard engine. In reporting the problem to Lieutenant Nelsen, I noted that there had been no increase in oil temperature and thought it was nothing more than instrument failure. However, a few minutes later, the engine became rough and unstable. Lieutenant Nelsen feathered it and we began a fruitless attempt to keep the PBY and beer in the air.

"The Lieutenant made a beautiful landing and we broke out a life raft, tying it securely to the port blister, in case we had to leave in a hurry. With nothing else to do, and since the plane was intact and going great in the not too rough water, we naturally broke open a case of beer.

"About the time we really didn't care — sitting on the wing drinking our beer — a ship was spotted on the horizon. We knew that we were nothing more than sitting ducks if it turned out to be Japanese. But our confidence was strong and the ship was the USS Taylor, a destroyer sent to find us. They spotted us and when they came alongside they sent over coffee and sandwiches. They took us in tow, making an all-night affair of it.

"It was about 0900 when they began attaching the beaching gear and pulling us up on the ramp. But word had traveled fast and the Captain of the island was there to greet me as I came out of the port blister.

'How much beer do you have aboard, sailor'? he asked.

'I'm not sure, Sir,' I replied. 'Ask Lieutenant Nelsen'.

"Well, the Lieutenant shared some of the beer with the Captain and everyone was happy for a short while.

"The old reliable PBY saved my crew's hide another time when we were patrolling the Indian Ocean off the west coast of Australia. At the end of our anti-sub track we blew number one cylinder in the starboard engine, with oil coming out all over everything. We were able to feather the engine and began throwing out equipment that wasn't required to keep the aircraft in flight. Off went the bombs, the guns and ammunition. We even dumped some gasoline to bring the weight down.

"Eight hours later, we landed at our advance base in Geraldton, Australia. My second Mech and I were able to salvage a cylinder from another failed engine and we had our Catalina ready to fly again in less than 24 hours."

George Poulos: "Men Belonga' You, Men Belonga' Me?"

Another experience involving the natives of Rennell Island was related in his last contribution to the PBY story by George Poulos.

"Although the U.S. Navy could not claim a victory at the Battle of Santa Cruz, we did blunt the Japanese sword in their attempt to retake

Guadalcanal and Tulagi. From that day forward, we were on the offensive.

"More and more PBY crews went on night bombing or other enemy harassment missions. We tried new innovations to lengthen our patrols by taking off from Espiritu Santo, flying 850-mile sectors instead of 700 miles, then landing at Vanikoro at dusk. The next day, we took off from Vanikoro, flew an 850-mile sector and returned to Espiritu Santo. We also made more flights with the express purpose of finding survivors of the battles and made open-sea landings to rescue them.

"Another method we employed, to extend the length of our patrols, was working with the submarine Argonaut. The Argonaut had made a reconnaissance of Sandwich Lagoon, but could not say, definitely, that PBYs could land and take off again. Our assignment was to determine whether the mission was feasible. To prove it we made two landings and takeoffs.

"The next day, my crew and I got the assignment for the first extended patrol from the Argonaut. We left Espiritu Santo at about 1600 hours and arrived at Sandwich Lagoon a bit early. We stayed away from the reef just in case there were Japanese submarines in the area that would jeopardize the mission.

"As the sun was setting, we made our approach to the lagoon; at the same time the Argonaut was surfacing at the entrance. We made our landing and dropped anchor, waited for him to locate himself and anchor, then we approached the stern to take on fuel. The Argonaut's crew had quite limited knowledge in fueling an airplane, so we instructed them what they should do henceforth to improve their technique. Having fueled the PBY, we taxied out again, dropped anchor and boarded the Argonaut for dinner and a night's sleep.

"The next day we made our takeoff before sunrise to enable the Argonaut to get out of the bay and submerge before daylight. Upon our return, as the sun was setting, the timing was perfect. The Argonaut was surfacing at the entrance and the PBY from Espiritu Santo, which would fly the next day's patrol, was just arriving. The trial run had been a huge success and the patrol range had been extended to 950 miles from Espiritu Santo.

"Unfortunately, the Argonaut did not survive to sustain this teamwork with the PBYs. The expanded activity by Japanese on Bougainville Island was jeopardizing some missionary camps and the Argonaut was ordered to rescue them. We received word that Japanese spotters had detected the operation and Jap dive bombers caught the Argonaut on the surface. The entire crew and its missionary passengers were killed.

"One special mission I undertook with two other PBY crews—one which I have fond memories of—was the ferrying of a group of eight Marines and an Australian coastwatcher, Andy Andresen, to Rennell Island to establish an observation and weather post.

"Rennell Island is situated about 140 miles south of Guadalcanal and has a fresh water lake in its center. In addition to providing a ferry service, we would be able to see how the PBY handled on fresh water for the first time.

"Within minutes after we landed on Lake Tungano and dropped anchor, native youngsters had rowed out in their outriggers and were climbing all over the airplane. Happy boys and girls in their loin cloths climbed in and out of the hatches, on the wing, dived into the water from everywhere, and climbed back on again. We had inflated life rafts to take our passengers and their gear ashore and the boys and girls were obstructing this effort.

"Adult natives arrived a little later but they were just as jubilant and playful as the children. Then, one of the natives pointed to an approaching outrigger and said, 'Chief!' I flagged his boat to the waist hatch and helped him aboard.

"He spoke first, in Pidgen English: 'Me Chief, you chief, we talk.'

"Not knowing what else to say, I repeated what he said.

'Men come!' (He could see the provisions being unloaded and knew he was being invaded.)

'Men come', I repeated.

'Men stay longa, men go day by day?' (How long is this invasion going to last?)

'Men stay longa,' I replied.

'Men belonga you, men belonga me?' (Who the hell is going to be boss around here?)

'Men no belonga me, men no belonga you. Belonga big chief far away.'

"At this time, Andy Andresen, who had flown in one of the other planes, was approaching us in a rubber dingy. 'You talka man belonga big hat,' I said, pointing toward the Australian.

"Immediately, the chief recognized the Australian by his dress and his Aussie hat and knew he was among friends. He offered his hand for a handshake, climbed into his outrigger, was assisted into Andy's boat, and the Pidgen English talk continued in earnest.

"After transporting the provisions to shore, we deflated the life rafts and undertook the almost impossible chore of getting the playful natives off the airplane. Even after we got them into their boats, or in the water, we did not dare start the engines for fear we would run over them. Suddenly, for reasons unclear, they all headed toward shore. We started our engines, made our freshwater takeoff, with no detectable difference from a salt water takeoff, and headed for home.

"My wartime experiences with the PBY ended where it began at Kaneohe Bay during a ferry of a crippled airplane.

"On January 14, 1943, we approached Kaneohe under stormy conditions with variable winds that looked like a small cyclone. I started my landing into the wind, but by the time the PBY made contact with the water, we were in a severe cross-wind which nearly flipped us over. It was my last water landing in a PBY and my worst ever.

"That night, as I closed out my log book and the PBY chapter of my career, I made an assessment of the 28 months I spent with that loveable machine. Since my first flight in a PBY on September 30, 1940, I had accumulated 2318 flight hours in PBYs. 1700 were during the 13 months we were at war and 617 during 15 prewar months.

"I had come to know the PBY and to admire it as a machine which completely served the purpose it was intended to fill. However, at times it appeared difficult to separate the man from the machine and the machine from the mission. This man-machine-mission combination produced the successful conclusion of our task. Perhaps it was because the machine was so well – suited to the mission that the man merged into the combination. On the other hand, man's proper use of the machine was necessary to successfully conclude the mission.

"Whatever the element, the combinations and the applications, I knew that my PBY service was, without a doubt, one of the highlights of my aviation career and one I would always remember fondly. A great experience with a great airplane."

17

Black Cats

Perhaps the most notable time slot of the Catalina's decade-plus naval service was that period between September of 1942 and the spring of 1945. While participating in all other war zones and contributing to each, the PBY, with its deadly accurate night bombing and elusive tracking of the Japanese fleet, was forcing the Pacific enemy out into the open — into daylight — a situation which eventually weakened his ability to stem the allied advance.

With their fighting confidence restored by the success at the Battle of Midway and the slowing of General Tojo's advance into New Guinea, Allied Forces began the long drive back to Japan and victory. But, in spite of a growing American military might, the Japanese whittled away at the Allied forces protecting our foothold on Guadalcanal. Historically, one well-executed attack, coupled with their strategic timing, could have slowed or eliminated American resistance.

However, the Catalina squadrons, compiling accomplishments far beyond their design expectations in other war zones, were beginning to show their worth in the Solomons. Their slow speed and light armament had presented small cause for concern on the part of the enemy and warranted little confidence from most Allied military leaders.

Relegated to the role of convoy duty, search and rescue, air ambulance and freight hauling, the PBYs had few opportunities to prove their aggressive ability. But by October the simple arithmetic of attrition in Allied aircraft presented them with the opportunity to play a major role.

PBY squadrons of the Solomons area were some of the first to receive the new airborne radar. The system lacked sharp, specific details but was capable of spotting ships and submarines within a 10 to-20-mile range.

The Japanese were using the cover of darkness to supply their Solomon Island garrisons and to move troops into forward staging areas of Guadalcanal. Since the PBY's 100-plus-per-hour speed handicapped its daylight actions, that same slow speed proved excellent when coasting in at masthead altitude in the dark of night. The Cats dropped their bombs on unsuspecting enemy vessels then slipped away, most often unscathed.

The "Black Cats," PBY-5 seaplanes and PBY-5A amphibious Catalina patrol bombers, were officially named on December 14, 1942 by Commander C.E. Coe. The honor of the first squadron so named went to VP12 who, along with VP11, VP91 and a detachment of VP51 Catalinas, began harassment raids on enemy held islands, supply barges and troop concentrations in the Solomons as early as September of 1942. Several of VP11 planes were painted black under the wings and hulls while beached at Espiritu Santo and flew "targets of opportunity" raids, beginning in early October.

Commander Clarence Taff, Commanding Officer of VP12, landed on Henderson Field, Guadalcanal on the 15th of December, 1942, piloting the first official Black Cat PBY. On December 21, four more of the dull-black

Patrol Squadron 12, second formation. Guadalcanal. (author's file.)

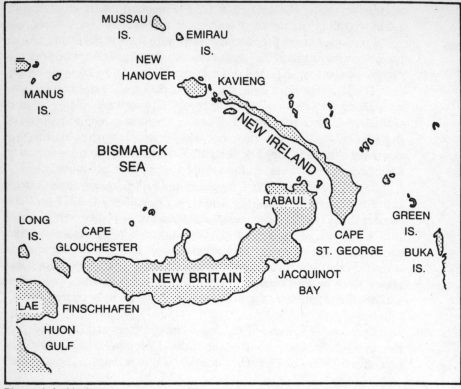

Bismarck Archipelago.

Catalinas joined him. It would be March before the sixth plane arrived but in that brief period of time the squadron flew 236 missions, logging 1660 hours. The greatest percentage of these flights were night raids and reconnaissance.

Normally, the Cats carried four 500–pound bombs, or one torpedo and two 500–pound bombs under the wing, plus highpowered illuminating flares and dozens of fragmentation bombs. In addition, the Catalinas that prowled the night used another weapon that must have struck fear into the hearts of enemy troops as they crouched in and out of shelters during air raids. This secret weapon was a couple hundred empty beer and coke bottles. Tossed from the blisters and tunnel hatch — hurtling toward the ground — they whistled an eerie, blood-chilling screech, a suitable cats-in-the-night serenade to give the Nips insomnia.

The Black Cat's worst enemy wasn't the Japanese, it was weather. The Solomon Island area presented the PBYs with some of the most violent weather fronts, with turbulence an almost standard condition. Thunderstorms bounced the aircraft around so severely that only the durability of the machine and its pilots brought it through. It was not uncommon to find a returning Black Cat with major sections of the wing and fuselage stripped of black paint from the effects of storms it had encountered.

In March of 1943, Patrol Squadron 54 relieved VP12 on Guadalcanal. Carrying on the Black Cat tradition, VP54 whetted and added to it as the Cats bombed the Japanese airstrips at Munda and Vila on frequent night raids. Among VP54's exploits, while serving the Black Cat cause, was the rescue of 52 pilots, crewmen and fleet sailors. Their commanding officer, Commander Carl Schoenweiss, and his co-pilot, Lieutenant Erhard, picked up a fighter pilot and eight dive–bomber pilots during one night of rescue operations off Rennell Island.

The art of night-bombing merchant vessels, tankers, barges and, on many occasions, vessels of war, was developed by combining the incredible capabilities of the PBY with the skills of young American pilots. The average age of PBY pilots during this period was 24. Their confidence and dedication to the job was buoyed by the all-forgiving aircraft they flew. The more they flew it, the more they trusted it.

With the successes of late 1942 to encourage them, the Black Cat squadrons of the South Pacific spread their operations to the Bismarck Archipelago, to the Marshalls and Gilberts, to the Marianas and Carolines. And, as the Allies captured key islands, while bypassing others on the way back to the Philippines, the PBYs, with their tenders and advance island airstrips, kept pace. Wherever enemy shipping of troops and supplies presented a danger to the Allied advance, the Black Cats set up operations.

Black Cats: Up-Moon, Stalking Their Prey

Swooping in up-moon, at masthead height, with the stealth and quiet of a cat stalking its prey, the Catalinas generally were over their target before the enemy detected them. With 500– and 1000–pound general-purpose bombs set to blow with a four- to five–second delay and with a Mark 103 nose fuse delayed by one-tenth of a second, the extremely low altitude rarely presented danger of concussion damage to the aircraft. To confuse and delay the enemy's response, a crewman dumped four or five high-candle-power illuminating flares out of the tunnel hatch just after passing over the target. The Cat's chances of escape were enhanced as the bright light shielded the plane from the ship's gunners.

In September of 1943, Fleet Air Wing 17 was formed to patrol the waters around New Guinea. Three Black Cat squadrons initially drew this assignment: VP11, VP52 and VP101. Their development of night operations against the enemy set the pattern for follow-on Catalina squadrons throughout the Pacific.

Japanese vessels of war were not exempt from Black Cat attacks. During the last two and a half months of 1943, while operating from New Guinea, Cats of VP52 damaged two cruisers, three destroyers and two

Bill Summers' PBY Black Cat Crew, Patrol Squadron 11. (courtesy Nellie Nelsen's file.)

submarines. They were also credited with sinking 10,000 tons of enemy merchant vessels.

The most effective attack procedure adopted by the Black Cat squadrons for night bombing of enemy merchantmen and barges was to begin the approach in a glide pattern from an altitude of 1000 or more feet. The bombs were normally released by an intervalometer which spaced their release at from 60– to 75–foot intervals. When the run was made across the center of the ship, bomb spacing all but assured one or more hits.

PBY pilots compared notes on various bombing approaches and developed the altitude levels by trial and error. Never had they trained, except on the job, in making low-level attacks.

Bright, moonlight nights were no deterrent to the Black Cats. In fact, an up-moon approach was regarded as safer than any dark-of-the-night attack. Conversely, an attack with the moon overhead was considered extremely dangerous. It became apparent in the early stages of Black Cat aggressiveness that the enemy could not pick up the Cats during their long, quiet approach. Enemy gunners' failure to bring anti-aircraft fire to bear before the drop was due in part to their belief that an attack was not imminent, or that they may not have been seen by the Catalina. The few seconds afforded the gunners to aim and shoot, after the drop, were lost in the blinding light of the flares.

Although the Japanese increased their air cover to reduce the effectiveness of the Black Cats, they failed to slow the growing losses of critical tonnage. The Catalinas merely flew extremely close to the water — making radical changes in course — leaving the faster land-based Japanese fighter and dive bomber without sufficient operating altitude to mount an effective attack.

During the period of Black Cat concentration on the Kavieng Harbor-Rabaul area of New Britain and New Ireland, the enemy began placing patrol boats across the mouth of St. George's Channel, the front door to Rabaul Harbor. He also increased aircraft coverage of the region during the nighttime hours, the hours he expected the Black Cats to come through. But these defenses were only partially successful. They were abandoned when the Cats simply found new routes.

Desperate to stop the destruction of critical shipping by the PBYs, the Japanese re-routed their ships dangerously close to the West Coast of New Ireland. They stopped forward progress of a ship when an aircraft was heard so as to eliminate the telltale wake of a ship under way. This action had the effect of reducing radar blips on the Catalina's radar screens and cutting back on visual observance. The enemy also developed small diversionary vessels with heavy armament which reflected radar blips, falsely indicating battleship-size targets.

But, by the end of December, 1943, the Japanese were sneaking ships out of protected harbors in the day time, in particular, when air cover was available. Destroyers, carrying cargo, used the North Coast of New Britain in these daylight runs. Clearly, the enemy was pressed to supply his many island garrisons with the material of war and survival.

When the Japanese increased their use of barges to transport goods in the Bismarck Archipelago, an innovative PBY pilot, Lieutenant William J. Lahodney, VPB52, devised a removable mounting for the bow of the Black Cat. He installed four, 50-caliber machine guns, each directed at an angle of nine degrees below the flight path. The installation did not interfere with operations of the bow turret guns and was fired by the patrol plane commander who sighted through ring sights, or by tracer path.

The only restriction these guns made on the aircraft was use of the bomb sight, a unit rarely used by the low-flying Black Cats. The increase in fire power against slow-moving and stationary targets proved quite valuable to the Catalinas, dramatically increasing their toll on enemy tonnage.

Wes Hicks: Patrol Squadron Fifty-Four

Wes Hicks piloted PBYs in patrol Squadrons 71 and 24 before completing his Pacific tour with VP54. He continues his story with anecdotes of service during 1943.

"After a short stint in February of '42 with VP24, I transferred to VP54, a Black Cat squadron forming for night flying out of Guadalcanal. Then, in March of '43, mine was one of four PBY-5As that landed at Canton Island en route to the 'Canal and were caught in a surprise night bombing attack by Jap 'Betty' bombers. All four Catalinas were flamed and destroyed.

"Press Maravich was one of the pilots. He had recruited all of us to buy chewing tobacco for his tour of duty down-under. Well, we lost all of our possessions that night, including Press's prized stock of chewing tobacco.

"The Japanese had been sneaking in close and shelling Canton but their shells had fallen harmlessly into the lagoon. Now there was suspicion that they were going to invade. So the 5000 Army soldiers based on the island prepared to defend it.

"An Army Captain, his silver bars shining in the moonlight, challenged my lack of assignment and ordered me to the beach to help defend the island. Since my only weapon was a 45 – automatic pistol, I decided the order was a foolish one and didn't go. When the attack failed to materialize, our group was flown back to Kaneohe to regroup and get new aircraft.

"One day in July, '43, we landed in heavy seas to pick up a fighter pilot who had ditched his aircraft. Then, with the fighter pilot still aboard, we picked up marine Colonel Linscott off the beach from our Bougainville invasion.

"Picking up Colonel Linscott was no easy trick. He had gone in with the initial wave and we were ordered to pick him up from a small boat just offshore two days later. To accomplish this, we had to land under fire from Japanese shore batteries and we were fighting the heavy seas. But, we got the Colonel aboard safely and out of there.

"On November 20, 1943, we flew to Sidney, Australia, for rest and relaxation. We had our parachute bags filled with American cigarettes to trade for booze and favors. Our Cabbie in Sidney accepted cigarettes for his fare, then sent some booze merchants to our room with 'fine' branded Scotch. We were so proud of swapping all but a few cartons of cigarettes for bottle upon bottle of top branded Scotch that we didn't bother to sample it until the deal was made and our 'benefactors' were gone. Then we learned the truth. Our premium Scotch had been watered down to where it was practically worthless. We took it back to Guadalcanal and gave it away.

"Liquor was hard to come by for the officers and next to impossible to obtain by enlisted personnel. After a mission, each officer received a bottle of brandy for 'medicinal' purposes. I didn't drink mine, preferring instead to give it to my enlisted plane captain, AMM/1st class, Bazelle. My reasons weren't all out of compassion for the enlisted men. I was so hyped-up about flying already; I might have been out on the line trying to go back up if I had anything to drink.

"Speaking of Bazelle, he was one outstanding plane captain. As First

Pilot, I made the decision as to whether we would accept an airplane for flight or reject it. I left the decision entirely up to Brazelle. If he said reject it, we simply didn't fly that aircraft.

"Flying the PBY was one of the greatest pleasures of my life. I learned how to do wing-overs with it and they were the most beautiful, graceful, gratifying maneuvers one could ever imagine. Flying on one engine was a snap. I used to check out Cadets for solo by cutting one engine and then turning the plane over to them. You could do anything within reason with a PBY."

Presidential Unit Citation: Patrol Squadron Eleven

VP11 was one of the first patrol squadrons in naval history to be awarded the Presidential Unit Citation. It was awarded for their attacks on Japanese shipping and for search missions in the Bismarck Archipelago.

Following is the text of that citation:

"For outstanding performance above the normal call of duty while engaged in search missions and anti-shipping attacks in the enemy Japanese-controlled area of the Bismarck Sea from 15 September 1943 to 1 February 1944. Rendering pioneer service in changing the passive, defensive search into a bold and powerful offensive, Patrol Squadron Eleven utilized the full potentialities of the PBY plane and its equipment, locating the enemy task force units, and striking dangerously by night in devastating masthead glide-bombing attacks to ensure vital hits on the target. Dauntless and aggressive in the fulfillment of each assignment, the gallant pilots of the squadron conducted daring lone patrols, regardless of weather, in a continuous coverage of the area, intercepting and attacking so effectively as to inflict substantial damage on hostile combat and other shipping, to deny the enemy the sea route between New Ireland and New Britain Islands, and thus prevent the reinforcing of important Japanese bases. The splendid record of this combat group is a tribute to the courageous fighting spirit of its officers and men, and reflects the highest credit upon the United States Naval Service."

Following are excerpts from a Navy Department news release on December 30, 1944:

"Combat Record of Patrol Squadron 11."

"VPB11's Black Cat operations inflicted the greatest damage on the enemy. In the 75,000 tons of shipping sunk or damaged were included: a cruiser, a destroyer, a 10,000 ton fleet tanker, a 7000 ton freighter, and smaller warships and merchantmen."

The news release continues.

"Lieutenant Walker E. Shinn, USNR, All American when he captained the University of Pennsylvania football team several years back, was patrol plane commander of a Catalina crew which seriously damaged Japanese shipping.

"Sighting a convoy between Kavieng and Rabual, when those waters were open to the enemy, Lieutenant Shinn's Catalina attacked and damaged a tanker. Then he saw a cruiser ahead. Again, he attacked and scored two direct bomb hits on the stern of the warship. 'Due to heavy anti-aircraft fire, retreat was hurriedly accomplished,' said Lieutenant Shinn, when asked if he saw the cruiser sink.

"A Catalina crew commanded by Lieutenant Goodwyn Rhett Taylor, USNR, executive officer of Patrol Bombing Eleven, also had their inning.

"Off the coast of New Ireland, their bombs straddled two enemy destroyers. Heavy anti-aircraft fire from the destroyers hit the Catalina but the plane got home. A few nights later the same crew bombed an 8000 ton merchantman off Rabaul, again encountering severe flak but forcing the vessel to beach. Three nights later Lieutenant Taylor and his crew made a torpedo attack on a heavily armed merchantman. Anti-aircraft fire knocked out the Catalina's port engine, but the pilot nursed the flying boat to its home base with one engine."

The log of dangerous, damaging, lethal, always tiring, often frightening action continues day by day.

"The Catalina commanded by Wesley B. Benschoten, USNR, served as air-sea-rescue escort for Army Mitchell medium bombers at Celebes and was attacked by four Zeros. Considerable damage was caused by bullets and cannon shells as the Zeros made a total of 15 attacks during a 25 minute, running attack. One Jap plane was shot down in flames by Melvin C. Hohnbaum, Aviation Ordnanceman, First Class, USNR, the Catalina's waist gunner. Another Zero was smoking badly when last seen. The other two enemy aircraft broke off the fight and the Catalina got home safely.

"Lieutenant Van Benschoten's crew bombed an enemy cruiser off Kavieng, sank an 8000 ton merchantman in attacking a six-ship convoy, sank a small tanker at Cebu in the Philippines and rescued three Army P-38 pilots forced down at sea.

"In November, 1943, a PBY piloted by Lieutenant Jack R. Penford, USNR, encountered a convoy of six ships between Rabaul and Kavieng. It left fires on a 10,000 ton freighter-transport which were visible for 30 miles. When last seen, the enemy ship was headed for the beach.

"In September, 1944, Lieutenant Penford and his crew came upon five small tankers, a barge and a sailboat in a harbor at Mindanao, Philippine Islands. Repeated low-level bombing and strafing assaults destroyed the barge and sailboat, left three tankers burning and sinking and two damaged. In a final run, the crew dropped float lights in an attempt to ignite oil on the water."

As Allied forces extended their campaigns in the Pacific West and North, more PBY effectiveness is related in the Navy news release.

"Lieutenant Lavern M. Nelsen, USNR, and his crew flew the squadron's first 'Black Catting' mission on 15 October 1943. A faster enemy plane which came upon the Black Cat that night fled when fired upon.

"Eight nights later, Lieutenant Nelsen and his crew found three Japanese destroyers in a bay at New Britain. Despite severe anti-aircraft fire from the destroyers and shore batteries, they made a masthead attack on one of the destroyers. Their bombs fired it immediately and 45 minutes later it sank. Lieutenant Nelsen was awarded the *Distinguished Flying Cross* for the achievement.

"This same crew had another big night on 29 August 1944 at a harbor in the Celebes, Netherland East Indies. It sank a small tanker, damaged a second, beached an enemy lugger, bombed a destroyer and left it badly damaged and listing.

"The Catalina crew commanded by Lieutenant Thomas L. Hine, USNR, bombed a vessel off New Britain in October, 1943. The bomb exploded prematurely, blowing off most of the Catalina's tail and forcing a water landing two miles off the enemy-held shore. Lieutenant Hine and his crew paddled 100 miles from New Britain in the three days before they were found and rescued.

"VPB11's most exciting air-sea-rescue mission involved the Catalina commanded by Lieutenant William A. Mason, Jr., USNR. On 30 October, an Army Mitchell medium bomber was hit by flak and forced to land in flames in a harbor at Zamboanga, in the Philippines. Despite heavy anti-aircraft fire, Lieutenant Mason landed his plane to pick up survivors.

"With shells landing all around the flying boat, Victor L. Killgore, Aviation Radioman Second Class, USNR, and Jake N. Stice, Aviation Ordnanceman, Second Class, USNR, jumped into the water to swim to the aid of the Army fliers.

"Killgore and Stice helped four badly burned survivors into the flying boat. Just as the Catalina took off, enemy marksmen found the range and bracketed the spot where Lieutenant Mason's plane had rested on the water a moment before."

Ken MacWhinney: General MacArthur's Navy

Ken MacWhinney, Osprey, Florida, spent the better part of VP11's first tour as an instructor for new PBY pilot recruits and didn't get a shot at squadron flying until VP11 began reforming for its second tour in March of 1943.

Ken offers a recap of his experiences beginning about the time the squadron was reforming.

"A lot of the pilots had just returned from the Guadalcanal action and thought they were headed for some rather soft duty in the Caribbean, after a lengthy leave, of course. So, it didn't help their morale to be recalled from leave and find they were reforming VP11 for duty in the same war zones they had just left. Some were further dismayed to find that a few of us 'stateside' instructors had more flight time and were made Patrol Plane Commanders ahead of them.

"We left the states in April, stopping briefly in Hawaii, then on to the west coast of Australia where we completed our training before heading north to Samarai, near the southern tip of New Guinea. From there we began our Black Cat searches in a northerly direction.

"On the night of September 16, 1943, we intercepted a Jap merchant ship just north of Wewak, New Guinea. We caught it about 300 miles up the coast. We slipped in on a bombing run, then strafed the vessel, repeatedly. It was hit after a couple of runs, but we continued strafing it until it flamed. We got the squadron's first kill; although Bill Mason got another on a like ship later that night.

"Naturally, we were not a skilled crew and Ensign Jim McGhee went up into the bow section where the forward blister had been, stood there with his body right out in the open, and manned the 30–caliber machine gun. We made a frontal attack to give him some direct fire and when he pulled the trigger, the gun muzzle-flash blinded us in the cockpit causing us to duck down behind the instrument panel and begin our pull-out.

"As we pulled up, we saw tracer fire coming past us and Jim McGhee became immortalized in the Southwest Pacific for his remark, 'Hey, my bullets are bouncing back past us!' When we assured him that those tracers weren't his, rather, the enemy's, he ducked down out of that fresh air so fast you would think he could outrun the bullets.

"During this period, we were working for MacArthur. He had asked for people to do night work because three or four of their B-24s had dropped into the water at night — killing all the crew — and the Catalina was a natural to take up the slack.

"The weather was so bad up there that most other aircraft flights during the day and evening were cancelled. But MacArthur kept sending out the communique mentioning that all other flights had been cancelled and 'Black Cat Eleven covered all sectors last night, as usual.' We got pretty proud of that. At which point, the Navy said, 'Okay, if MacArthur's going to decorate you and give you all the credit himself, then rotate with the Army!' With that, they kicked us out of the Navy Officer's Club. But guys from the Fifth Air Force came over and split their beer rations with us.

"We got along famously with the Fifth Air Force pilots but we did have to rotate with them. That caused our squadron to stay out almost 20 months when other Navy squadrons were being relieved after about six months.

"On September 15, 1944, we were en route to Morotai, flying along over this vast expanse of sea — expecting nothing at all — when the radar operator said, 'Hey, there's a blip on the radar!'

"I said, 'There's nothing out here!'

"He said, 'It's a great big one!'

"Just as I was repeating my 'nothing out here' statement, we were surrounded by fighter planes. About then we came up over the horizon upon a major unit of the United States' Seven Fleet.

"Quickly, we turned on our IFF — Identification, Friend or Foe — to keep those trigger-happy fighter pilots from shooting us out of the air. Then we looked again. As far as the eye could see, there were ships of the line and supply ships: battle wagons, carriers, cruisers, everything and everywhere. We sat there awe-struck and began to realize the immensity of the force behind us, the enormity of the fighting force that was ours. It gave us a great thrill knowing that with such might, there was no way we were going to lose that war."

January of 1944 brought a new plateau for the Black Cat squadrons operating night offensive reconnaissance missions in the Bismarck Sea. In that month they sank an estimated 52,500 tons of Japanese merchant shipping while damaging an additional 5500 tons. Quite impressive was the combined totals compiled by the Black Cats operating in the area from August of 1943 through January, 1944: 112,700 tons sunk; 47,000 tons damaged. In addition, they damaged, without known results, seven destroyers and three cruisers, each hit by 500 – pound or 1000 – pound bombs or both. They received credit for two probable sinkings of enemy submarines. But more damaging to the enemy than the tonnage sunk was the total disruption of his shipping routine.

January, however, also brought stronger defensive measures against the Black Cat attacks. Air cover became a near constant accompaniment of convoys; more escorts were provided, their anti-aircraft fire beefed up. Single Catalina attacks on convoys were discouraged by squadron leaders except where additional help could not be called up in time to make a combined attack. Coordinated attacks by two or more Black Cats often confused the enemy, causing ships to disperse, permitting attack.

One such coordinated attack meeting with outstanding success was executed by five Black Cats, two of which were carrying a torpedo with a TNT head under one wing and two 500 – pound bombs under the other. The other three carried the normal complement of one 1000 – pound and two 500 – pound bombs.

This group of agitators attacked a convoy consisting of a cruiser, a destroyer and two torpedo boats which were escorting four merchant vessels. The first torpedo missed but apparently was heard by the sound gear of the escorting vessels, causing them to disperse in an attempt to locate the source. Left unattended, the four merchantmen were attacked by the Black Cats and three were left burning and dead in the water. B-24s verified their condition the following day.

Lavern M. "Nelly" Nelsen: Power-Dive Approach

Lavern M. "Nelly" Nelsen, Scottsdale, Arizona, piloted a PBY Catalina for VP11 from January of 1943 to December, 1944. In the thick of just about everything going on around them, Nellie and his crew virtually challenged the law of averages and won. Their activities were varied and rarely boring.

"With our PBY painted black, flying our first battle tour, we were sent to the South tip of New Guinea to operate night patrols. The Navy had given us instructions on glide bombing, however the pilots thought it over and said, 'That's just fine for bombing submarines but when you go in on warships, you want something besides a glide attitude with the plane. You want to get in there as fast as you can and out as fast as you can.' So we devised what we called our power-dive approach. We would climb to 3500 feet after flying just off the water as we homed in on the target. After reaching our desired altitude, we held it until we were close enough to tip the plane over and dive at a speed past the red line, the maximum speed marker of the PBY. In that diving attitude, we dropped our bombs on the target and had high air speed to pull out and get away.

"The first occasion we had to use this attack approach was one night on patrol at Jacquenot Bay, New Britain. We had some of the earliest radar gear called, 'Easy,' and my radioman, Tom Gilliam, called in from the radio compartment that he had picked up some blips, right off Jacquenot Bay. Flying in close enough to see them, we spotted a couple of destroyers, a destroyer escort and a couple of tankers, or merchant ships.

"Realizing the Japs had seen us by this time, we decided to retreat back to sea 50 to 75 miles and make a run right off the water into Jacquenot Bay, hoping for the element of surprise. During our briefing before takeoff, we had heard that the Army had cleared the entire Jacquenot Bay beach line of enemy installations by heavy bombing. But somebody forgot something.

"We felt that by flying directly into the bay, if we did have any Zeros rising to intercept us, we could duck over the mountains and fly the valleys out of there, giving us the best chance of losing the Japs. So we came straight in, zooming up to 3500 feet and over into our power-dive, right after the number two destroyer.

"At that time, the number two destroyer lay hard to port, so we switched our target to the lead destroyer and straddled it with two depth charges. But as we approached the shoreline of the bay in our planned retreat, the whole beach opened up on us. We quickly changed our strategy and winged the Catalina back over the bow of the destroyer, then high-tailed for the open sea. The destroyer was burning amid-ships and we learned later that it sank. The depth charges must have blown the ship's boilers.

"Coming out of that encounter as well as we did, we felt the PBY had performed sheer magic, so the crew and I named the plane, Black Magic. Sully Sullivan, my co-pilot, who was quite a singer, composed a song that followed the tune of 'Black Magic' and we sang it frequently throughout the remainder of our tour.

"One night, while flying out of Morotai, we were training a new squadron which had recently moved into the area. Our patrols were extending into the Celebes Sea and, in particular, there was a heavy concentration of Jap ships at Manado Bay, Celebes Island.

"We decided to hit Manado Bay that evening, and to demonstrate our flight plan, a crew from the other squadron was to take a similar patrol sector but was scheduled to arrive at Manado Bay exactly three hours after we had been there. Again, we were planning to fly out to sea and come back just off the water from 50 miles out.

"What we didn't know was that the other plane misjudged his navigation and had arrived right in the mouth of the bay, saw a small ship, worked it over and was gone before we got anywhere near. We didn't know it as we approached but our element of surprise was gone.

"We came into the bay and noticed, as we passed along the shore line, that a light would go on up on the hillside; another mile, another light and so it went. We thought this was rather odd. But when we found our target in the bay and began our run, the Japs threw everything at us from ships and shore batteries. We pressed our attack on the tankers or freighters and left one listing and one afire.

"Flying at night had its good points but when the weather was nasty, we depended on our primitive radar and the skills of our radiomen. I believe we were fortunate to have one of the very best in Tom Gilliam. He developed a skill in reading the radar screen which brought us through close calls on many occasions.

"We had been training a new second radioman in the crew for a couple of months, when we hit a terrible storm on the way back from a night attack on Jap shipping in the Halmaheras, off the Northwest tip of New Guinea. We had threaded our way through the turtle – neck of New Guinea on the way out and now had to go back through in a storm.

"I decided this would be a good time to test the new radioman under heavy stress conditions, so I had him sit the radar, instructing him to report a constant status of radar blips and formations showing on the radar screen.

"He began calling out radar readings and I was carefully monitoring just about everything he said. Suddenly, something I never could explain told me he was reading it wrong. I flipped the Catalina up into a 180 – degree flipper turn and about this time, there was a flash of lightning. There, just below us, were the tree tops; they were right under our wing tips. If we had flown on for a split-second longer, we would have crashed into the side of a mountain. Anyway, we backed out of there. Tom took over and guided us through as if he had the eyes of a cat."

Blackcats Of Patrol Bomber Squadron Fifty-Two

VPB52 was no stranger to action when it arrived in the South Pacific. It had been on duty in the Atlantic, flying "Neutrality Patrols" as early as

1940, and had served in the Caribbean and Canal Zone until spring of 1943. Patrolling and sub-chasing from Bermuda, Guantanamo Bay, San Juan and Natal, Brazil, Catalinas of VPB52 were more than ready for duty in the tropics of Milne Bay, New Guinea.

VPB52 Catalinas became Black Cats in the late summer of 1943, and became pioneers in the night low altitude glide bombing attacks made famous by Catalina squadrons for the remainder of the war.

Lieutenant William J. Lahodney, who devised the multiple 50-caliber bow guns, commanded a Black Cat crew on November 24, 1943, which attacked a Japanese cruiser escorted by three destroyers some 70 miles north of Rabaul. In the darkness, Lieutenant Lahodney was handicapped by the convoy having just sustained an attack from another aircraft, and having been alerted, anti-aircraft fire was intense and close-by. But the Lieutenant pressed his glide bombing attack to within 150 feet of the cruiser before releasing his bombs. Two of his charges hit the target. The Catalina also sustained numerous hits but Lieutenant Lahodney nursed it back to base. For this action, he was awarded the Navy Cross.

William J. Pattison commanded a Black Cat on the night of November 30, and spotted a large convoy heading south between Kavieng and Rabaul. As did Lieutenant Lahodney the week before, Lieutenant Pattison braved heavy anti-aircraft fire and attacked a 15,000-ton tanker, scoring with two bombs and sinking the vessel. He was awarded the Silver Star.

VPB52 ended its specific Black Cat duties as 1943 came to a close. Their toll of Japanese shipping was impressive: sunk, two submarines; damaged, two cruisers and three destroyers; sunk, 34,000 tons of merchant vessels and probably sank 10,000 more tons of enemy shipping.

The squadron covered a number of naval bombardments at Gamata, New Britain, and the invasion of Arawe on December 14, 1943.

18

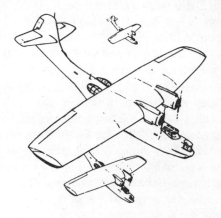

The Dumbos

The Black Cats of the South Pacific were not limited to harassing Japanese shipping and troop concentrations. As in the other war zones, the Catalinas were performing almost daily missions of mercy.

With key islands of the South Pacific war zone inhabited by friendly natives led by brave Australian and New Zealand coastwatchers, the Catalinas were called on to slip in — sometimes under fire — to pick up survivors of air crashes and ship sinkings. They were asked to transfer the wounded and seriously ill from advanced bases and ships-at-sea. Mass evacuation of islanders and military personnel was not uncommon.

One such mass evacuation earned elements of VP11 the undying respect and appreciation of 219 Aussie Commandos and police workers. Surrounded by the Japanese, and virtually assured of annihilation or capture, this hell-raising group was ordered withdrawn. Believing at first that the PBYs had two to three weeks to complete the withdrawal, the task appeared routine. But the enemy closed in faster than expected and completion time was reduced to five days.

Vernon Koenig: Rescue The Aussies

Vernon Koenig, a radioman with VP11, was assigned to one of the participating PBYs taking part in the evacuation-rescue. As he tells it:

"The biggest evacuation or rescue mission that VP11 was involved in was in December of 1943 when 219 Australian officers and men, including

New Guinea native trackers, and about 25, 000 pounds of machine guns and other equipment were air-lifted from a jungle camp on the Sepik River near Wewak.

"Each PBY made two to three trips a day across the Owen-Stanley Mountains. On each trip we brought out between 18 and 20 men, plus hundreds of pounds of supplies. We battled the thin air of high altitude, crowding our service ceiling. We sought valleys and canyons to ease the strain of crossing the mountains.When we approached the Sepik River to land, the target was barely two and a half times the width of the giant Catalina wing. On the water, it meant dodging hidden logs and debris.

"The evacuation went well until the last Catalina's starter jammed and the plane couldn't take off. They camouflaged the Cat with tree branches and Lieutenant Ragsdale stayed with it overnight while the rest of the crew returned to Port Moresby in another Catalina.

"I was chosen as the radioman to assist on the repair and rescue of the ailing Cat. In order to replace the starter, the generator had to be removed. These generators were the responsibility of the radiomen.

"We were working against time, since the trackers had told us the Japanese were four, maybe five miles away. Expecting to hear a machine gun at any moment, two mechanics and a radioman worked furiously to get the job completed so we could get airborne and out of there.

"With the starter installed, the propeller turned freely. We loaded the remaining personnel and gear, cleared away the camouflage, and taxied out into the midstream of the river. The Australian service boat was tied to the back of the aircraft and, after chopping a hole in the bottom so it would sink, we cut it loose. No further delays. Opening up the throttles, the pilot jockeyed the PBY around a small bend and along a straight stretch until we were in the air.

"I was too busy to dwell in the urgency of that last flight until we found most of the squadron waiting for us at the dock at Port Moresby. Naval Intelligence told us we had made it out with but a few minutes to spare."

Not all PBY rescue attempts were successful, though their frequency of failure was very low. Quite often they became the carrier, or holding medium, while awaiting additional help from other aircraft or fleet vessels.

Robert Corlett: A C-47 Transport On A Coral Reef

One such rescue-failure, turned successful, involved Lieutenant Robert Corlett. Lieutenant Corlett's PBY and two others were searching for a downed C-47, Missing for over a week.

"On October 29, 1942, while tender-based on the USS Curtiss at Espiritu Santo, I was dispatched in charge of three PBYs to search for a missing C-47. It had taken off from Guadalcanal 10 days earlier, loaded with sick and wounded, headed for Espiritu Santo. There had been no word from it since it left. However, a report was received that a weak signal had been heard from a certain area, triggering our response.

"We located the C-47 on a reef, all but submerged, with a number of survivors waving at us. It was getting late in the day, but we landed in the open sea close to the reef and tried to work our way to the downed plane. One of our other PBYs landed while the third returned to base.

"We broke out rubber rafts and tried to send two or three of our crew over the reef to the C-47. This met with only limited success. They reached the aircraft and loaded the most severely injured, then tried to make it back through the reef. But the wind blew the boats, scattering the men. We had a very serious situation to deal with since darkness was approaching.

"We made numerous unsuccessful attempts at taxiing close to the reef and throwing them a line from the wing, but finally had to beach the PBY to round up all the men. They never could have returned to the C-47 because it was well up-wind of them. We finally managed to get all hands aboard my plane — 10 in my crew and 25 from the C-47 — most of whom lay out on the wing overnight. We cracked open all of our parachutes to provide cover for the survivors. My crew remained inside the aircraft all night, some standing in waist-deep water. The hull had caved in when the Cat beached on the reef.

"The second PBY that landed drifted all night, unable to get off the water. As I recall it sank the next day but the crew was picked up.

"We were all rescued by the USS Barton, DD-599. Before picking us up, the Barton had plucked 200 or more men from the water who had survived sinking of one of our carriers, the Hornet. Our 24 – hour cruise into Noumea was wall-to-wall bodies.

"The rescue mission we had set out upon was, in a sense, a dismal failure since we lost two PBYs and managed to need rescuing ourselves. On the positive side, there was no loss of life in the rescue attempt and we located the downed C-47. Its survivors lived to tell their story even after their 10 – day ordeal at sea."

John Byrd: Treated To A Can Of Spam

Flying for VP11, John Byrd was aboard a PBY returning from patrol near the Stewart Islands when they spotted people waving from an island beach.

"They fired a flare-pistol and we thought they were shooting at us. But as we got closer we could see khaki shorts on some of them, so we landed.

"It turned out to be a PBY crew from VP14 that had tangled with eight Zeros. They had battled the Zeros until running out of ammunition, then managed to get away. Most of the crew had been wounded and the old Cat was badly shot up, but the Zeros hadn't been able to knock her down. Besides, the crew claimed one sure kill and possibly had more.

"Somehow, they managed to make a landing at this little island and the natives had torn what was left of the PBY to shreds to hide it from the Japs. A third class mechanic named Sollitt had been shot through the chest, with the bullet going all the way through and out his back. His crew kept him alive with sulpha powder and band-aids from the first aid kit and fed him turtle eggs. Although we had to pass him by hand through the waist hatch he never made a sound.

"Once we were airborne, the VP14 crew was 'treated' to a $4 \times 4 \times 12$ inch tin of Spam. You would have thought we were feeding them New York steaks the way they devoured that Spam. I learned much later that all these crew members, including Sollitt, survived and returned to duty. This was a PBY crew that eight Zeros could't bring down, was given up for lost and rescued by one of their own."

Chuck Rich: Reluctant Rescue

Chuck Rich flying for the second formation of VP23, picks up his story after the squadron returned to the South Pacific and was patrolling from a base on Tulagi.

"In August, 1943, we were looking for a B-25 reported missing and last heard from approximately 100 miles south of Tulagi. The weather was clear and the sea fairly smooth. I was section leader of three Catalinas. We had just started our search when my radioman, who had been trying to pick up emergency radio signals on 500 KCS with his loop antenna, called that he had raised a signal but that it was too brief to locate.

"I asked if he could tell me what quadrant it was in, within 90 degrees, and he did. Looking at the chart, I saw a small island named Rennell about fifty miles away. We decided to take a look.

"We came over the island, circled it, and saw an emergency balloon holding up the antenna of an aircraft survival transmitter. I figured we had found our B-25 crew, or somebody. We made a landing at the atoll — no small chore with all the coral heads around.

"As we anchored, natives in canoes came out to great us. One canoe carried the chief's son who handed us a letter from his father to Admiral Nimitz. It was written in rather broken English but we could make out that they needed some rice seed. They had suffered a drought and were without seed for crops. As an aside: the letter was delivered and another PBY took them seed.

"The chief's son told me the Americans on the island wouldn't be able to leave at that time. Suspecting the Army survivors were behind this ploy, I told the chief's son to advise the Americans that it was absolutely necessary that they be ready to leave in 30 minutes since we had to be back at Tulagi before dark.

"He left to deliver the message and soon six dark-skinned maidens were rowed out and delivered to the aircraft. They climbed aboard and were ready to leave with us. Much to the dismay of my crew, I instructed them to order the girls off the Catalina, and to throw them off if they refused. The maidens were unhappy, but left. My crew was unhappy. And the Army Air Forces crew, who finally came aboard, was unhappy. But we did our job, nonetheless."

PBY Dumbo: Open Sea Rescue

In 1943, as America's home front reached high gear producing all forms of war materials, the PBY squadrons were relieved of some duties which had been necessary when a shortage existed in freight aircraft, torpedo bombers and personnel transports.

Although they continued performing these services in all zones, their time was found better directed toward night black-catting and to flights as angels of mercy in rescue operations.

Some squadrons were assigned the primary duty of rescue and were dubbed "Dumbo" in honor of the Walt Disney elephant character featured in cartoons of that era. The Dumbo squadrons wrote an exciting new chapter in the annals of open sea rescue, literally snatching hundreds of men and women from death by drowning or heat exhaustion.

The ongoing struggle between the Allied and Japanese forces to sway the island resident's support was often tipped in favor of the Allies by acts of human kindness and understanding of the islander's needs by Dumbo squadron commanders. When word came down that a particular group or village was having trouble with food rations, the commanders would arrange drops of rice or other staples, then coastwatchers made sure the natives were aware who sent it.

Tom Benton: A Ton Of Rice

Tom Benton was dispatched from Tulagi to pick up a PV pilot and his crew who had been secreted by villagers to a certain point on the northern tip of the Japanese held island of Choiseul. Stacked in the hull of the Catalina was a special thank you for the islanders responsible.

"On a rainy day, October 17, 1943, I picked up a PV lieutenant and his complete crew on the enemy island of Choiseul. When we got the call we were supposed to have a P-38 escort but the weather was so rough they turned around and went back.

"Coastwatchers had said they would have a fire burning on this certain point on the northern tip of the island. But on that day, they couldn't have lit a fire if they had had butane, it was raining so hard. We circled for quite a while, trying to see some sign of life, but there were no fires. Then we saw four big war canoes, with high bows sticking out of the water, appear out of nowhere and head for the outer bay. We landed and made our way to their selected point of rendezvous. After some maneuvering, the canoes made their way in from the stern. Their bows were too high to go under the wing.

"Each canoe had one or more survivor. We guided each man aboard and to the forward part of the aircraft. We then began unloading one ton of rice into the long war canoes. The entire operation, from landing to takeoff, lasted just ten minutes."

Milton Cheverton And Jeff Blackman: Rescues Under Fire

Milton Cheverton and Jeff Blackman have told of their activities while piloting Catalinas in the early months of VP23's Pacific tour. They now cover some of their Dumbo activities during the months of June through November, 1943.

Jeff: "There was a big naval battle off Vella Lavella in the first week of October and Milt and I took separate Dumbo flights to rescue fleet survivors. I took the morning search and Milt picked up in the afternoon.

"I started my day out by landing among a bunch of Jap survivors who were so covered with oil we had to get up close to identify them. We cranked up and got out of there, leaving their rescue to the PT boats which were better able to handle prisoners. But we followed the lead of a bunch of P-38s and rescued a total of eight sailors that morning."

From VP23's war diaries the following report expands the modest brevity of Jeff Blackman's air-sea rescues that day.

"From: Report of Dumbo Mission to rescue survivors in water, 24 miles from Bagga Island, off Vella Lavella, bearing 315 deg.

"Pursuant to orders from COMAIR, New Georgia, PBY-5 plane of VP23, on Rendova standby, under command of Lt. (jg) G.A.L. Blackman, took off from Rendova Harbor at about 1000, 7 October 1943, to search for survivors of friendly destroyers reported on the water — bearing 315 degrees from Bagga Island, off Vella Lavella, 24 miles distant.

"According to plan, a rendezvous was made with 12 fighters west of Munda and a direct course was taken to the area to be searched.

"Arriving on station at 1110, 12 additional fighters were circling an area in which there was much debris and oil. There appeared to be 24 to 30 men clinging to debris and covered with oil. Float lights were dropped immediately to mark the spot and a landing was made. The plane taxied into the debris and the engines were cut. A closer examination showed that the survivors in the area were all Japanese. All guns were brought to bear and engines started again. The PBY taxied through the entire group in search of Americans, and finding none, took off a few minutes later.

"The P-38s of the fighter escort then led the plane to a spot about three miles away where there were six Americans in a life raft. Lt. (jg) Blackman landed at 1130, took the six men aboard, then sighted two more men in life jackets bobbing in the water about two miles away. He taxied over and picked them up, taking off again at about 1140."

Milt: "I was on patrol on November 23, 1943 supporting a B-25 raid on Bougainville. The Army raiders had bombed their targets but one of their planes had been shot down and the Japs left the crew in their life raft as decoys, I guess. We were ordered to go in and get them.

"Twelve Australian P-40's went with us and strafed hell out of the enemy shore batteries and small-arms fire. Man! They were something.

"I sat the Cat down in Shortland Harbor and, without knowing it, found we were right at the end of a Jap landing strip. They opened up with every gun they had. At least it seemed that way.

"When we pulled up alongside the raft, it seemed to be taking an extremely long time in getting the all-clear to taxi for takeoff. So I went aft to the blister and found some of the B-25 crew arguing to bring their raft aboard. Well, it took only a short time to convince them that those were real bullets and shells splashing ever closer and that rubber rafts were quite expendable.

"As we taxied out of the harbor, the Japs began firing 'four inchers' and cannons and the works at us but never touched a man or the plane.

"The B-25 skipper said, 'I've always thought the PBY was the ugliest airplane I had ever seen until I saw you coming in to pick us up — then I decided it was the most beautiful craft in the world!'

"I got a 'Well Done' from Admiral Halsey, a Distinguished Flying Cross, and went to the top of the "good list." But two days later I was sent to another island to pick up a sick coastwatcher. I was all shook up because one of our planes had been shot up, all the pilots wiped out, and it had crashed because none of the crew knew how to fly the thing.

"Because I didn't want the same thing to happen to my crew, I had Brownie, my radioman, in the cockpit showing him how to make a landing. Somehow, as we came in, I missed the planned landing spot and hit a swell. It was all I could do to keep the plane going. If Brownie had been a co-pilot, he could have given it power and let me down. But we went up and down, up and down, until part of the tail broke off.

"The coastwatcher was ready to come out, so they called and some-one else picked him up. We finally came up on the beach, took our anchor and wrapped its line around a tree, then when the tide went out, we folded up the floats and leaned the Cat on one side. We put nuts and bolts on 200 rivets we had popped. Later, they sent out a horizontal stabilizer; we put it on and flew home.

"When we arrived back at base, I learned I had gone from the top of one list to the top of another."

Jeff: "We used to follow the fighters when they went out, then picked them up if they dropped. One guy was returning to Rendova when he went down. We picked him up with seemingly routine dispatch. But when we got back to base and I was being debriefed, the Intelligence Officer said, 'Exactly where did you pick up that pilot?'

"I pointed to a spot on the map, 'Right there.'

"He said, 'You sure that's it?'

"I said, 'I'm positive that was it.'

"He said, 'You know, don't you, that's a Japanese mine field?'

Leon Freeman: F6F Pilot To The Rescue

Leon Freeman was a Lieutenant (jg) on his second South Pacific tour. He adds now to his colorful PBY story with some of his Dumbo experiences.

"On the afternoon of December 26, 1943, I landed at Cape St. George, New Ireland, where we rescued six B-25 crewmen. Japanese fighters were trying to strafe us as we struggled to bring the crewmen aboard. The co-pilot of the B-25 got up on our wingtip float and refused to leave. We were about to leave him out there when he started swimming toward our blister through a hail of fire from the beach. At the same time, a Japanese Zero was diving on us. We had several F6Fs strafing the beach and as one completed his strafing run, he pulled up and there was the Zero. He shot him down, so close to us that the Zero crashed in our wake.

"After we were airborne, the F6F pilot came alongside, perhaps expecting three cheers from us. He moved right up under our wing and my co-pilot, Lieutenant (jg) Goodey, looked over and said, 'That's a fraternity brother of mine from Northwestern!' The F6F pilot recognized him with a wide mouthed exclamation, 'Goodey!,' then a wave and he was gone.

"Some of the B-25 crewmen were in pretty bad shape so I played doctor most of the way back to Barakoma, Vella Lavella, administering blood plasma and sulpha drugs. We left them at the hospital and returned to Rendova.

"We had been operating from the seaplane tender Curtiss at the time and one day a short while after the rescue, I had just finished taking my shower when the Duty Officer came down and said, 'Hey, there are three Army Generals up in the Admiral's quarters looking for you!'

"I thought he was kidding and told him to get out but my squadron Commander, Ernie Simpson, came down and escorted me up to the Admiral's quarters.

"The Generals were there and said that the rescue did more for the bomber people's morale than anything since their arrival in the war zone. That the Dumbos would land under fire and pick up their people was really appreciated. They also wanted to know if I had been recommended for any medals.

"I said, 'Not to my knowledge.'

"But then the old Admiral came sputtering over and said, 'Yes! Yes! Yes! We have recommended him for the Distinguished Flying Cross.'

"Up until that time they weren't going to say a hell of a lot about it; a guy almost had to get killed to get a medal out there.

"We flew Dumbo for attack aircraft over Rabaul Harbor many times.

We had as many as 30 airplanes covering us—with the Marines, Army, New Zealand and Australia doing their thing. If they were Australian or New Zealand P-40 pilots, two would go under the Cat and two overhead. No matter how low you got, they stuck like glue. That was great! We could go out and never worry about our cover. They had dog fights and we set down just off the water, watching for survivors.

"Our PBY crew was at Torokina, Bougainville, operating Dumbo flights a few days after the Marines had landed. When we arrived they gave us a brand new tent, cots, mosquito netting and the whole bit. They even dug a fox hole for us alongside the tent. Nearby a mortar battery was banging away.

"Unbeknown to us, during the night, the Japanese came down and overran the mortar position. Then the Marines pushed them back again. We slept through the whole thing. When we came out in the morning, stretching and scratching, they said, 'Oh! Have you guys been in there all night?'

"We said, 'Yes.'

" 'Well,' They said, 'you were lucky. The Japs were here last night but just didn't come into your tent.' "

Nathan G. Gordon: Medal of Honor

Nathan Gordon flew a PBY into Kavieng Harbor on February 15, 1944. The day began as a routine Dumbo mission, but before it ended, that brave pilot and crew, with their incredible aircraft, made four landings in and from Kavieng Harbor, rescuing 15 airmen in the process.

For this courageous deed, Lieutenant Nathan G. Gordon was awarded the highest honor of the United States: the Medal of Honor.

Following is his personal story:

"In May of 1941, I enlisted in the Navy V5 program and was sent to New Orleans for preliminary training, then on to Jacksonville, Florida, where I became a PBY pilot. In time, I was commissioned an Ensign and in the latter quarter of 1942 was ordered to Norfolk, Virginia, where squadron VP34 was forming. In July we arrived in the Panama Canal Zone to perform search missions, submarine patrols and convoy protection in the Caribbean.

"VP34 served in the Caribbean until June of 1943 when we migrated West, eventually arriving at Perth, Australia, where we continued training and backup service until December of 1943. Finally, on December 29, we arrived at Samarai Island, off the southern tip of the Papuan Peninsula, New Guinea and began Black Cat operations in the area of the Bismarck Sea.

"We were trying to keep the Japanese from supplying their bases at Rabaul and Kavieng by executing low level bombing and torpedo attacks on enemy ships as they attempted to sail under cover of darkness. The success of our effort is reflected in the numbers: four destroyers and one escort vessel damaged, 73,700 tons of merchant shipping sunk or destroyed, 12,250 tons of merchant shipping damaged and 50 to 75 barges destroyed.

"I was awarded the Distinguished Flying Cross for attacks on Japanese shipping, particularly destroyers and barges, during that period of time.

"Also, our squadron was engaged in rescue work in this area, rescuing Army flyers who were shot down on day missions over various Japanese bases in the Bismarck zone.

"On February 15, 1944, I was ordered to standby for air-sea rescue work in connection with an Air Force raid on Kavieng Harbor, New Ireland. We were in the vicinity of Vitu Island when we received a message from one of the planes on the raid that a plane had been shot down and was located at a certain latitude and longitude.

"We plotted it as down in an area some 40 miles from Kavieng Harbor and proceeded to that point. We found nothing and decided that the person calling for a 'Dumbo' was mistaken as to the aircraft's location. Then, shortly after arriving at the first location we received word that an aircraft had been shot down in Kavieng Harbor. We flew to that location, finding it within the harbor and about a mile offshore. After a brief search, we spotted dye markers in the water and some partially inflated life rafts. We were unable to see any survivors in them or in the water.

"It is extremely difficult to locate objects in the sea. But we knew someone had been shot down at this spot because of the dye markers and rafts. Since landing and taking off from open sea under the best of conditions is hazardous, we were reluctant to land unnecessarily. Deciding that we needed a closer look, we made a pass over the rafts, dropping two smoke bombs to line ourselves up for a landing near the area where the plane had gone down.

"We attempted a 'full stall' landing but stalled too high so that when our plane hit the water we popped a number of rivets. This created a slight leak in the hull that was nothing to be alarmed over. Those Catalinas could take an awful beating and quite frequently popped rivets in full-stall landings.

"We cruised around in the area where the dye markers were but found no one. After a few more minutes of searching we took off. No sooner were we airborne than we got another message from one of the fighters telling of another Army aircraft that had been shot down. This one was located much closer to Kavieng itself. The fighter pilot said he would fly over the spot to help us locate any survivors. We were apprehensive because we were very near the Kavieng shore installations.

"We followed the same procedure as in the first landing but this time saw six men in the water, either in or hanging onto one life raft. I ordered my strongest men to the aft section of the plane with Ensign Jack Keeley, who was my senior co-pilot and most knowledgeable person aboard in administering first aid.

"We taxied to the life raft and threw a rope to its occupants in an attempt to pull them alongside the aircraft. But with both engines running we just couldn't get the raft close enough. Besides, the Air Force personnel were pretty well banged up and weren't able to assist. I finally realized that if we were going to get the men out, I would have to cut my engines. That, of course, entailed some risks because sometimes the engines, under such conditions, simply wouldn't restart.

"Before making a final decision, I called my plane captain and said, 'Wiley, if we've got to stop the engines, can we get them started again?' He said he was pretty sure we could. So we stopped them and were then able to pull the raft alongside where we lifted the six men into the plane. While this was happening, fire from Japanese shore batteries became more intense and was getting closer.

"With the survivors safely aboard, and the engines started, we took off again. Again in the air, we received yet another call from an Air Force fighter pilot reporting another plane down in the harbor and even closer to shore. Once again, the fighter pilot guided us to the place where the second plane was down and we found three men in a life raft.

"After dropping our smoke markers, we made our landing even closer than before. We were getting considerably more enemy fire but somehow it didn't worry me. I had too many other things to think about. We taxied up to the raft, threw them a line, and again had to cut the engines before being able to pull the men into the plane.

"We took off and headed back toward base. We had flown some 20 miles when another call came in from an Air Force plane that had found still another plane down in Kavieng Harbor. We returned to that point but by now two of the four planes flying cover for us had left due to low fuel supply.

"When we arrived at the spot indicated by the fighter pilot, we saw six men in the water, in a life raft, or hanging on to the sides. They were approximately 600 yards from the shore in Kavieng Harbor. Now we were presented with a new problem. To make the approach for our landing, it was necessary to actually fly over the shoreline. We couldn't approach from any other direction because, when making landings in heavy swells, you have to land along with the swells. Crosswise landings tend to make the plane's nose dig in.

"We made our approach and landing, again having to cut the engines after throwing the line to the life raft. Enemy fire picked up considerably and we did become alarmed with the possibility of being hit. But we got the men aboard, carefully handing them through the blisters to avoid further injury, all the while with a wary eye toward the shell splashes coming closer and closer.

"Again we started the engines. And again we headed for base. When we had flown about 20 miles, the air cover had to leave us, searching for a safe place to land before running out of fuel. But there were no enemy aircraft around.

"We flew to a little bay near the Army Air Force base at Wewak, New Guinea, where we unloaded the Air Force personnel onto a seaplane tender.

"I was awarded the Medal of Honor and each member of my crew received the Silver Star. The awards were presented in Brisbane, Australia, by Rear Admiral T.C. Kinkaid, USN."

Following is the full text of Nathan Gordon's Citation.

"The President of the United States takes pleasure in presenting the Medal of Honor to:

LIEUTENANT NATHAN G. GORDON
UNITED STATES NAVAL RESERVE

for service set forth in the following:

CITATION: "For extraordinary heroism above and beyond the call of duty as Commander of a Catalina Patrol Plane in rescuing personnel of the United States Army Fifth Air Force shot down in combat over Kavieng harbor in the Bismarck Sea, February 15, 1944. On air alert in the vicinity of Vitu Island, Lieutenant, then Lieutenant Junior Grade, Gordon unhesitatingly responded to the report of the crash and flew boldly into the harbor, defying close range fire from enemy shore guns to make three separate landings in full view of the Japanese and pick up nine men, several of them injured. With his cumbersome flying boat dangerously overloaded, he made a brilliant takeoff, despite heavy swells and almost total absence of wind, and set a course for base, only to receive the report of another group stranded in a rubber life raft 600 yards from the enemy shore. Promptly turning back, he again risked his life to set his plane down, under direct fire of the heaviest defenses of Kavieng, and take aboard six more survivors, coolly making his fourth dexterous takeoff with 15 rescued officers and men. By his exceptional daring, personal valor and incomparable airmanship under most perilous conditions, Lieutenant Gordon prevented certain death or capture of our airmen by the Japanese."

The Citation was signed: Franklin D. Roosevelt.

Convairiety: "Send Catalinas Out To Meet Them"

"An excerpt from *Convairiety,* a house organ published by ConVair, the manufacturer of the PBY Catalina, defines the activities of Fleet Air Wing 17 Catalinas during the months of the Allied drive back to the Philippines.

"As the New Guinea campaign opened forward bases, elements of Air Wing 17 moved northwestward, until by late summer of 1944 the tender Wright was stationed at Owl Island near Biak, whence her Catalinas could range as far as Philippine waters or the Celebes on patrol, anti-shipping and Dumbo missions.

"When Liberators of the Fifth and Thirteenth Air Forces raided Borneo oil refineries from new Guinea that fall, the rescue Cats performed brilliantly. The 307th Bombardment Group lost four B-24s in the Balikpapan strike of September 30, but PBYs picked up the complete crews of three, and half the men from the fourth.

"Major General George C. Kenney, Commander, Allied Air Forces, has reported that 50 P-38 fighter pilots volunteered to accompany B-24s to Balikpapaan, knowing they would run out of gas on the return flight, 'if I would just send six or seven rescue Catalinas out to meet them.' The pilots were confident they could simply parachute down and get picked up by the Cats.

"Rear Admiral Frank D. Wagner, who as a Captain was in command of Patrol Wing Ten at the outbreak of war and during the retreat from the Philippines, took command of the Seventh Fleet, Aircraft in July 1944. When the Philippines were recaptured that winter, it seemed fitting that he should return to Manila Bay flying his flag in the seaplane tender Currituck, mothership to many a Catalina."

Tex Foret: One–Hundred–Fifteen Survivors Picked Up

Tex Foret closes his contribution with the story of the PBY rescue that never got off the water, but didn't have to.

"While we were at Tacloban, Leyte, Philippines, one of our destroyers was torpedoed after getting separated from the rest of the fleet. There were a lot of men in the water and a Catalina from the squadron next to us — I think it was VP34 — was coming back from a long hop, when they saw the tin-can going down. All those fellows were in the water with no help in sight.

"They landed the PBY and loaded 114 or 115 men inside the plane, on the struts, on the turtle–back, on top of the wing and everywhere they could hold on. Then they simply taxied until they contacted an American ship, which promptly took the survivors off their hands.

"I thought that was one of the rarest occurances. This old, old Catalina, bless her soul, was able to snatch over 100 sailors out of the water and hang on to them until help arrived."

William A. (Bill) Barker: Winding Down Their Service

Bill Barker served two tours of duty in the Southwest Pacific flying for VP11. He is typical of the many hundreds of Navy men who served their country as crewmen in the PBY Catalina patrol plane. Four decades after his first flight, his enthusiasm and devotion to the Catalina has never wavered. He writes of the closing months of VP11's Pacific service.

"In July of 1944, we moved up to Biak where we operated as Dumbo, ASW night patrol for the fleet, and still did our Black Cat operations up into Ceylon and into the lower Philippines. We worked our way up to Morotai and our last operation was off of Tacloban, Leyte in the Philippines. Some of our squadron planes were in on the Philippine landings.

"We were scattered from Manus Island to New Guinea, to Biak, in the Schouten Islands, to Morotai and all the way up to Tacloban. We operated off of three or four different tenders; everyone was doing something different.

"It was winding down for us. By late November-December, we knew our time was about up. We were going home as soon as some squadron could relieve us. In October, a PBM squadron came into Morotai to relieve us and couldn't. Their planes wouldn't stay in the air. A PV-2 squadron tried to relieve us in November but couldn't cut it. So we had to stay until December. We ended up with quite a lot of action in the Philippines before being relieved.

"From March of 1942 until December of 1944, I flew 3000 combat hours. Granted, many of those hours were those slow, routine patrols out of Guadalcanal, Espiritu Santo and later out of Morotai and Biak. But they were combat patrols in enemy territory where we were subject to attack, or were finding targets to go after.

"They were something else, those Catalinas. I still believe that if it weren't for the slow, lumbering old birds and their ability to remain airborne in all the adverse elements of nature, and to overcome every manmade challenge, the war would have been a little slower in coming to a climax. Also, literally hundreds of men returned home to their families because of the PBY Catalina."

Bill Barker's facts are accurate. The war was winding down for many PBY squadrons serving in the Southwest Pacific. Between November 1944 and early February 1945, VP101, VP11, VP33, VP34 and VP52 were all relieved from their stations and aircraft tenders at Morotai, Schouten, Manus, Biak and Leyte. All had served many months in the Southwest Pacific. Now it was time to back off and let fresh squadrons finish the job.

But some of the replacement squadrons were far from new. VPB71 moved to Morotai in November 1944. This squadron had been serving various areas of the Pacific war as VP71 since Christmas Day, 1941.

VPB23, formerly VP23, was one of the unfortunate Catalina squadrons to have their aircraft wiped out at Ford Island, Pearl Harbor, on December 7, 1941. Their service had been almost continuous since replacement PBYs arrived in the early months of 1942.

VPB44, VPB53 and VPB54, formerly VP squadrons, were veterans. They were dispatched to various bases in and around the Philippines where they continued the awesome tradition of PBY Catalina Black Catting, reconnaissance, transporting and air-sea Dumbo rescue.

As Allied forces in Europe closed in on Hitler's shattered Wehrmacht, more offensive forces were brought to bear against the rapidly crumbling empire of Japan. But along the way, the Japanese would exact a heavy toll on the Allies with the introduction of suicide assaults by fanatic troops and Kamikaze "Divine Wind" attacks by specifically trained pilots.

In the war with Japan the end result was no longer in doubt, but as Allied forces drew closer to the island fortress of Japan itself, the problem of bringing that proud nation to its knees without horrendous loss of life became of paramount concern to all military leaders of the Allied movement. Of course the solution chosen, however tragic, is now history.

Atlantic Fleet PBY squadrons patrolled the waters of the Northern, Mid and South Atlantic, searching for the German U-Boat, until the cessation of hostilities with Germany on May 8, 1945.

In the Pacific, Catalina squadrons searched and patrolled, raided enemy shore installations, attacked and sank Japanese shipping and rescued friendly survivors of downed aircraft and sunken ships right up to the war's end.

Total tons of enemy vessels sunk, or permanently put out of commission by PBY Catalina patrol bombers, in all war zones, has not been compiled for this writing. Neither has a total of aircraft downed by the lumbering bird, nor total combat hours flown been assembled. But two totals have been calculated, and their numbers alone tell much of the reason this incredible aircraft is yet held in reverence by so many military and non-military survivors of World War II.

The combined air-sea rescue totals, as listed in a 1951 Department of the Navy statistical summary of World War II, "Fleet Air Wing's Accomplishments," has 2,957 men and women rescued by the Catalinas and their sister aircraft, PB2Y and PBMs. In addition, more than 1069 people were evacuated from hostile situations on islands and land masses around the world.

Before the war, and for a while after it began, the PBY was ridiculed and laughed at for being ugly and ridiculously slow. Among its many nicknames were "Blue Goose" and "Ugly Duckling." But German U-Boat crews in the Atlantic, Japanese freighter crewmen, the bivouacked soldier — even line sailors of the Japanese fleet — as well as fighter pilots, didn't ridicule the PBY. They feared and respected it.

The Australian and New Zealand coastwatchers, the downed airmen — floating around in giant oceans with nothing but a small rubber raft or a life preserver — the fleet sailors, merchant crewmen, the sick and injured requiring air transport to stay alive, the soldier, the marine, the islander and the missionary, desperately praying for evacuation, sometimes under the guns of the enemy, didn't call it an ugly duckling. To them, it was an Angel of Mercy.

Glossary

Glossary

AA Salvo — Concentrated anti-aircraft fire.
Aft — Rear. In back of.
Aldis Lamp — Signal lamp. Used to transmit morse code.
AP — Aviation pilot.
Awash — Object just above water surface.

Bearing Down — Full spead toward an object.
Belted-Four Ball & Tracer — Belted machine gun bullets; fifth bullet is tracer.
B.O.Q. — Bachelor's officer's quarters.
Buck Ensign — Newly commissioned naval officer.

'Canal — Abbreviation for Guadalcanal.
Cherry-Picker — Heavy-duty lifting crane.
Close(d) — Shortening distance between an aircraft or vessel and another.
Cocked Hat — Slang term for upset plans.

Darken Ship — Shut off lights; prepare for night flying or sailing.
Dead Ahead — Directly in front of.
DD — Naval Destroyer.

DFC — Distinguished Flying Cross.
Divine Wind — Japanese military logo.

Eyes of the Fleet — WWII term for PBY patrol aircraft.

Fan Tail — Rear of ship.
Flotsam — Floating ship wreckage.
Full Alert — Prepared for enemy attack.
Fuselage — Body of aircraft.

Ground Swells — Large rolls of ocean water.

Heading — Navigational direction of flight.
Hedge hogs — High-arch depth charges.
Hung on Props — Remaining airborne slightly above flying speed.

Jaygee — Naval lieutenant, junior grade.
Jetsam — Discarded cargo to lighten ship load.
Jury-rigged — Pieced together.

Meat Ball — Slang term for Japanese rising sun insignia.
MO's — Radio signals repeatedly keyed by continuous-wave transmission to allow homing by other vessels.

On My Wing — Another aircraft flying alongside.
On the Step — Last point of water contact on hull of PBY before lift off.

Pad-eyes — Hooks in dock for aircraft tie-down.
Patron 52, 94 — PBY patrol squadrons
P-Boat — Patrol seaplane.
Pitot tube — Device to measure air speed.
PPC — Patrol plane commander.
Preflight — Check of instruments and operating status of aircraft prior to flight.

R&R — Rest and relaxation.

Scramble — Emergency command for aircraft take off.
Skeleton Crew — Varied on PBY. Normally, two pilots, one mechanic, one radioman, and one ordnanceman.
Slot — Ocean waters between certain Solomon Islands.
Smoke Markers — Locating devices floating on water and emitting smoke.
Sono-Buoys — Signal emitting floating buoys.

Sons-of-Nippon — WWII slang term for devout Japanese military personnel.

Straits — Abbreviation for the Straits of Gibraltar.

Tin Can — Naval destroyer.

Tracers — Machine gun bullets trailing fire or smoke, marking their path.

Turtle Back — Blisters on PBY fuselage.

Wake — Track left in water by a moving ship or boat.

Wing — Patrol aircraft headquarters squadron.

500 kcs — 500 kilocycles on radio band. Used for emergency calls only.

Index

Other Bestsellers From TAB

☐ **AERIAL RECONNAISSANCE—The 10th Photo Recon Group in World War II—Tom Ivie**

A fascinating overview of World War II from the unique perspective of the aerial photographer. You'll find dozens of photos chosen from the more than 18,000 taken by these recon photographers, plus details on aircraft, the group's adventures, and more! You'll discover how these secret photos helped turn Germany's last offensive. 208 pp., 366 illus.

Paper $9.95   **Book No. 28900**

☐ **THE LADY BE GOOD: MYSTERY BOMBER OF WORLD WAR II—Dennis E. McClendon**

What happened to the B-24 bomber nicknamed "The Lady Be Good," and its nine young American crewmembers when they vanished without a trace in 1943? An exhaustive post-war search produced no clues. Then—16 years later—the B-24 was found deep in the Sahara desert. Step-by-step the author pieces together the solution to the bomber's fate. 208 pp., Illustrated

Paper $12.95   **Book No. 26624**

Send $1 for the new TAB Catalog describing over 1300 titles currently in print and receive a coupon worth $1 off on your next purchase from TAB.

(In PA, NY, and ME add applicable sales tax. Orders subject to credit approval.   Orders outside U.S. must be prepaid with international money orders in U.S. dollars.)

*Prices subject to change without notice.

━━━

To purchase these or any other books from TAB, visit your local bookstore, return this coupon, or call toll-free 1-800-233-1128 (In PA and AK call 1-717-794-2191).

Product No.	Hard or Paper	Title	Quantity	Price

☐ Check or money order enclosed made payable to TAB BOOKS Inc.

Charge my ☐ VISA ☐ MasterCard ☐ American Express

Acct. No. _____ Exp. _____

Signature _____

Please Print
Name _____

Company _____

Address _____

City _____

State _____ Zip _____

Subtotal	
Postage/Handling ($5.00 outside U.S.A. and Canada)	$2.50
In PA, NY, and ME add applicable sales tax	
TOTAL	

Mail coupon to:
TAB BOOKS Inc.
Blue Ridge Summit
PA 17294-0840   BC